The
Radical
Spinoza

THE
RADICAL
SPINOZA

Paul Wienpahl

New York • New York University Press • 1979

For
Jan and Mark

Library of Congress Cataloging in Publication Data

Wienpahl, Paul.
   The radical Spinoza.

   Bibliography: p.
   Includes index.
   1. Spinoza, Benedictus de, 1632–1677.   I. Title.
B3998.W63   199′.492   78-65448
ISBN 0-8147-9186-7

Manufactured in the United States of America

Contents

Preface

Ten years ago I undertook a book on Baruch Spinoza. Ten years prior to that I began a practical association with Zen Buddhism by being taught to sit in meditation in Daitoku-ji, Kyoto. The book was undertaken because I believed that I could best relate that practice to Western philosophy by writing about Spinoza who seemed to me to be *the* modern philosopher. Baruch, in Latin Benedictus de Spinoza (1632–1677), will hereafter often be called by his initials, "BdS," or simply by "Sp."

The undertaking failed. I failed in it because, as I realized when it ended, I did not understand BdS. The book failed because it was fifty percent quotations from BdS. It is a poor book when 300 of its 600 pages are in the words of one other than its author.

This aspect of the failure had two sources. There is no complete translation of Spinoza in any language, and the translations in English are for the most part unbelievably bad. They are, furthermore, philosophically unsound, which was one of the reasons for my failure. The result was that whenever I had to quote BdS I could not do so by referring to a page in any of the English texts. I had to do so by providing my own translations. There was, then, nothing to do but shelve the "book" and set about preparing a complete translation of Spinoza.

Translation is arduous work. Because the writings of BdS are of relatively small compass I was able to translate them all. This issued in two complete re-translations. No sooner had I arrived at the end the first time than it was apparent that the whole had to be redone. Words had appeared in different contexts, and what had at first appeared as reasonable renderings of them turned out not to be. This what-became-constant reworking was complicated by the philosophical clarities and profundities it revealed. The insights that came themselves required changes in vocabulary. Consider some examples.

Any translation, no matter how scrupulously made, is interpretive. Therefore, I decided that my work should not be so much a translation as a bridge to the original. (Any sound edition of BdS should bear the original Latin or Dutch on pages facing the English. This is true of any writer, but particularly is it true of BdS because of the novelty of his thinking.) To aid readers in the task with which this would confront them, I selected as a principle of translation from the Latin, in which the bulk of Sp's work is written, the principle that, wherever possible, the word in English rendering a Latin word should be one with a Latin root. Employing this procedure would in addition preserve to some extent the purity of Sp's language, as well as further reduce the interpretive aspect of translating. Thus where BdS had, say *educo* (rear, educate), I would use "educate."

This principle proved extraordinary. For one thing, whereas sixty percent of the words in English have roots in Latin (the rest are of Anglo-Saxon and Teutonic heritage), ninety percent of the words on any given page in English are of non-Latin provenance. The result is that a translation based on this principle sends its readers constantly to the dictionary.

In the second place, and far worse, is the fact that philosophically the principle drove me to doing the opposite of what it required. Thus I found that the Latin noun *intellectus* (past participle of the verb *intelligere*, "to understand"), which can be translated "intellect," had to be rendered with "understanding" if Sp's usage was to become clear. Even more fundamentally I found that the Latin participle of the verb "to be" (*esse*) *essentia*, which is commonly translated with "essence," simply had to be rendered with the non-Latin-rooted participle "being."

In view of the fact that BdS had no influence on the development of philosophic thought from 1650 on, the question

arises: Why spend so much time and effort in translating him?
The Biblical exegesis of the nineteenth century had its foundation in Sp's *Theological-Political Treatise.* However, his great
philosophical piece, the ETHIC, remained virtually unread
until it was seized upon by the poets of Goethe's day, and even
after that its language did not become part of our philosophical
currency.

Aside, then, from the value for scholars of a thorough and
complete translation of Sp's writings, and aside from the intrinsic value of performing such a task, what reason can there be
for spending years of daily labor at it? A full answer to the
question will, I trust, be apparent to those who read the present
volume. Here, however, is a brief answer; for the question has a
reader's form: Why bother with a work on a philosopher of the
seventeenth century?

The twentieth century has been experiencing a revolutionary
alteration in outlook. Nietzsche expressed the change at the
century's opening with the cry that God is dead. There followed
the philosophies of pragmatism, positivism, and existentialism.
In England, Russell and Moore moved from idealism to logical
atomism and common sense. Auden called ours the "age of
anxiety," and Wittgenstein spoke of "the darkness of this time."
Most recently in *The New Yorker* Hannah Arendt expressed her
despair by announcing that she had "joined the ranks of those
who for some time now have been attempting to dismantle
metaphysics, and philosophy with all its categories, as we have
known these from the beginnings in Greece until today." She
added "that the thread of tradition is broken and that we shall
not be able to renew it." All the names used to describe the
change suggest its nature ("dead," "pragmatism," "anxiety,"
"darkness"), and the word "wisdom" is not among them. A
striking fact, because philosophy is the love of wisdom.

Consider one example. John Dewey found that the influence
of Darwin on philosophy was that of causing us to rethink completely our notions of what science and knowledge are. As he
put it, a whole new logic was required. Under the influence of
the Greek thinkers we had believed that science as a method

[ix]

was the discovery of the unchanging forms or species that lie behind or within the constantly changing appearances of our world. As the result of this procedure science was also the body of the knowledge of these forms, the expression of the unchanging realities. The mere title of the work that influenced Dewey, *"Origin* of Species," suggests a totally altered view of the nature of science. It indicates that there are no fixed and unchanging forms or species.

The "new logic" was, of course, accompanied by a new view of human experience, one quite different from the Greek. The latter depended on the distinction between appearance and reality, where by "appearance" is meant that which constantly changes and by "reality" that which is unchanging. The "new logic" is that science does not give us a knowledge of reality. It gives us pragmatic devices (concepts, theories) for dealing with the constantly changing which is all that there is in the new view of human experience. All stability, all reality, it seems, disappears from view in this new outlook.

The experience of this alteration of outlook has had many manifestations. There has, for example, been a marked but curious resurgence of a religious interest. Westerners have turned to drugs, to Buddhism, to Zen Buddhism, and to the Buddhism of Tibet and to Tantric Buddhism. Another form of this development is the interest in the so-called "expanding of consciousness." The most recent aspect of this manifestation is a growing awareness that technology and laws may not be of as much avail in the crises of energy and pollution as a fundamental change in our attitude toward nature will be. From Bacon on the cry has been that knowledge is power, that it provides control over nature, and that nature is to be brought to heel for the benefit of mankind—a cry that is not far from Dewey's. We are beginning to see that another attitude toward nature may be indicated: an attitude of reverence, an attitude in which we see ourselves as integral with nature instead of as set over against her.

In his work on the new logic Dewey once remarked that the influence of modern science on philosophy could have been felt in the seventeenth century and the step he took taken then. Unbeknownst to Dewey, whether the influence was felt, the step was taken: by BdS.

This would be no reason for reading pragmatism in a seventeenth-century garb, however, were it not for the fact that BdS moved on from the step in far profounder and wide-ranging fashion that any contemporary philosopher has. The philosophic move that BdS made included that of the new theory of science or reason. It brought him to the attitude to-ward nature which has just been mentioned. As he made the move, BdS outlined an instrumental theory of rational knowledge. He went on, however, to speak of another mode of per-ceiving or knowing things. This is a kind of knowing that differs radically from that of reason, though we come to it by the exercise of reason. It is a kind of knowing that has been called "mystical," and as we know in this way we come to love. In this manner the other attitude toward nature develops, and there is in this knowing that which satisfies the interest in expanded states of consciousness. In making his move BdS in effect brought science and religion together. He broke with the old duality and identified Nature and God.

I have said that he was not read. Partly this was because those who did read him misunderstood him and said that he was an atheist. People turned from him, then, because to them he ap-peared as the anti-Christ. The truth is in fact just the reverse. A German poet saw it when he described Spinoza as *"ein gottbet-runkener Mensch"* (a god-intoxicated human being). I shall have occasion to remark later that Sp's ETHIC is the seventeeth-century version of the Bible.

The reason, then, for expending time and effort on BdS is that he is a grand spokesman for our time. He has not only seen further than most of us do. He also provides us with a lan-guage, there are no doubt others, for forming and articulating our awareness of ourselves now in this period of revolutionary change. In becoming acquainted with this language and perhaps learning how to use it a little we can understand our-selves better.

[xi]

In this book I have attempted to reflect the essential and the essentially novel aspects of the thinking of BdS. I have tried to avoid scholarship, though I have not shrunk from it where it seemed necessary. In this connection I deliberately mention no secondary sources or books about Spinoza, at least those from recent or near-recent times. That is, my concern is solely with BdS.

From this work, if readers are interested, they should turn to Sp's writings themselves, possibly return to them. As noted, the extant translations in English are poor. They confuse works which are already apt to confuse by reason of their novelty. But until more adequate translations appear, these are there.

For this reason I have provided aids for dealing with any translation of BdS where it seems to me that translation is apt to go astray. There is also the possibility that the deeply interested reader can turn to the original texts in Latin. This is a chore, but not a terribly difficult one. The aids provided for dealing with translations will also be of some assistance with the originals.

The latter advice is mainly for graduate students in philosophy. I am more concerned with the general reader and suggest that he or she turn to whatever translation is at hand. You will be able to decide after you have read this book which of the various writings you may try first. However, in the Appendix of the present volume a feature of Spinoza's ETHIC is used to provide assistance even to the general reader, both with available translations and with occasionally consulting the Latin text.

The use of this feature has the additional advantage of giving in brief compass the general outlines of Sp's thinking. I refer to the so-called geometrical manner in which the ETHIC was written. This consists of a division of the work into five parts. Each, except the fifth, commences with a list of definitions and axioms or postulates followed by propositions. The propositions are in turn accompanied by "demonstrations," occasionally by corollaries, and frequently by scholia or notes which further explicate the propositions. (The "demonstrations," by the way, are not what we would call "proofs" of the propositions. They serve to unfold the propositions.) Some of the parts have prefaces and/or appendices which present subjects in the essay form.

By extracting the propositions and presenting them in the order in which BdS wrote them we are confronted with the skeleton of his thinking which he fleshed out with demonstrations and scholia. Adding the Latin versions of the propositions on facing pages gives the reader the aids in reading available English texts and in turning to the Latin when this is wanted.

Thus the Appendix also presents Sp's thinking in his own words in a very small space. It has a further feature of which I was unaware until I prepared the Appendix. It sheds light on this thinking which reading the entire ETHIC curiously does not provide. The reader will see what is meant here as the Appendix is read, especially if it is read with care: by taking the Latin version seriously. Indeed, this feature may have been one of the reasons why BdS wrote the ETHIC in the geometrical manner, a reason which has not to my knowledge been offered in the literature on Spinoza. He used the manner for clarity, precision, and brevity; perhaps also with a pedagogical purpose in mind. However, the technique gives a view of the ETHIC, contained simply in its propositions, which is unique.

In this connection it should be added that the Index has been carefully prepared so that it becomes a part of the reading of the book. It reveals connections between lines of thinking which are not explicitly indicated in the text.

I wish in conclusion to express my gratitude to Mrs. Muriel W. Ponzecchi and Mr. Philip F. Siff for their kind assistance in making the publication of THE RADICAL SPINOZA possible.

Paul Wienpahl
Santa Barbara

[xiii]

CHAPTER 1

Some Background

In *Before Philosophy* Henri Frankfort alludes to the thinking before philosophy as mythopoeic. Before people in the West began to think abstractly, critically, and methodically, around 600 B.C., they thought poetically in terms of myths. Examples of this kind of thinking occur in the ancient myths of Egypt and Mesopotamia, in the *Iliad* and the *Odyssey*, in some books of the Old Testament, and today in our dreams. It has several characteristics.

One of these is that ancient peoples felt at home in nature in a way that seems impossible for us now. The realm of nature and the realm of human beings were taken to be one. In so far as humans made a distinction between themselves and nature they did so in terms of "I" and "thou." Nature was not an *it* for them. She was animate.

Related to this characteristic is a second: The distinction between appearance and reality did not play a role in this thinking. Thus, for ancient peoples dreams were no less real than waking experiences. This in turn involved a "failure," if it can be called that, to distinguish between the subjective and the objective. One of the things this means is that there was no objectivity in such thinking. People could not be, and were not, objective about themselves or their world. They reacted to it primarily emotionally.

In the logic of mythopoeic thinking abstract categories like causality, space, and time had no place. Where we see merely associations, they saw connections. For us space is abstract, con-

[1]

tinuous, and homogeneous. We can locate objects in it and believe that two objects cannot be in the same place at the same time. This was not the case for ancient peoples. They did not separate the abstract concept of space from the experience of space. Any temple could be the same place as the original primeval hill which first emerged from the chaos of the waters. Much the same can be said for time. The future and the past were interchangeable; or rather, there was no future and no past in the way that we with our abstract concept of time can think about them.

Generally speaking, in mythopoeic thinking there was no consciousness of self. This helps to explain the importance of the dictum which Socrates took to be central to philosophy: Know thyself.

Philosophical thinking emerged from mythopoesis when people began to make distinctions. Possibly the most basic distinction that was initially made was that between the self and nature. Given this, speculation about the nature of nature could occur. And it did so in the persons of the Greek cosmologists, from the time of Thales around 600 B.C. till the time of Protagoras (480?–410). During this period almost as many views of nature as there were philosophers appeared. Amongst other things this required that a distinction be made between appearance and reality. Each philosopher could then think that he was onto the reality that lay behind the appearances.

Another consequence of this multifarious speculation, though by no means was the latter its sole cause, was that thinkers turned to the nature of the human being as the object of their thinking. Whereas the object had been *Being,* or what is, it now became human being; at first human being, and then gradually this human being, or I. This is the period of the Sophists. In very short order philosophical thinking came to include both *Being* and human being. In this Golden Age of Greek thought Socrates and Plato became aware of thinking itself and the Platonic theory of Forms or Ideas appeared on the scene. The culmination of this reflective effort was Aristotle's definition of man as the rational animal. He developed this definition throughout his *Nichomachean Ethics* in which he depicted the good life as the life of reason.

Making distinctions and reflection had given the Greeks considerable awareness of themselves. Science had been born. There is the natural world with the human being in it. It is in the nature of a human being to know. The object of knowledge is the forms or structures of the natural world, of what is. The Greeks were not clear about these forms. Plato thought that they were in a realm of their own and that the individual things which we experience in various ways somehow took on the forms, making each thing what it is by some process of imitation. A swan became a swan by taking on the form of swanness. Aristotle was inclined to the view that the forms or ideas ("idea" being a Greek word for "form") are in the things and that there is no separate realm of forms. Thus, for example, in each thing that would become a swan there was its essence, the form of swanness. As that thing grew and developed it gradually realized this form. It was the essence of the human being to know these forms of the things; in other words, to get ideas of them.

The death of Aristotle in 322 B.C. roughly coincided with that of Alexander the Great. These events marked the end of that civilization of Greece that so influenced the development of the Western world. The civilization had been based on the political institution of the city-state. Indeed that institution had given the Greeks and other peoples their civilizations. "Civilization" is from the Latin *civitas* (city) and "political" is from the Greek *polis* (city).

In the person of Alexander a movement was begun toward the development of a new "political" unit: that of the empire. Alexander's attempt to form an empire failed. The people of the city of Rome continued the attempt and succeeded in it. The period from 300 B.C. till the time of Christ was that in which this success occurred. It was also the period of two other developments: an inner and an outer development, the latter being an aspect of the growth of the empire. The two developments influenced each other. The one was philosophical: the

[3]

growth of scepticism; the other was social: curiously the growth of anti-socialism and a turning away from the outer world of society to the inner world of the individual human being.

Aristotle had defined man as the rational animal. As reflection on this notion continued, people thinking philosophically began to doubt it. During the next 300 years they came upon a series of arguments which, taken in their entirety, made the reflective individual sceptical about the possibility of rational knowledge. For example, men became aware of the relativity of the senses. Objects, they realized, appear differently to us depending on the distance and positions from which we view them. Which distance and which position give us the true picture of a thing? Objects also vary in their appearance to us with the varying moods in which we perceive them. A man in love sees his beloved as the most beautiful of her sex. After five years of marriage he may lower his newspaper one morning, glance at his partner, and ask himself: "God, what have I done?" Gradually it came to seem impossible that we should ever know the real nature of anything.

This philosophical development coincided with the establishment of the Roman Empire. Politically and socially speaking, this meant that all of the peoples where the empire spread became disenfranchized. They became stateless peoples. True, they could become members of the new civic body, the Empire, but in doing so they lost their citizenship in the *polis* or city-state in which they had been born. Economically speaking, the civilizations of the ancient world were based on the institution of slavery. It was a recognized and accepted fact of life. With the development of the Empire a new kind of "slavery" was added to the old: the bondage of the stateless person. The lot of the masses of peoples in the Empire, except that of the Romans, became a desperately sad one.

This outer development, as I have said, fitted with the inner development of philosophical scepticism. Despair and hopelessness with the world in which Western peoples lived became the attitudes, especially of those who reflected on their lives. There seemed to be nothing in which they could place

[4]

their trust. The familiar social institution of the city-state had lost its weight in the bestowal of rights on individuals; and reason itself had been called into question. That is, that which people had come to believe constituted their very essence was seen to be without hope of success. The result was a further turning within. The outer world of nature and society provided no promise of security, and, if reason herself tottered, what was left. Was there anything else, perhaps deep within each individual, on which a human being could depend?

Beside the Greek development from mythopoesis to the concepts of nature or *Being,* there was in the ancient world another strangely similar and at the same time dissimilar development: the Hebrews'. One of the most illuminating accounts of it is Spinoza's analysis of their own history of it, the Old Testament, in his *Theological-Political Treatise.* Escaping from bondage by the Egyptians, the Hebrews left the civilization by whose rights they had been living. In the desert they had both the opportunity and the need to develop their own civic body or civilization. In this they were aided by the prophets, one of the greatest of whom brought them the Law, the Ten Commandments. These codes for living were to be the foundation of this civilization. Basically, as Christ was much later to make clear, they came down to one law: to love thy neighbor as thyself. That is to say, if you observed the Commandments, your behavior would in fact be that of being diligent toward or loving your neighbor. The key word is "neighbor." In the early Biblical sense it meant your fellow citizen, that is, your fellow Hebrew. And it is clear that such behavior would indeed guarantee the smooth functioning of a civic body.

Given human beings as they are, however, the operation of this law presented a formidable problem: Why observe it? One must remember here that the ancient Hebrews, like all ancient peoples, were a rude people, and when they left Egypt an uncivilized people (i.e., a people without a city). They were, in fact, as children. Their imaginations may have been great (witness the myths), but their understanding was minimal. Furthermore, what was true of the people was true of those who became their leaders, the prophets. Faced with the question about obeying the law and faced with a contumacious or stiff-necked people and being a man of particularly strong imagination, Moses answered the question out of the depth of his being in a highly imaginative manner. You obey the law because it is the word of God. Of course the people backslid from time to time. But the answer was repeated from prophet to prophet and from time to time: It is the word of God.

The force of this answer can probably now be only dimly felt, though it may intellectually be deeply appreciated. The answer's force comes with God's other names or appellatives (and particularly with his proper name, especially his proper Hebrew name): The Father, *Eloah, Elohim, Deus, Dieu,* and *Gott.* But it is *the* proper name, the one that for a long time the Hebrews would not pronounce, and even now pronounce only on special occasions, *the* proper name which provided the full force: *Jehova,* or in another form *Yahvey.* With it we came to the parallel in the Greek and Hebrew developments. For *Jehova* is a tenseless form of the Hebrew verb "to be." Moses' concern was with *being,* even as the Greeks' had been. The concern is with *what is* (to use a phrase instead of a word). *Being* tells you this. To be is to love thy neighbor.

In the dim past, of course, it did not come out like this. The thinking then was mythopoeic. For the Hebrews, God is what is, was, and ever shall be (in a way a tenseless verb includes all the tenses). He was also the Father of the People, their Legislator. He was Moses, and all the other prophets. Today we make distinctions. Then they did not. And God's message was wonderous. It helped the Hebrews to build The City. When it was destroyed and they were led away again into captivity, the message helped them to endure. Again it helped them to rebuild The City. And when the Romans finally took it, the defense was beyond belief.

At about that time the two civilizations that have done so much since to form the human development in the West came together. In their despair, which was articulated in Greek scepticism, the peoples of the ancient world heard the message: the good word, the Gospel. Love thy neighbor, but in the Gospel "neighbor" came to mean fellow human being.

Mythopoeic thinking was not immediately replaced by philosophy. There is still a lot of it today. Certainly in the year 50 A.D. its language was a large part of the intellectual currency of the day. The message, then, had many forms. It was not only to love thy neighbor. It was to the effect that there is another world, a world to which we shall all finally go; the world of the Father where all God's children are brothers and sisters. The turning from this world that was Greek scepticism became a turning to that world. Here we may be slaves and stateless. There we will be free and in God's Kingdom, the highest state of all.

The notion of the political or civilizing unit had been vastly expanded. And here I will caution the reader. I am not encapsulating the history of Western thought. I am, in Wittgenstein's phrase, "assembling reminders" for a particular purpose: that of providing context for Spinoza's thinking. Consider, then, the ambiguity in "the highest state of all." In the next line there is "civilizing unit." That gives one meaning of the term "state." Another occurs in the phrases "a state of the union message" and "a state of being." What did the people in 50 A.D. have in mind when they thought of the highest state of all? A kingdom or dominion (and "dominion" can mean either a rule or that which is ruled), or a state, or way of being?

The period from the birth of Christ till the Renaissance used to be called "The Dark Ages." Users of the phrase, historians for example, had in mind that during that period the light had gone out of Europe: the natural light, the light of reason, science. The Renaissance was the rebirth of the Greek spirit, or the period when modern science began. Later with more knowledge of the history of Europe the time of the *Dark Ages* was reduced to 1 to 800 A.D., for around 800 the Arabians brought some of the Greek science to Europe. Still later a further breakdown of the ages occurred. From 1 to 400 (the

[7]

time of Augustine) came to be called the "Religious Period." The Dark Ages were reduced to the years between 400 and 800.

In a way, however, the original designation of the Dark Ages was correct. The light did go out of Europe from the time of Christ to the Renaissance. It went instead into the 'hearts and minds of the human beings living there. For with the Christian message the peoples found themselves confronted with a remarkable new question. In terms we have been using the question was: What is the highest state of all? The Greeks had defined man as the rational animal. The Romans had accepted this definition. The Hebrews had defined human beings, that is, the Hebrews, as "God's Elected" (the "chosen"). The impact of their civilizing influence on that of the Greeks became the realization that in addition to being rational the human being is also spiritual. The Religious Period could have as well been called the "Spiritual Period." As a consequence, we might think of this other dimension of the human as the religious. A new task became that of understanding the human religious or spiritual aspect. The light of reason was used for this task. It turned within because Greek thought had become introspective and because surely the Kingdom of God or the highest state of all was not to be found in this world. The fall of the Roman Empire had begun. The Universal or Catholic Church became the civilizing force.

What, then, and where is spirituality? For twelve centuries, with many interruptions, reflective men and women worked on these questions. Under the Greek influence the gradually developing answers to the questions were conceptualized. The simple Christian message was formalized. Theology or the science of God (the Spirit) developed. It became more and more abstract until by the thirteenth century men despaired of understanding God.

On the other hand, a simple and unified world view was gradually firmed up, a view that not only included God, or the element of spirituality, but that also took into account the prevailing notion of the movements of the heavenly bodies, the

Ptolemaic. According to this view the world was God's creation. At its center was Earth, the hub of the now-called solar system. Around Earth moved the planets and beyond them lay the fixed stars. Earth was the stage on which the human drama of salvation took place. To accomplish God's unfathomable purposes we come into this world, that is, our souls or spiritual beings enter our bodies. There they, we, enact the drama. Tempted, we fall. We lose our innocence, our unknowing, and come to know good and evil. The drama is overcoming evil, expatiating for our sins, and going on to immortal life.

There are glimpses of the spiritual throughout this view. Unfortunately the things the glimpses reveal are either seen as through a cloud, or they are so naively simple as to seem occult. Of the first things are God and his purposes, of the second the temptation and the life immortal. God was finally defined as Perfect *Being* or the Perfect *Being* (Latin, the language in which the definition was given for Christians, has no articles; so it is difficult to say which God was). This seems to make God incomprehensible. *"Being"* is not even a noun, that is, not the name of anything. (The Latin for "noun" and "name" is the same: *nomen*. Remember we are still in something like the Roman Empire, in which the common language was the Roman: Latin.) What this being's purposes may have been, then, also seem unimaginable. I can think of this person's purpose in something, but what would being's purposes be?

On the other hand, temptation seems quite clear, as does immortality. However, when we focus on them the clarity vanishes. Temptation by whom? The snake? This is at best a slippery answer. It is in fact mythopoeic. Immortality? But what is that? Non-mortality, that is life after death? But that is self-contradictory. The picture of the spiritual in the thirteenth century was simple, but confused, as one painted by a child.

Although the gulf between the educated and reflective minority and the great uneducated majority in Europe at that time was huge, this lack of clear understanding of the spiritual no doubt played a role in the transition from the Middle Ages to the Renaissance. Simple unreflective folk could accept and live by the picture of their lives which had been drawn in the 1200 years since Christ. This was not so with the philosophically and scientifically inclined. There were also other forces at work: Large economic, political, and social changes were occurring. Europe was moving from a primarily agricultural economy to a bartering one. Cities reappeared on the scene and with them a new class of people: the city-dweller, the bourgeoisie. Gradually the nation-states began to form, still another kind of political unit.

People turned from an interest in the spiritual or religious to an interest in nature. This was at first satisfied by a revival and reading of the classical writers, who had been so long forgotten: the Greek and Roman poets, the historians, and the dramatists. The Greek philosophers came into vogue, especially Aristotle, the materialist Democritus, and Plato. The printing press was invented, and with it came the proliferation and propagation of books. Minds were freed from the shackles of the Church's dogmas, shackles that centuries had forged.

The next phase of the Renaissance, after the Humanist interest in books and the classical authors, was the Religious Reformation. Beginning to think for themselves, men turned from the authority of the clergy, and there was a renewed and individual interest in the original Christian message. A cry for the simplification of ritual and the structure of the Church went up. The Universal or Catholic Church split into two sects, a shattering blow to the Medieval foundations of European thought.

To change the metaphor, the picture of the life of humankind was further rent by the third phase of the Renaissance: the scientific. For our purposes we can consider this as beginning with Copernicus' work on the revolutions of the heavenly bodies. Copernicus was primarily a mathematician. As such he found the Ptolemaic theory unsatisfactory. According to it Earth was at the center of the system of the planets which revolved around it in perfect circles. In order to account for their positions on successive days and nights, the theory had to include the notion that some of the heavenly bodies not only

[10]

moved in large circles about Earth, they also moved in small circles on the large. These small circles were called "epicycles," and the theory required that there be some 52 epicycles. The complications that this introduced into the mathematics of the system were large, bothersome, and inelegant.

Copernicus found that, if we supposed that the sun instead of the earth was the center of the system, the number of epicycles with which we had to deal was reduced to thirteen. The simplification this introduced was considerable. Solely on this ground, then, and on the authority of Plato and William of Occam Copernicus believed that his new hypothesis was justified. From Plato men like Occam had acquired the view that nature operates in a well-ordered, that is, roughly simple fashion. Thus Occam had proposed the scientific principle that, other things being equal, the simpler of two hypotheses was likely to be the true one. The empirical evidence at the time was against Copernicus' and in favor of Ptolemy's hypothesis. We still say on the basis of visual evidence that the sun rises and sets. The method of authority, however, which had become the method of acquiring knowledge in the Middle Ages, still prevailed in men's minds. Given this, and the mathematical simplicity of the new view, there was justification in accepting the new astronomy.

The next step was taken by Kepler. He too was primarily a mathematician. As such, and in the climate of the times, he was inclined to accept Copernicus' view. Curiously, however, he had another justification for the hypothesis. He was a sun-worshipper. He was therefore emotionally as well as intellectually committed to Copernicus.

However, there were still the thirteen epicycles. Furthermore, on the basis of the mass of observations which the Danish astronomer, Tycho Brahe, had accumulated during years of patient star-gazing, Kepler knew that the Copernican hypothesis did not accurately account for the positions the heavenly bodies had occupied night after night for a number of years. Kepler finally saw that, if he violated the Aristotelian dictum that the circle is the perfect figure and supposed that

[11]

the planets moved in ellipses, he could reduce the number of epicycles to zero. He also had a formulation that accounted for the positions of the planets far better than the Copernician. Observation had come to play a role in science. The method of the scientists was becoming empirical.

This became all the more so in the work of Galileo, Kepler's great contemporary. On the basis of "news" from Holland (actually the telescope had been invented ten years earlier), Galileo constructed a telescope. With it he observed the motions of Jupiter's moons about the planet. Here was observational evidence for the system of Copernicus as modified by Kepler. Galileo went on to a further development in the scientific or empirical method. He investigated the problem of motion by asking *how* bodies moved instead of *why* they move, and by constructing inclined planes and using a new accurate water clock to measure the speeds of bodies "falling" down these planes. The outcome was the first law of motion. Galileo had also introduced experiment into the new science.

The culmination of this development of the physical and astronomical sciences came in the work of Newton. He not only unified our ideas of local or earthly motion with those of sidereal motion. He also insisted that his work was descriptive solely of observable phenomena. I do not feign hypotheses, said Newton. He was concerned solely with observable facts. The turn from the spiritual and the supernatural to the natural, usually taken to characterize the Renaissance, was apparently complete. That Newton spent the last half of his long life writing obscure theological and Biblical treatises has been regarded as an aberration or the result of declining mental powers.

We are at the end of the scientific Renaissance. Before it occurred, however, the philosophic Renaissance had begun. By 1600, the year that Giordano Bruno was burned at the stake, roughly 150 years after Copernicus' work, one of the philosophic implications of the latter had become apparent. Although it was earth-shaking in more ways than one, the implication is very simple to state. In substituting the sun for the earth as the center of the planetary system, Copernicus had without realizing it removed the keystone of the arch of the worldly outlook of Europeans. The earth could no longer be regarded as the center of creation. In fact, as the new astronomy was being accepted, the earth was no longer regarded as that center. With this and the development of reliance on the empirical method for acquiring knowledge, the whole edifice collapsed. The drama of salvation was called into question. The immortality of the soul was, if not ridiculed, at least disproved (by the monk Pompanatius). Even the existence of God came to be questioned. Scepticism and then gnawing doubt, as well as great hope became the new marks of the Renaissance.

Descartes characterized the situation in a Medieval metaphor: the tree of knowledge. According to the metaphor knowledge is like a tree. There is the trunk, science, the branches of science, and the fruits of knowledge. What, however, of the roots, asked Descartes, without which the tree has no life? We in the seventeenth century are in the position of not knowing them. As a philosopher Descartes' task was that of uncovering them.

Others than Descartes had accurately assessed the situation. With the men in the schools, the Scholastics, Bacon vaguely felt that the roots were in the ground of Aristotle. But Bacon was early in the game and was more interested in understanding the new method that was appearing with such success. It fell to men like Gassendi, the Frenchman, and Hobbes, the Englishman, to seek more consciously for an awareness of the roots.

They found them in the thought of the ancient materialist, Democritus, which had tended to dominate pagen thinking from 300 B.C. till the time of Christ. Democritus' metaphysics was simple and clear. Being or reality is composed of tiny indivisible particles of matter which differ from each other only in quantitative ways: in size, shape, speed of motion, etc. The soul or breath of life is composed of distinctively round and very fast particles. All the things that we experience are made up of various combinations of these atoms, and the qualitative differences we "find" in things are due to changes atoms produce in

[13]

us when they act on us. On something like this basic materialism Hobbes was able to construct a psychology, an ethics, and a political philosophy. In his work Hobbes had done something from which the Renaissance gets its name. For in his work the thought and spirit of one of the greatest of the ancient Greeks was reborn. Hobbes was furthermore giving expression to the temper of the times. Despite the growing scepticism the interests in the Renaissance were Epicurean and materialistic.

CHAPTER 2

The New Philosophy

Although Hobbes was superficially successful in grounding knowledge anew, and although the upper reaches of his thought, his political philosophy, became influential, his efforts did not satisfy the deeper needs of reflective individuals. This failure has two sources. In returning to Democritus for his inspiration Hobbes had not employed the new method, the empirical. He had instead employed the old. He had turned to an authority. Furthermore, he had ignored what was new in Western thought after the Greeks: the development of the idea of the spiritual dimension of human being. It was not just that he ignored what had been thought about this dimension, for example the work of Augustine, the towering figure of the early Middle Ages. In his view everything was material. He ignored the seemingly essential duality of the spirit and the flesh, of thought and thing.

It fell to Descartes (1594–1650), *the* philosopher of the Renaissance and the later-styled Father of Modern Philosophy, to write the new philosophy. He did this in the *Meditations,* though he restated it in a different form in Part I of his *Principles of Philosophy.* In performing his meditations for writing the *Meditations* Descartes employed the new method. He turned away from the authorities to his own experience. This, probably as much as anything he said, stirred his contemporaries. The move was a breath of fresh air in the stale atmosphere of Scholasticism.

Descartes also concerned himself mightily with the spiritual and gave it the most important place in his philosophy. The full title of the *Meditations* is "Meditations concerning First Philosophy, in which God's existence, & the Human Soul's distinction from the Body are demonstrated." In the Dedication of the work to the "Illustrious Gentlemen of the Sacred Faculty of Theology of Paris," Descartes noted that "I have always estimated that the two questions, concerning God & concerning the Soul, are the principal of those which are to be demonstrated by Philosophical rather than by Theological effort."

Thus Descartes avoided the two faults in Hobbes' work, and produced a philosophy that was strikingly original. So original was it in method and at least in the form of its expression that it became *the* philosophical foundation of modern Western thought. The content was not new. The *Meditations* gave new form to the basic dualisms of both ancient and medieval thought: form and matter, and the spirit and the flesh.

It is the fashion in the schools today to treat extensively of Descartes. It is also the fashion to use principally the *Meditations.* Finally, it is the fashion to treat these not as meditations, but as though the *Meditations* were a logical document. In this way it is easy to refute Descartes, to consider philosophy as though it were a matter of logic rather than of understanding, and to give students practice in logical analysis. This makes everyone happy and disturbs no one. Professors and students can remain Cartesian without ever indulging in the sort of reflections which gave Descartes something new.

Spinoza, who wrote a book formulating Descartes' *Principles* geometrically, was onto something very like this, by the way. In a short preface to Part I of the Appendix of that book he wrote: "The end and object of this Part is to show that common Logic and Philosophy only serve to exercise and strengthen the memory; so that we retain well the things which, wandering upon us, are shown through the senses without order or connection and by which we can only be affected through the senses; but they do not serve to exercise the understanding."

There is, of course, logic in the *Meditations;* and Descartes was one of the leading mathematicians of his day, the inventor of analytic geometry. However, the *Meditations* are, particularly when taken together instead of piecemeal, primarily a paradigm of philosophical thinking. For their principal function is the resolution of doubt. They do not solve problems. They resolve doubts. Their function is exemplified in the Zen Buddhist koan: Before I studied Zen mountains were mountains and rivers were rivers; while I studied Zen mountains were not mountains and rivers were not rivers; when I finished studying Zen mountains were mountains and rivers were rivers. (The rest of the koan, the question, is: How does the first condition differ from the third?)

René Descartes was born into a Catholic family of wealthy landowners. He remained a practicing Catholic till his death. When he was three his mother died of consumption, the disease that carried BdS off. After consequently being indulged at home by his father, Descartes was sent to a college at La Fleche in Touraine. There he received the finest formal education possible in those days, at the hands of Jesuit fathers. He travelled thence to complete his education in Paris. Although this should have meant, for a young man in his station, learning the courtly life, Descartes spent the next two years consorting with mathematicians and Augustinian monks. Eventually finding Paris too distracting for the reflective life he had come to find necessary, he joined a Catholic army which was setting off to stamp out Protestantism in Bavaria. After a winter in that country, during which he spent much time meditating and in the course of which he seems to have had some crucial experience, he journeyed to Holland where he settled down for much of the rest of his life. It is important that, although Holland was then predominantly Protestant, Descartes always lived close enough to a Catholic church to be able to attend mass regularly.

The nature of the crucial experience in Bavaria is not certain. It may have been the discovery of analytic geometry. It is more likely that it was the beginning of the resolution of the doubts Descartes had come to feel as a child of his time. For, as he reveals in the First Meditation, he had come to doubt the basic grounds of all that he had been taught and of all that

[17]

which he had taken to be matters of the firmest belief. He had found, that is, that he had come to doubt whether he really existed, whether the world exists, and, perhaps worst of all, whether God exists. These are extremely fundamental doubts. For if neither God nor the world exist, all the rest of his beliefs concern nothing.

The reasons Descartes states for his doubts are three and straightforward. He is aware that his senses sometimes deceive him, as when a tower seen round at a distance turns out to be square. How does he know that his senses do not always deceive him? He is also aware that dreams can be as vivid as waking experiences. How does he know that he is not dreaming all the time? Finally, he has always supposed that he was created by God. How does he know that God did not so create him, that he is deceived, for example, into believing that $2 + 2 = 4$ when it really equals 5? Or, if you prefer not to think that God could deceive him, how does he, Descartes, know that he was not created by an evil genius who so made him that he is always deceived?

When we reflect on these reasons for doubting, noting first that each is a question, we find that they are in order of increasing depth: that the first leads into the second and the second into the third. The first enables Descartes to doubt *what* things he perceives are. (For example, Is the tower round or square?) The second enables him to doubt *that* things are. (If all his experience is a dream, then there are not mountains and he has no body.) However, the second question leaves certain very simple truths indubitable, for example, the truths of mathematics. The third question then puts these too in the sphere of the doubtful. We find, thus, as a result of these questions that there is nothing that Descartes cannot doubt. That there are mountains in China is, of course, to be doubted since there may be no China. And so on.

In the depths of his doubts, however, Descartes finds one thing that he cannot doubt. This is that he doubts. If he doubts that he doubts, he is nonetheless doubting. Doubting he takes to be a mode of thinking. Thus he comes to see in one stroke

[18]

lieve what they found when they turned to their own experience. (Visalius, the anatomist of their time, actually remarked in his notebooks as he turned from the authority of Galen to the actual human anatomy: I can scarcely believe my eyes.)

The second thing that Gebhardt did in preparing his edition was to restore a system of capitalization which is found in the Latin text of the ETHIC in the OP, but not in the Dutch of the NS. This system of capitalization was dropped in Bruder's edition of 1843–6, and it appears only in one translation of the ETHIC in any language (Charles Appuhn's French translation). The system did not appear in the Latin of any other of the items in the OP.

Capitalizing the initial letters of words was extremely haphazard in printing and publishing in the seventh century. However, in the Latin text of the ETHIC a system is carried out with great rigor. In the first place BdS used three names for God: "God" (*Deus*), "*Being*" (*Ens*), and "Nature" (*Natura*). These three words are almost invariably capitalized in the initial letter when they are used as synonyms. (It is an extraordinary fact that the Latin words are respectively of the masculine, neuter, and feminine genders. What we call "God" is, therefore, genderless for BdS. I have "*Being*" in italics to distinguish it from "being" which is used to translate the other participle of the Latin "to be," *essentia*.)

In the second place, two other words invariably have the initial letter capitalized when they are used adjectively *even though* they may be the subjects of sentences. These are "Mind" (*Mens*) and "Body" (*Corpus*). This occurs when they are used where we would ordinarily employ "mind" and "body" in referring to a human mind or a human body. They come to stand respectively, therefore, for "a human being mentally considered" and "a human being corporeally considered." When BdS is using "mind" and "body" in any other connection, the words are not capitalized, when, for example, he is referring to animals' minds or to physical bodies. He also uses the word "mind" in the sense of "meaning"; as when we ask, what was Descartes' mind here, intending to ask, what did Descartes

[51]

mean here. When that is its use, "mind" is not capitalized.

The significance of this device will become clearer as we proceed. It may be said briefly here that it was part of Sp's outlook to regard the human being as made up of a mental aspect and a physical aspect instead of being constituted by having a mind and a body. This was in keeping with his insight that there are not substances. There are consequently not minds and bodies. Wittgenstein once said that a great source of philosophic bewilderment is the tendency to look for a thing that corresponds to it whenever we have a substantive (i.e., a noun; *Blue Book,* p. 1). In the ETHIC this tendency was diminished by the device of capitalizing "Mind" and "Body."

In the third place all the names of Affections or emotions are capitalized in the ETHIC. Thus we find Anger, Love, Joy, Hate, etc. instead of anger, love, joy, hate, etc. The reason for this is Sp's view of the Affections. He does not regard anger, for example, as an emotion in the way we ordinarily think of emotions. For him it is a kind of activity or behavior. Thus, people behave angrily, lovingly, etc.

There is one other word in the ETHIC that is capitalized: "Individual" (*Individuum*). *Individuum* is the Latin word that corresponds to the Greek-rooted "atom." It means *an indivisible thing.* Greeks like Democritus regarded atoms as the ultimate building blocks of reality. BdS also took individuals to be the building blocks of reality. But he so defined "individual" that it referred to things that are *divisible.* He, so to speak, reversed the definition of the atom. Leibniz once wrote that BdS had "a strange metaphysic, full of paradoxes." This is one of them.

With the exception of capitalizing for proper names, we see from the foregoing that the capitalizing in the ETHIC generally serves the function of notifying the reader that the word in question is being used in an extraordinary way. It has its customary meaning, but its *use* is radically different from the ordinary one. This will be fully appreciated as you read the Appendix in the present volume.

There is some mystery about this system. As I came to appreciate its significance and power, my admiration for BdS leapt higher. Then I saw a letter in his own handwriting, thirteen of them in fact. (These letters are the only holographs by BdS that we have. There are no extant manuscripts of anything else he wrote.) Like most seventeenth-century manuscripts these are shoddy in the extreme in the matter of capitalization. Sentences are begun without capital letters. Proper names are often not capitalized. Sometimes they are. And so on. The chances were, then, that the manuscript followed for printing the ETHIC did not have the system in it. This inference gains weight from the fact that the words in question are not capitalized in the NS. That is to say, the manuscripts Glasemaker used to make his translations did not have the system. Furthermore, the printing of both the Latin and the Dutch versions were done by the same man: Rieuwerts. Surely he and the editors of the volumes would have agreed to put the system in both versions of the ETHIC. (Bear in mind that the EU, the TP, and the letters do not have it.)

My own guess is that Lodewijk Meijer was responsible for the system in the Latin text. This, of course, does not explain why it was not used in the Dutch, for it fits the thinking in whatever language it occurs with great philosophical accuracy (or something like it does—in German all nouns are capitalized). However, Meijer, besides his contacts with BdS and his circle, is better known in Dutch history as a literator. Orthography and lexicography were his specialties. (Copies of his signature show that he always insisted that his name was spelled "Meijer," when in Holland "ij" and "y'" were used indiscriminately.) Given the first-rate understanding that he shows of Sp's thinking in his Preface in *Descartes' Principles,* then, he could have been the author of the device. It is a natural for anyone who saw clearly what BdS was doing and who was interested in and sensitive to the appearances of words. Of course, BdS himself might have had marginal indications in his manuscript, though why in that case is the capitalizing not in the NS? He may have been the author of the device. In a way it does not matter. The thing is there in the first edition of the ETHIC, it makes superb sense, and it is too good to abandon.

CHAPTER 4

The Notion of Unity

All of Spinoza's thinking centers about the notion of unity and his life was one of atonement or at-one-ment. When his editors went through the correspondence he left, they apparently omitted for publication letters that would be of purely biographical interest. At least we have very few statements from his own hand which inform us directly about himself, though in Chapter 6 it will be found that many of the propositions about God may be read to be about BdS. Fortunately there is one, and it provides one of the many possible ways of expressing the notion of unity. It occurs in the opening four pages of the little unfinished essay on understanding. These pages are wholly autobiographical, the only such in all of BdS, and the expression of unity occurs at their end.

Having examined the three traditional goals that have been taken as the highest good by humankind: riches, fame or honor, and the satisfaction of our libidos, or basic drives, and having found from experience that they finally serve only to distract us, BdS expresses his view of the highest good. However he prefaces this by noting that "good" and "ill," and "perfect" and "imperfect" are said of things only relatively. That is, the same thing can be said to be good and ill under different circumstances. Thus music is good for him that is melancholy, ill for him that mourns, and neither good nor ill for him that is deaf. The same is true for "perfect" and "imperfect"; and no thing looked at in itself, without comparison with others, will be said to be perfect or imperfect, "especially as soon as we shall have known that all things that happen, happen according to an eternal order, and according to Nature's certain laws."

BdS is now ready for his statement about the highest good. Since in our weakness we do not attain to this eternal order in our thinking, we conceive a nature far firmer than our own. Then, seeing that there are no impediments to acquiring this nature, we seek means for arriving at such perfection. All these may be called "true goods." "The highest good however is to arrive" at such a nature so that we enjoy it "with other individuals, if it can be done." What exactly this nature is, says BdS, we shall show elsewhere. Briefly, "it is knowledge of the union, which the mind has with total Nature."

The notion of unity is expressed in other ways in the ETHIC. Before turning to these, let us have a general look at this work, which is 264 pages long and divided into five parts. Part I is on God; Part II on the nature and origin of Mind; Part III on the nature and origin of Affections (Joy, Sadness, etc.); Part IV is on Human Servitude, or the forces of Affections; and Part V is on the potency of Understanding, or Human Freedom. The whole is written in "the geometrical manner," occasionally also called "the mathematical manner." (See Preface.)

In the early days of writing the ETHIC and sending copies of it to friends, BdS was asked by one of them about the difference he made between definitions, axioms, eternal verities, postulates, and propositions. His reply is Letter 10. Generally he did not see substantial differences between them. That is to say, he did not use the terms as they are used by logicians and mathematicians today. As the latter usages developed, they gave rise to the view that the ETHIC is a deductive system. It is not.

Descartes and BdS thought that there are two ways of writing philosophy which *they* called the "analytic" and the "synthetic." The *Meditations* and the EU are examples of the former, the demonstration at the end of Descartes' Second Response and the ETHIC of the latter. Descartes found the synthetic way generally unsuitable for writing philosophy and used it only once. BdS seems to have disagreed, since he employed the synthetic way for one of his major works and treated Descartes' *Principles* in this way. And to my mind it does seem to be the better way for clarity and precision. It also serves well for cross-referencing. However, it will be noticed that over half the ETHIC is in the analytical style: the scholia, appendices, and prefaces.

While we are on the subject of their views on writing philosophy, mention should be made of another distinction Descartes and BdS employed in relation to writing and reading philosophy. (Note that these distinctions do not concern doing philosophy, or thinking philosophically.) They were of the opinion that a philosophical statement was either understood at the outset or at first, that is, *a priori* in the language in which they wrote; or it had to be understood later (after much talk), that is, *a posteriori* in their language. Some statements require such perspicuity to be understood at the outset that most of us have to have them, so to speak, unpacked, unfolded, or explicated. *God exists necessarily* is an example of such a statement. Hence the "proofs" or demonstrations of God's existence. They are all in the language of Descartes and BdS *a posteriori*. They are not, to put it otherwise, what we would call deductive proofs. The ETHIC may be regarded as follows: The scholia unfold the demonstrations, the demonstrations the propositions, and the propositions the definitions. (The axioms and postulates were also called "common notions," or propositions that were held in common belief by all people. A typical example of an axiom or common notion is: Bodies either move or are at rest. When you think about it, it comes to feel like a definition—of "body.") There is, then, no question of anything's being proved in the ETHIC. There is only the matter of understanding the definitions. On the whole this is the matter of getting clear about unity. We return to this notion.

There are two common misunderstandings of BdS. The first is that the basis and starting point of his thinking was Cartesian and that his philosophy is an attempt to solve the problems of dualism. The second is that Sp's conception of God differed radically from that in the Christian-Hebraic tradition. Of the

[56]

first it may be said that, although BdS couched his thinking in terms of the "new philosophy," it was not the starting point of his own. The misunderstanding may have arisen because it is also the case that the problems of dualism do not appear in Sp's work. This, we will see, is because they are typically human problems and not because they are peculiarly the result of Descartes' way of thinking.

The second misunderstanding arises from failure to take proper account of the influence of the Hebraic tradition on BdS, including the language of that tradition, and of BdS himself. If we can trust Lucas' biography of BdS, he was voicing views that express the germ of his philosophical work long before he read Descartes. These in turn led to his excommunication which was the occasion that resulted in a thorough examination of his tradition that finally produced the TTP, a book on which he worked longer and more assiduously than he did on the ETHIC. The starting point of Sp's thinking was the idea of God, the central idea of the tradition from which he came. Further, as we have observed, in his meditations with this idea BdS did not depart from it nor radically change *it*. He profoundly deepened his *understanding* of it. The God of BdS was the God of his fathers. Any change that he made was in himself. He so came to understand God that he, as we might say, experienced God. The expression of this experience, together with the life which it formed, occurs in statements about unity, for there is unification in the experience and the life. The experience of God is the experience of unity. Thus Sp's definition of "God" in the ETHIC is *Jehova*, that is, *"Being,"* with some modifications which signify his deeper understanding of God. Here is that definition (the reader is reminded that all the definitions and the propositions of the ETHIC are in the Appendix):

"By means of *God* I understand *Being* absolutely infinitely, that is, substance being established in infinite attributes, of which each expresses being eternally, & infinitely." In Sp's terms this runs: *Per* Deum *intelligo Ens absolute infinitum, hoc est, substantiam constantem infinitis attributis, quorum unumquodque aeternam, & infinitam essentiam exprimit.* Of the Latin terms only

[57]

one requires special notice at this point: *constantem* (being established). It is the present participle of the verb *consto*, which is formed from the verb *sto* (I stand) and the preposition *con*. It therefore differs only in the preposition from the verb for "I exist" which is *exsto* (*ex* and *sto*), and one of the definitions of *consto* is "exist." Thus, we might read in the definition of "God" that he is "substance existing in infinite attributes." *Consto* can also mean to become clear or manifest, so that we might think of God as becoming clear or made manifest in infinite attributes. Finally, BdS himself defines the verb in the *TTP* (p. 20, not in Elwes) as meaning "rising up."

Posed before our eyes now are two statements of the notion of unity: this definition, and that nature which is the knowledge of the union of the mind with total Nature. At first or at the outset they seem neither clear nor related to each other; much less equivalent, as they must be if each is a statement of the notion of unity. Furthermore, by this time you may be asking yourself, the notion of the unity of what? To reply, the unity of God, and to refer you to Letter 34 is an answer but an unhelpful one. Therefore, as a starter let us see how BdS proceeded in the ETHIC by first clarifying the notions of substance and attribute, the only two main new terms in the definition of "God." (*"Being"* for BdS is simply God's *proper* name.)

Definition 3 of Part I is: "By means of *substance* I understand that which is in itself, & is conceived by means of itself." This was a definition of the term current in Sp's day and was the one stated by Descartes in *Principles* I, 51: "By means of *substance* we can understand nothing other than a thing which so exists that it needs no other thing for existing." Definition 3 was the only definition of "substance" employed by BdS. Descartes, in contrast, always had in mind a second. This was a version of the common notion or axiom that no property or attribute is of nothing (see above p. 20): a substance is that to which properties or attributes are attached, or which is the agent of actions (the thing that does the running; again see p. 20). One of the ways of seeing the basic difference between BdS and

[58]

Descartes is by realizing that BdS abandoned this definition of "substance."

From Letter 2 of 1661 we know that in an early version of the ETHIC the present first four propositions were among the definitions and axioms. The present Prop. 5 was Prop. 1,* the first proposition of the ETHIC, and Pierre Bayle in his entry on Spinoza in his *Dictionary* took it as the central proposition in the work. It is difficult to get into English, and in various demonstrations and scholia in Part I it is stated in various ways. When the thing is finally reasonably clear, you appreciate the difficulty of stating it in any language. The most commonly accepted translation of Prop. 5 runs: "In the nature of things there cannot be given two, or plural substances of the same nature or attribute." A simpler version of the proposition occurs, for example, in the demonstration of Prop. 13: It is absurd that there be given plural substances of the same nature. "Plural" in both cases has its strict meaning of "more than one." It gradually becomes apparent that the proposition is difficult to state because it comes to abandoning the traditional notion of identity. Since this move is at the heart of Sp's thinking, I will consider it before turning to a demonstration of the proposition.

There is a very old principle that goes back to the time of the Stoics, the Epicureans, and the Greek Sceptics. Leibniz finally gave it a name: the principle of the identity of indiscernibles. It too can be stated in various ways: Two things cannot differ solely in number (*solo numero*). That is, given that a thing is a substance plus properties, two things cannot differ solely with respect to their substances. Why? Because we distinguish things on the basis of their properties. This is different from that because it is taller than that, etc. Thus, another version of the principle is if two things have indiscernibly different properties, they are identical; or, if two things have the same properties, they are the same thing (and hence not two). That, however, comes to saying that a thing is its properties; which, in turn,

---

* See Bibliography and Abbreviations.

[59]

amounts to saying that there are no substances,—only collections of properties.

Few philosophically minded individuals have been able to accept this, for it means that there are no identical things; that is, there is no such thing as identity. But this seems impossible, since we do believe that it was (the same) Socrates that talked day after day in the market place. Simply because his properties changed daily does not mean that there was a different man there day after day. No, his properties changed, he grew older, weaker, wiser, etc., but *he* did not change. That is, his substance did not change. The belief that there are substances seems or is logically required for the notion of identity. Prop. 5 is a version of the principle of the identity of indiscernibles. BdS accepted it, and all of the consequences of accepting it, which, as we shall find, are both numerous and paradoxical.

At the risk of repetition but in the interest of clarity the foregoing will be restated. The traditional notion of identity is that a thing has an identity when there is something in or about it so that we can say absolutely or without qualification that it is the same thing today that it was yesterday. I am speaking of identity in its sense in the dictionary (the state of being identical or absolutely the same), not any particular notion of identity held by some philosopher. If we regard a thing as composed of a substance which does not change, to which properties which may and do change somehow adhere, we can understand a thing's identity. Consider again the example of Socrates: It is the same or identical Socrates day after day because, although his properties change, his substance does not. In Prop. 5 BdS is abandoning this notion of identity because he is saying in effect that there are not substances. So-called "things," therefore, are just collections of properties.

The principle of the identity of indiscernibles (and, therefore, Prop. 5) comes to stating that no thing is ever identical with another. For if two things have the same properties, that is, are identical, we could not distinguish between them because we distinguish things by differences in properties. That is, according to the principle a thing is simply a collection of change-able properties (it has no substance).

There is, however, a double aspect to the principle. It involves seeing that if it be accepted, no thing is identical with any other thing, and no thing is identical with itself, that is, has an identity. It is primarily with the second aspect that we are concerned when we say that Prop. 5, in saying in effect that there are not substances (in the plural), comes to abandoning the traditional or definitional notion of identity. However, this also involves the first aspect. There cannot be plural identical substances. Thus of any one thing it cannot be the case that it retains its identity or sameness over a period of time (that is, it has no identity). Nor are there any plural identical things. (We can allow that there may be plural identical things in a weak or relative sense of "identity," such as strong resemblance.) This in turn comes to realizing, or trying to, that each thing is unique, *and that all things are constantly changing.* Indeed, to see each thing as unique is to see all things as constantly changing. The two insights come to the same thing (that is the relative sense of "same," for their expressions are clearly different).

Lest this seem impossible, let me say that we can *think* that a thing has an identity. For practical purposes we can *assign* an identity, as we do with proper names. Or we can take some property which changes imperceptibly and treat it as constituting a thing's identity (as we do with fingerprints). You can, that is, take it that BdS is changing our *minds,* not saying something new about reality. Try to see that we can think of a thing's having an identity; but we can also think of it as constantly changing, i.e., as not having one. In practice it is useful to be able to establish an identity when cashing a check. In fact it is part of that process. However, it is often apt to lose one's identity, or to identify with someone else, as in loving: to become one with that other. One unfolding of Prop. 5, then, reveals that it is an expression of an acceptance of the reality of change.

What BdS called the "demonstration" of Prop. 5 is a further unfolding or explication of it. He also explicated it in Scholium

2 of Prop. 8, for it is enormously difficult to understand; and in Prop. 11, the proposition which states that God exists necessarily and which in turn has its own three "demonstrations." He also demonstrated it in a single sentence in Letter 12 and unfolded it at some length in Letter 34. There is also a demonstration in *Descartes' Principles* in P. I, Prop. 11 (plural Gods are not given).

This last is close to a demonstration I will now give, but my demonstration as such does not occur in BdS. Prop. 5 states in effect that two or plural (i.e., more than one) substances cannot be given. From the definition of "substance" (see above p. 58 or the Appendix) it follows that a substance has independent existence; that is, a substance does not depend on anything else for its existence (as, for example, properties do). This is clear in Descartes' version (p. 58), but BdS makes it clear in the second half of his definition (only the first half was given): a substance is that "a conceiving of which does not need conceiving another thing."

Now, suppose that there were two substances, call them "A" and "B." It is impossible to conceive A without conceiving B, for one of the things we mean by "A" is that it is not B. Similarly for B, "B" in part means something that is not A. Thus the supposition that there can be two substances, or more than one, leads to an absurdity (which, namely the *reductio ad absurdum,* was Sp's favorite mode of demonstration). Therefore, two or plural substances cannot be given. This is equivalent to (for our purposes) there are not substances, i.e., in the plural.

In Schol., Prop. 36, P. V BdS says that all these things can be demonstrated beyond reasonable doubt, but demonstration does not affect the mind with the force that experiencing a thing does. The demonstration of Prop. 5 surely admits of no doubt. It is a logical consequence of the definition of "substance" that there cannot be more than one substance. Indeed, the definition seems to be equivalent to saying that substance is unique. Let us consider an aspect of that last statement, as BdS does in Letter 50.

Saying that there are not plural substances or that there is not more than one is not equivalent to saying that there is only one or that there is one substance. This may be seen by considering the other version of "there are not plural substances": namely, "there are not substances." For if there were one, it would be true that there are substances, but as it happens only one. Thus BdS says in Letter 50 that either he does not understand God or he speaks of him improperly who says that God is one or unique (remember that God is defined as substance). To say that there is one or only one substance, therefore, is either to speak improperly or to fail to understand the idea of substance.

For this reason BdS cannot, except improperly or without understanding him, be called a monist. Hobbes is a monist. He said that all is made of matter. Hegel is a monist: All is mind, or everything is spiritual. But beyond saying that God is *Being*, BdS attributes no properties to him. Regard Def. 6 above or in Appendix. BdS agrees that there are certain things that we can properly say of God, for example, that he is eternally (again see Def. 6, as well as pp. 68 ff. for use of the adverb), but is of the view (see below) that we only improperly or without understanding attribute properties to God. For this reason a term we get from Buddhism is advisable if we wish to label BdS: He is a non-dualist. Some who have realized this have felt that "non-pluralist" is perhaps more apt. However, strictly it is the case that "plural" means more than one, i.e., two, so that "non-dualist" is the more correct label. It is not multiplicity or large numbers that are involved. Only the question of there being more than one is.

These considerations may prepare us for realizing what is further involved in Prop. 5. One thing is that substance exists necessarily, which is Prop. 7 (Prop. 6 is that one substance cannot produce another, which also clearly follows from the very definition of "substance"). That is, when we are talking of substance we are talking of that which exists. BdS exhibits a way of seeing this in Letter 12 (p. 54; 116 in Wolf). It is that "substance" and "existence" are verbally the same though prepositionally different. That is, "stance" stems from the Latin verb *sto* and so does "stence." The two words differ only in prepositions entering into their makeup: *sub* and *ex*.

[63]

However, since God is defined as substance, an understanding of Prop. 5 involves seeing that God exists necessarily, which is Prop. 11. If you persist in thinking of God as *a* being (who, for example, created the world or has the property of having done so), this will not be at all clear. If, on the other hand, you can think of God or substance as *what is,* or *Being* (to use a single word rather than a phrase), it will be somewhat clearer than it may have been before you do this. However, it will still not be very clear. Even if, unlike Descartes, you have not been raised as a Catholic, the idea of God as *a* being is in all the literature you have read and it is in your language. Consider the atheist who once said, "I'm an atheist, thank God." The thing is extremely hard to get clear on. For example, readers of the ETHIC have felt that Props. 1 through 8 clarify the concept of substance, Props. 9 and 10 that of attribute, and Prop. 11 with its demonstration proves the existence of God. Whereas in fact, or at least as I am suggesting, Prop. 5 and Prop. 11 are simply different versions of the same—what, "proposition?" or *insight.*

An early way of conveying this insight that BdS employed was to distinguish between "being" and "existing." In fact he employed this means in *Descartes' Principles,* but he tells us in Letter 34 that he had to abandon it. Descartes also employed the distinction in Meditation V, except that in existing translations it comes out as the distinction between "essence" and "existence" (the Latin terms are *essentia* and *existentia*). The distinction is that between the verbs "to be" (*esse*) and "to exist" (*existere*). The idea is that to exist properly applies to particular things. It is used improperly with "God." As BdS remarks in Schol. 2, Prop. 8, great confusion arises when God is confused with particular things. Thus the question whether God exists is, strictly speaking, an improper question. If we do use "exist" with "God," BdS figured, we should qualify it; and he does, for example in Prop. 11, which says that God exists necessarily. No particular thing exists necessarily. Since God is *Being,* of course he *is.* He is what is, and to wonder whether he is (exists) is at best very odd.

BdS found himself forced to abandon this means of explicating his insight. A reason why is the reason why it does not work.
In virtually all the Indo-European languages the verb "is" is
fatally ambiguous between "to be" and "to exist." Curiously,
BdS himself revealed this when he translated *Jehova* in the TTP
(see above p. 6). He rendered it with the phrase "to be existing"
(in the Latin the word *existendi;* p. 38 in Gebhardt; 36 in Elwes,
who has "existence").

We must now pause to be scholarly as well as, I trust,
philosophical. The Latin verb for "to be" is *esse.* From it are
formed the present participles *essentia* and *ens,* and the gerund
essendi (though the latter does not occur in classical Latin. It
became a tool of the Churchmen.). *Essentia* has almost universally been rendered into English with "essence" and *ens* with
"being," the present participle of "to be." In fact, of course,
"essence" is not a translation of *essentia.* It is a transliteration.
That is, it is the Latin word Englished. As a translation it is all
right when "essence" is taken to mean being. However it has
rarely been so taken. Far more often it is taken to mean something like the connotation of a class-name. Thus, for example,
the essence of man is that he is rational (and see pp. 2–3 above
where this use occurs).

The amount of philosophical confusion that centers about
the translation of *essentia* simply cannot be overestimated. Nor
is this the place to go into that. I bring the matter up to point
out that wherever in English translations of BdS you come
across the word "essence" you should substitute "being" for it.
Enormous amounts of confusion will thereby dissolve. The active character of Sp's thinking will become more apparent. And
you will be surprised what this will do for your own thinking.
Since *essentia* is translated "being," it is fitting to translate *existentia* by "existing" rather than by "existence." This looks odd initially, but it gets one away from thinking that existence is something God has instead of something he does, or better, is.

Although this is not the place to discuss the confusion about
"essence," I will say that one cause of it is the Aristotelian view
of things according to which a thing is a substance plus

properties. With this view people went on to believe that some one, or a few of all its properties made a thing what it is. The rest were accidental. Thus, being rational makes a human animal what it is. That any human animal is five feet ten inches tall rather than six feet is an accident in the sense that it is not necessary for that animal to be what it is, namely a rational one. Thus, the distinction was made between necessary properties and accidents. The necessary property became the defining property of the thing, that is, was taken to constitute its very being. Hence *essentia* became "essence" or the word that refers to a thing's essential being as distinct from its accidental being. Then to have the essence of a thing become confused with its definition was an easy step, for we are prone to confuse words or ideas with things. I point this out because a feature of Sp's thinking is that he came to abandon the distinction between necessary and accidental properties. For him *all* of a thing's properties, including the temporal, are necessary for it to be what it is. Change one of them and you change the thing. As you see, identity once again comes into the picture.

That *all* a thing's properties are necessary for it to be what it is, is probably the main aspect of what has been called Sp's "determinism" (all things happen of necessity). When this determinism is understood, it is a far cry from what is ordinarily regarded as determinism. All that it amounts to is: Change one of a things properties and you change the thing. As I said, identity is again involved but now in a manner that includes, almost paradoxically, great emphasis on individuality. A given woman is not merely a woman. She is *this* woman, differing in all these enormously varied ways from that woman. Every single thing about her, every property, no matter how seemingly insignificant, distinguishes her from the other. To know her, then, is to overlook nothing about her.

We have now observed that what BdS calls God's unity, that is, to speak improperly, his uniqueness is equivalent to his existing necessarily. Or, to see that he *is* is the same as to see that he is uniquely; that is to say in terms of Proposition 5 that there are not plural substances. Speaking improperly, there is only one substance. An immediate consequence of this is that it implies that the mind and the body about which Descartes talked cannot be substances, in common parlance: things. If mind and body are substances, there would be more than one substance, which, as we have now seen, is absurd.

BdS faces this issue in Prop. 14: "Besides God no substance can be given nor be conceived," and its corollaries. Corollary 1 reads: God is uniquely, that is, in the nature of things only one substance is given, and it is absolutely infinitely. Corollary 2 is: The extended thing and the thinking thing are either God's attributes, or affections of the attributes of God. Talking simply about a human being, this is to say that the so-called "mind" and the so-called "body" are not separate things by which that human being is constituted. They are two distinct attributes of that human being. That is, "mind" and "body" are aspects of the same thing. In the terminology of the ETHIC, Mind and Body are attributes of the same thing. We examine this important notion of attribute in the next chapter. I will only say here that with it we have another facet of the notion of unity: So-called "mind" and "body" are one and the same thing looked at in different ways. A human being is not two things, but one with different attributes.

Before leaving the notion of unity I want to describe it in one other way. Before doing that, however, I want to note that we are referring to it as the *notion* of unity. Why not the *idea* of unity? Because BdS had a special use for the word "idea," namely for referring to something very clear. This in turn is related to a way of knowing or being conscious which none of his immediate predecessors discussed as a way of knowing. We shall talk about it and as we do you will feel much better about the notion of unity. I wanted to interject this here so that readers will be aware that I am aware that they will feel dissatisfaction with this chapter. It all seems so verbal. There is an air of sleight of hand about it, which can be cleared by some realization of this other way of knowing (concerning which there is a hint three paragraphs back, on determinism).

Descartes in his "new philosophy" departed from the Aristotelianism in the schools. BdS with his insight into unity departed completely from the Aristotelianism in all Western peoples' minds. This Aristotelianism is reflected in our language, and consequently in our speech and thoughts. I refer to a character of the subject-predicate structure of our grammar. We talk in sentences, or at least our grammar has it that we do, and our sentences consist of a subject plus a predicate. The latter is either a simple verb (e.g., in "Paul runs") or it is a form of the verb "to be" used as a copula to link an adjective to the noun which is the subject of the sentence ("Paul is tall").

We tend to assume that this linguistic structure reflects or represents the structure of the world. In the latter, we think, are things which perform actions and/or have properties. These things are the substances which satisfy the second definition of "substance" Descartes employed (see above pp. 20 and 58). Because of the first definition, which was the one that BdS used (that a substance is an independent thing), we also tend to think that the things have relations to each other but they somehow always remain distinct from each other. The tendency to think this seems to be supported by our experience. A man and a woman get married, but they remain two human beings (and it surprises us to find that the long-married begin to "read each other's thoughts").

Spinoza's insight into unity is in effect a requirement that we see our grammar differently, and with that our experience. The required difference can be stated quite baldly and simply. That is, the verb "to be" should never be used as a copula. Or, when speaking either properly or philosophically (that is, with understanding), it should never be used as a copula. When speaking philosophically or properly, the verb "to be" should always be used as an active verb. Thus, for example, in Corollary 1 of Prop. 14 (p. 67 above or Appendix) we properly read: God is uniquely, not that God is unique; and that the one substance "is absolutely infinitely," not that it is infinite. The adverbs rather than the adjectives indicate that the verb, "is," is active (properly: is actively).

Taking a more concrete example, we should say that a given

table is brownly rather than that it is brown. The table's mode of *being* is brown; still better, its being is brownly. Ah, ah, ah, you may say, that last "is" is (sic) a copula. Very well, I may be speaking improperly, but you get the idea. Furthermore, there are times when speaking improperly is perfectly all right (you may have noticed that BdS himself did in Corollary 1: "Only one substance is given"). I have said that, speaking properly or *philosophically,* the verb "to be" should always be an active verb and never a copula. Usage of it as a copula is related to Descartes' second definition of "substance" (that which properties are of). That definition has been of great service in the development of science; indeed it was at the foundation of that development, though we may now be at a point in science when it can be abandoned. In the scientific context BdS himself used the definition: to indicate that there is no vacuum (see Letter 13, p. 64; 126 in Wolf: the impossibility of a vacuum clearly follows from the fact that no properties are of nothing—in Wolf, nothing has no properties). [Note that this paragraph is related to that other way of being aware mentioned four paragraphs back. The scientific is the common way, the philosophical (i.e., with understanding) the other.]

Properly the verb "to be" should not be a copula (and in speaking with understanding is not) because that supposes that things are substances which have properties. Therefore, they can be related to each other, and their properties can be related to them. Given the view that there are not substances, the function of "to be" changes. So does the notion of a property, for "property" has been defined in terms of "substance." (In fact, it gradually becomes apparent as one reads BdS that all our philosophical terminology either gets redefined or re-used. We have already seen this with "mind.") A whole new way of looking at "things" begins to unfold.

BdS helped with this explication by taking over the term "mode" (*modus*) which was coming into current use at that time. (He was faced continually with the problem that, to express himself, he had to use the language of his day while at the same time adapting it to his insight. See the Explication of Def. 20 in the Definitions of the Affections in P. III.) "Mode" is defined in Def. 4 of P. I as "a substance's affections, or that which is in another, by means of which also it is conceived." You will recall that a substance is that which is in itself. Now we have it that a mode is always in another (mode or substance) and that it is an affection of substance, or something that is happening to substance. Since all things which are, are either in themselves or in another (Axiom 1 and note that both "are's" are active), all that is, is either a substance or a mode. Since there is not more than one substance, all that is, is substance and its modes or affections of it (Prop. 4). Finally, since substance is *Being* (Def. 6: God is *Being* or substance), another way of putting this is: All that is, is *Being* and modes of *Being*.

"*Being*" is only grammatically different from "being," so we may speak of modes of being. For BdS and in this new view of things, what are commonly called "things" are referred to as modes of being. I am a mode of being, you are a mode of being, BdS was a mode of being. What we commonly call a "tree" is an arboreal mode of being, that is, an arboreal being (remember that that last word is active). And so a ship is a navicular being. With this new terminology we come to feel the oneness of all things. The notion of unity becomes more like an idea of unity. It becomes a part of our being in a way that it has not been.

Then we realize that loving and knowing are also modes of being. There are not, as we commonly think, things or people that love and know. Or, if we want to look at it that way, we can also see that there are lovings and knowings. We have thought that a loving is simply an action, something that some thing does. Now we see that that thing becomes or can itself be seen as an action. The so-called "knower" and "known" become a knowing. This, too, is part of the insight into unity (which, as we are also seeing, is an insight in *Being*). The Aristotelian view has it that reality is the static and unchanging beneath the changing appearances. With BdS we see the distinction between reality and appearances dissolving. Reality is what changes (again the accustomed notion of identity is threatened). Linguistically speaking, all becomes adjectival or adverbial. Nouns or substantives come to seem queer. Or rather, we find that there is only one true substantive: *Being,* and its variations God and Nature; and as the proper name indicates, even what it names is not substantial.

In the Preface I said that I would make suggestions for assistance in reading current translations of BdS. We have noted that, where "essence" occurs in them, "being" should occur. Now we note that, where adjectives are used to modify "God," "*Being,*" or "Nature," they should be changed to adverbs. In "God is uniquely" (p. 68) the Latin is *"Deum esse unicum." Unicum* is an adjective, but I render it with the adverb. In Latin the accusative case is often used adverbially, so there is even grammatical precedence for this. However, BdS also used the nominative case this way, that is, as an adverb (the careful reader may consult, for example, Prop. 8 and its demonstration). Even without grammatical justification, however, the thinking or philosophy involved requires the adverb instead of the adjective. Without the adverb we do not understand BdS. What is more important, we do not depart from or in any way change our conventional way of thinking. Reading BdS then becomes an exercise in memory and imagination instead of one in understanding.

CHAPTER 5

The Attributes

Of all the notions that are novelly used by BdS, the one that has possibly caused the most difficulty and is the most important is that of an attribute. Here again he had to take a term in current use with a meaning suggestive of that which he wished to accomplish with it and attempt to provide a new use for it. The new use derives from the old, but, as is true of all the terms BdS used, the old use can subtly prevent accomplishment by the new. Throughout the correspondence until almost its very end, the notion of an attribute proved a stumbling block to even such an acute writer as the mathematician Tschirnhaus (see, for example, Letter 70). Since then through the years the same has been the case, to the extent that phrases involving the word *attributum* have been seriously mistranslated. The notion is absolutely essential to understanding non-dualism.

Descartes used the word more technically than others had in his new philosophy. He used "attribute" to refer to the essential characteristic of a substance in the sense of "substance" as "an independent thing." He was also of the view that substances had only one attribute. The attribute of minds was thinking and the attribute of matter was extension (see *Principles* I, 53).

As soon as BdS understood this concept of substance and realized that there are not substances, the concept being, like that of God, one of those rare ones that dissolves, when you get the idea, he was confronted with the question: How then to talk about minds and bodies? Certainly thinking and extension seem quite different. Furthermore, people have been aware of things somewhat similar to the difference for a long time, though they may have talked about them in different ways. Plato was close to the distinction when he demonstrated that we think of strength though we never see it (see above p. 19), and he talked about something like it as the distinction between Forms or Ideas and individual things. Aristotle spoke of the distinction between form and matter. In the Middle Ages there was the distinction between the spirit and the flesh.

Sp's answer to the question came in the form of the notion of an attribute. Instead of regarding mind and body as substances, he came to see them as attributes. That is to say, instead of regarding them as independently existing things, he came to see them as rather like aspects of things. Descartes had said that, although we ever only perceive the properties of things and never their substance, we know that where there are properties or attributes there must be a substance because it is a common notion that no property is of nothing (*Principles* I, 52). He went on: "And certainly a substance is known by any attribute whatever; but nevertheless there is one principal property of each substance, which constitutes its nature or being" (I, 53). You will observe that Descartes used "attribute" and "property" indiscriminately. BdS selected "attribute" from the pair and, using Descartes' definition, gave it a subtle twist, thereby introducing a quite new notion based on an older one. Def. 4 of P. I of the ETHIC is: "By means of *attribute* I understand that which an understanding perceives concerning a substance, as if constituting its being." The subtle twist lies in the phrase "as if." Otherwise the definition is nearly the same as Descartes'. It is characteristic of Sp's thinking that it only departed from the thinking that had already been done in the sense that it deepened it by clarifying it.

In the notion of an attribute, the clarification occurs mainly in relation to the notion of substance. We see from Descartes' Principle 52 an essential peculiarity in the notion of substance, as he and most of us think of it. The peculiarity is that, as substance is defined in that principle, it is admittedly something that we never perceive. We see its properties but never it. Believing that there are substances, then, is what is today called a logical requirement. As Descartes put it, we know that there must be substances because of the common notion that a property must be a property *of* something.

It might also be said that the belief in substances is a grammatical requirement. In every sentence there is a subject as well as a verb or a verb and a predicate. The subject-word must refer to something, even as the verb and predicate do. You cannot think of running without a runner because you cannot say, for example, "Paul runs" without "Paul," otherwise the notion of substance expressed in Principle 52 is unnecessary. The clarification introduced by Sp's notion of an attribute consists in abandoning the otherwise unnecessary notion of substance.

(I remark parenthetically that I have just said "consists in" rather than "consists of," because it sharpens what I am saying and bears on the definition of "God" and "attribute." "Consists in" is an obsolete usage in which "consist" means the same as "exist." In Elwes' translation of the ETHIC, the most widely used of the English translations, the definition of "God" runs: . . . "a substance consisting in infinite attributes." Compare this with the definition on pp. 57–58 above. That is, Elwes has it that God exists in infinite attributes, not that he consists of infinite attributes as though they were properties. Elwes' usage, though now obsolete, was accurate. So too I am not saying that the clarification consists *of* abandoning the notion of substance, but exists or is in abandoning it.)

We have already realized with the notion of unity that there are not *substances*. Indeed, it may be said that the idea of unity occurs with the realization that reality is substanceless. Now we see that the belief in substances or that there are substances has in part been a requirement of thinking (a logical one) or of grammar. It is, of course, required for many other reasons; for example, as we have noted, by the notion of identity—and we may now add by the sense of personal identity, which we all feel very strongly in some form or other. But the belief is at least a grammatical requirement. BdS dealt with this by seeing that we could treat "mind" and "body" as adjectives or adjectivally or attributively instead of as nouns or substantively. Instead, then, of thinking that these words refer to substances or things, let us regard them as referring to some one thing in different ways. But let us nonetheless allow them to function as subjects of sentences. So at the end of Letter 9 BdS says: "I understand by means of *substance* that which is in itself [etc., he states Def. 3 of the ETHIC]. I understand the same by means of *attribute,* except that it [substance] is called *attribute* with respect to an understanding, when it is attributing such and such a nature to substance."

In the letter the quotation is in italics. BdS wished to emphasize that attribute-words ("mind," "body") refer to the same thing that substance-words (*"Being,"* "God," "Nature") do, but they have a different use, or we might say, a different meaning. There is little doubt in my mind that BdS came to this marvellous linguistic device partly as a result of his philological and philosophical study of the Hebrew language. However, we need not wonder about the source of the device. It is the device that counts. In the scholium to Prop. 10 BdS tells us what it enables us to do, namely, to think of two things as really distinct without at the same time thinking that they refer to two *beings* or two different substances. (His exact words are: "From these things it is apparent that, although two attributes are conceived as really distinct, that is, one without the help of the other, we cannot nevertheless conclude thence that they constitute two beings, or two diverse substances.") It may be repeated here that Props. 1 to 8, P. I explicate the notion of substance, and Props. 9 and 10 that of attribute. The point of Prop. 9, by the way, is that, unlike Descartes, BdS is so thinking of an attribute that substance can have more than one (i.e., plural) attributes. Descartes had said that a substance has only one.

In the first edition of the ETHIC the linguistic device of the attribute was made a part of the printing by the additional device of capitalizing the initial letters of the attribute-words when they are used in relation to human beings (see pp. 51–2 above). Thus, *Mens* and *Corpus* appear where in later editions, except Gebhardt's of 1925, *mens* and *corpus* appear. Readers can become well acquainted with both it and the notion of an attribute by introducing the capital letters in their own copy of the ETHIC. You will find that great care must be taken with this, for "body" as it is used for all bodies except a human Body should not be capitalized, and BdS often used "mind" in the sense of "meaning." (The first three chapters of the TTP are helpful with Sp's use of "mind.")

We have now to notice that BdS defined an attribute by saying that it is that which an understanding perceives concerning a substance *as if* constituting its being. In translations of the ETHIC that I know this always comes out: as constituting its essence. Not only is the confusing word "essence" used, the Latin adverb *tanquam* (which can mean either "as" or "as if") is mistreated. This mistreatment is probably due in part to mistaking what BdS means by "attribute" for what is conventionally meant by "property." It is also due to failure to realize that beyond saying that God is *Being* we can, strictly, say nothing about *what* he is. As Descartes defined "attribute" we can say that extension is the attribute of matter and thinking that of mind. As BdS defines the word, we can only say that it is as if God were a thinking Being. That is to say, we can talk about things this way, or we can talk about them as if they were extended. Furthermore, we do talk and think this way. But these are mere modes of speaking and thinking. In other words, we are not saying *what* God is when we attribute thinking or extension to him.

All the foregoing is abstract and technical. Let us notice for a moment what the notion of attribute does for us in thinking and talking about human beings. Principally and simply it enables us to think about them in a unified way—a way, incidentally, that fits our view of them when we are not thinking philosophically about them. Thus it enables us to think of them as individuals which think, and do physical things. That is, we do not ordinarily see them as made up of minds and bodies, but as individuals who behave in two characteristically different ways, the ways that we call the mental and the physical. In other words the notion of an attribute enables us to think philosophically about people as we ordinarily think about them. It brings our philosophical thinking into line with our everyday thinking. In this way too the notion of an attribute is related to that of unity.

With the non-dualism that the notion of an attribute makes possible, we come to understand what is meant by means of "the union of the Mind and the Body"—a point that BdS makes in the scholium to Prop. 13, P. II of the ETHIC. As long as the mind and the body are thought of as substances, that is, as substantially distinct from each other, this unity is incomprehensible. In the Preface to P. V Sp discusses this with specific reference to Descartes' attempt to understand the union through the device of the pineal gland in the brain (the mind affects the body through this gland, Descartes said, and vice versa the body the mind). BdS covertly scoffs at this attempt because of its manifest absurdity: The pineal gland is material, so that it provides no understanding of the union of the material and the mental which is so obvious a fact of experience. When the so-called "mind" and "body," however, are thought of as attributes of the same thing their union is understood because their dis-union is thereby dissolved.—The reader may turn here to the EU, p. 11 (9 in Elwes), where in the second footnote BdS explains how people have mistakenly come to misunderstand the union. Remember, however, to turn "essence" into "being" if you look this up in Elwes. However, much of the note is reproduced below.

You may be tempted to say that the notion of the attribute gives me no *positive* understanding of the union. However, room is made for understanding by removal of misunderstandings. Feelings of dissatisfaction with Sp's remark in the scholium to Prop. 13 are largely due to the lurking preconceptions of dualism. One wants still to understand the union in *terms* of *mind* and *body*. One scarcely notices that little if any question about it arises when we think in terms of the mental and the physical. Nevertheless, there is a far greater blockage in the way of understanding the union. It was there with under-

[77]

standing the notion of unity, but it becomes much clearer with the notion of an attribute. I am speaking here of a logical difficulty. There is not much we can do in a book about the psychological difficulties, such as the sense of identity in each of us.

In Def. 6, of God, BdS says that God is substance which is established or exists in infinite attributes. In Prop. 14 and its corollaries we realize that these are the attributes of thinking and extension (see p. 67 above). In Prop. 4 we find that all that there is, is substance and its modes, which are affections of it. It becomes clear, then, that every mode of being is expressed in these attributes. That is to say, as BdS does in the scholium to Prop. 13, P. II, *all things in Nature are of the mental as well as of the physical attribute.* In his words: "For the things, which we have shown up to now, are quite common, and pertain no more to human beings than to the remaining Individuals, all of which, although in diverse degrees, are nevertheless animate."

The things that BdS has shown "up to now" in P. II are mainly that neither attribute can exist without the other (Prop. 8) and that a human Mind is the form or idea of the human Body (Props. 11 through 13); put slightly differently: the object of the idea which constitutes the human Mind is the human Body. However, a consequence of the notion of attribute is that *all things are mental* as well as physical, and we see by this means something else that is involved in the notion of unity. We human beings are at one with all things in that all that is, is alive. Unity was with us in the mythopoeic age. We simply were only very vaguely conscious of it. Put the other way around, BdS has brought to consciousness something that was in the being of our ancestors, though it was little of their mental being.

Grand as this conception is, and however much it further unfolds the notion of unity (the union of Mind and total Nature), it confronts us with a paradox: It makes the inanimate animate. In effect BdS seems to be telling us that things like stones have "minds." We find that we may grant that animals are in some sense rational or can think. We may even grant the same for plants in the respect that they can feel. But it seems impossible that a stone can feel, or think in any way whatever.

The resolution of this paradox is the subject of the first thirteen propositions of Part II of the ETHIC, which concern the attribute of thinking, first generally and then specifically for human beings. The chief clue to resolving the paradox is the key term used in speaking of the mental: "idea." When you look this word up in a dictionary of Latin, you are either likely not to find it or you find a disappointingly short definition: " = idea [in the Greek alphabet], a (Platonic) idea, archetype." (Speakers of Latin used "notion," "image," "thought," "conception," etc. for mental units.) Turning to a Greek dictionary for "idea" you have: form; generally the look or appearance of a thing. We used the word in this sense in Chapter 1 when we spoke of Plato's Ideas or Forms. BdS was able to understand that stones "have" ideas by thinking of the root-meaning of the key mental term (see Def. 3, P. II in the Appendix). Nowadays, except when talking about Plato, we think that the word refers to a psychological unit. BdS went into the matter more deeply. Then, of course, he saw that all things have a form, which is to say, using the root-meaning of "idea," that all things have an idea.

In the scholium to Prop. 13 BdS says that all Individuals are animate *"though in diverse degrees"* (emphasis added). The proposition states that the object of the idea constituting a human Mind is the Body (I paraphrase; the proposition can be consulted in the Appendix). That is, the object of the idea which is a Mind of a human being is that being's Body. Given what has been said of "idea," this comes to: The form of a human Body is that Body's Mind. By extension, the "mind" of a stone, say, is the stone's form. Roughly, it is that by which that stone is distinguished from other pieces of matter, including other stones, for we are not thinking of defining properties here. But the stone's mind is vastly simpler than a human being's. A stone is animate to a far less degree than is a human being. Plants and animals (as the latter word *shows*) are also animate; less so than human beings and more so than so-called inanimate modes of being like stones. Thus all Individuals in *Being* are animate, that

[79]

is, are formed, have a form, or have a mental or thinking aspect, as we might now use these terms because of what we have seen in the term "idea."

I said that a chief *clue* to the paradox that the inanimate is animate lies in the term "idea." Reflection on the word does not fully resolve the problem. BdS was fully aware that helping readers to understand this consequence of the notion of unity was an almost insuperable task. In the first thirteen propositions of P. II he either admonishes the reader or confesses inadequacy no less than four times, things that occur nowhere else in the ETHIC. Thus, in the scholium to Prop. 3 he says: "I only ask the reader again and again to perpend once, and again the things that have been said in the first part from Prop. 16 to the end concerning this thing" (that in God there is an idea of his being as well as of all things; i.e., the attribute of thinking is infinite, it is expressed in all things). In Chapter 6 we will look at Prop. 16 to the end of P. I and see that BdS tells us there how we have to be, or the way we must look at things if we are to understand unity and the consequence that the inanimate is animate.

In the scholium to Prop. 7 BdS says at the end: "and for the present I can not explicate this more clearly." (That is, Prop. 7 that order and connection of ideas is the same as order and connection of things. See Letters 17, 70, and 72. It is likely that this scholium was added to Prop. 7 after Letters 70 and 72.) In the Scholium to Prop. 8 there is another confession: If anyone wants an example to illustrate this I shall "be able to give none which would adequately explicate [it], in as much as it is unique" (namely, that thinking cannot exist without extension, Prop. 8 and its Corollary). And finally the scholium to Prop. 11 is entirely an admonition and a most important one. Without doubt, says BdS, readers "will stick fast here" and think of many things that will cause delay. "I ask them for this cause to continue slowly and gradually with me, and not to bear judgment concerning these things until they have read everything through."

This admonition is vitally important because the whole

ETHIC is about the notion of unity, not simply Part I. We think that BdS is describing a system of the world, and try to imagine that system. But he is developing an insight. Thus, we look at the titles of the five parts and think that P. II is about the human Mind and that we are finished with that topic when we turn to the Affections, Slavery, and Freedom (Parts III, IV, and V). But this is dualistic thinking. The full explanation of knowing, for example, a topic of Prop. 40 to the end of P. II, is not realized till the last twenty propositions of P. V, which deal with a way of knowing that is only sketched in P. II: knowing intuitively. So accustomed are we to dividing things into neat compartments (the body, the mind, for example) that we are baffled when we encounter things non-dualistically as we are in the ETHIC.

We have stepped into Part II of the ETHIC, whereas the notions of unity and the attributes are the explicit subject matters of P. I. The step was made for the purpose, however, of further explicating the notion of the attribute (and the first thirteen propositions of P. II are actually midway between the main portions of Parts I and II). We have seen that the attributes of thinking and extension are aspects of the same thing: generally of *Being* or God, and specifically of each singular mode of being. It may now be seen that there is a sense in which they are aspects of each other, a bit like the opposite sides of a coin. A Mind is the form of a Body, and a Body is the object of a Mind. Thus, though different, the two attributes are, we want to say, inextricably linked to each other, but that implies that they are different *things* that are closely connected. They are not. The one is the form of a thing, the other its extension. We have to be very careful here because, as I have just intimated, the normal dualistic way of thinking tends to block understanding things non-dualistically, that is, thinking of things in terms of substances interferes with thinking of them in terms of modes.

In the days of "the new philosophy" there was a singularly handy division of distinctions into the real, the modal, and those of reason. Descartes discussed it in *Principles* I, 60–62. BdS did so in his Appendix to his *Descartes' Principles* P. II, Ch.

5. A real distinction is one between two substances (for Descartes there was a real distinction between God and the world, and between a mind and matter, as well as between individual minds). A modal distinction is one between a substance and a mode of a substance, or between two modes of a substance. A distinction of reason is a distinction that we make in thinking about things, as, for example, when we distinguish the heart from the lungs for anatomical purposes.

Non-dualism can be put in these terms and the notion of attribute further clarified by means of them. Non-dualism, then, is the view that there are no real distinctions. There are only modal distinctions of the second sort, and rational distinctions. There is also the distinction between the two attributes. This is to be expected because the original tripartite classification of distinctions was made from the dualist point of view. With non-dualism we see that in addition to modal and rational distinctions there is the distinction between attributes (Sp's version of the real distinction, if you will). Sp. did not name it, but it might be called the "attributive distinction." It is real in the sense that the attributes are conceived as really distinct. It is not real in the sense that the attributes cannot be conceived to exist independently of each other. As Spinoza said, we can really distinguish the attributes, but this should not lead us to suppose that we are talking about two things or substances. As he further said, he understands the same by "substance" and "attribute"; although attributes provide us with a way of understanding what "substance" and "attribute" refer to, namely *Being*. Thus, the attributes are really distinct from each other, though attribute-words do not refer to separate beings.

There is another way of coming to a better understanding of the unique notion of the attribute. In the definition of "God" we have it that God is substance "being established in infinite attributes." The phrase "infinite attributes" is ambiguous. It can mean that the attributes are countless in number, or it can mean that each attribute ranges, so to speak, throughout *Being*. This ambiguity has been involved with more misunderstanding of BdS than any other single factor in his thinking. Thus, the

French translations of the phrase *infinitis attributis* have it that God is constituted by "an infinity of attributes." And even where it is correctly rendered in translation as "infinite attributes," the most common, if not the only view of the number of attributes has been and is that it is infinite. Confusing the notion of attribute with the ordinary notion of properties, people reason that, since God is the infinite Being or the Perfect Being, he must have an infinite number of attributes.

In fact, of course, there are only two: thinking and extension. You have only to remember why BdS introduced the notion of attribute to realize this. Furthermore, BdS himself tells us in Letter 64, in response to a question (Letter 63) about the number of attributes, that besides these two "no other attribute of God can be concluded or conceived." Such, however, is the force of the dualistic outlook that the response to this has been: Ah, we may not be able to infer or conceive another attribute from these two, but that does not affect the possibility that there *may* be other attributes. And unfortunately there is Prop. 9 in P. I which is regularly translated something like Elwes' version of it: "The more reality or being a thing has the greater the number of its attributes," from which it seems to follow that God must have an infinite number of attributes since he is infinitely real.

Another possible translation of Prop. 9, however, is: "To the extent that each thing has more reality or being, plural attributes appertain to it." Notice of this, first, that the reference is to the reality of a thing, any thing, not God. Notice, second, that where Elwes has "the greater the number" we have "plural attributes." The Latin phrase is *plura attributa,* or, strictly speaking, "more than one attribute." It is significant, finally, that the demonstration of Prop. 9 is excessively succinct: "It is patent from Def. 4," which is the definition of "attribute" (see above p. 73 or the Appendix). Nothing about number is involved in the definition. I have said that Props. 9 and 10 explicate the definition of "attribute." BdS took the term from Descartes, according to whom a substance had *one* principal attribute. I submit that Prop. 9 simply distinguishes Sp's notion of attribute from

Descartes' (of which everyone was reading in "the new philosophy"). Prop. 9 says in effect that I, BdS, am so conceiving of an attribute that a substance or any thing can have more than one attribute. Prop. 10 then tells us that the two attributes are really distinct from each other, but that this does not mean that there are entities which correspond to them.

The point, again, is that in Descartes' loose phraseology "attribute" and "property" were alternated, even though he finally tended to take the former to signify the principal property or attribute of a substance. Stemming his work as well as he could from the terminology in "the new philosophy," BdS introduced the novel notion of an attribute. It comes out of the idea of a property. However, the latter is commonly conceived in terms of substances. A property is a characteristic or quality of a substance. Having seen through substances, but finding the notion of qualification or modification useful, BdS thought in terms of attributing things to what is, or *Being*. Since substances have dropped out of this picture, so have properties. Thus, an attribute, though the conception of it derives from the original notion, is not, nor anything like, a property. Clinging to the confused idea that it is, however, an idea which is confused because of its relation to dualism, readers of BdS have found themselves forced to believe that the number of attributes is infinite—and this despite the fact as BdS himself told us, that no other attribute than thinking and extension can be conceived. Ordinarily we relate the inconceivable to the impossible, but in this case readers of BdS have not done so.

If further demonstration of the fact that attributes are not properties is necessary, you have only to reflect that we commonly distinguish between things in terms of differences in properties. A horse is not a dog because it does not have the properties that characterize being a dog. It is, however, a consequence of the notion of attribute that every thing has the two attributes; more strictly, is expressed in both attributes. "Has" is a word that goes with "property." Thus, every thing is both mental and physical. As BdS conceived attributes, then, they do not serve the common function performed by speaking of properties.

We have returned again to the notion of unity: All modes of being are expressed in or by the attributes. There are no real distinctions between modes of being. We are all in *Being*. We have our being in the same thing. It may be said that Sp's great insight is into *Being*, or God, to use the Biblical term. It is an insight in which philosophy and religion come together or are unified.

One further thing may be said about unity, union, oneness or atonement in relation to the attributes. I have found that it helps enormously with understanding them. We call the one attribute "thinking," a word that suggests activity. The word comes into English from the Latin participle: *cogitans,* from *cogito* (I think). Descartes had called a mind *res cogitans,* a thinking thing. And BdS employed the word when he defined "idea" as referring to "a Mind's conceiving, which the Mind forms [sic], on account of the fact that it is a thinking thing" (Def. 3, P. 11). He then explained that he used the word "conceiving" rather than "perception" because "the noun *perception* seems to indicate that a Mind is passive with relation to its object. But *conceiving* seems to express an action of the Mind." He thereby stressed the activity of this attribute.

[I must remark parenthetically that Sp's explanation hinges on the language he was using. The Latin for "conceiving" in "a Mind's conceiving" is *conceptum,* which is commonly translated "concept" or "conception." The word is, however, the past participle of the verb *concipere* (to conceive), that is, it is a verbal form. Hence, "conceiving" is the proper translation if we are to accept Sp's explanation. The word for "perception," on the other hand, is *perceptio,* which in Latin is a true nominal form, that is, not a verbal one. We have here another hint about existing published translations of the ETHIC; where they have "concept" or "conception" replace it with "conceiving."]

Our name for the other attribute commonly if not universally is "extension." This comes from the Latin *extensio* which, like *perceptio,* is a true nominal form and suggests inactivity. The translation of Descartes' phrase, also employed by BdS, for a material thing, *res extensa,* reflects this: an extended thing. The

[85]

phrase further suggests, not only that matter is inert, but that it is or has been acted on.

In terms of Sp's explanation of his definition of "idea" we immediately see another manner of regarding extension. In *res extensa,* as in *res cogitans* the modifier is a participial form, that is, a verbal form. True, like *conceptum* (nominative: *conceptus*), it is the past participle of a verb, *extendo,* whereas *cogitans* is a present participle, and this suggests "extended" as its translation. Nevertheless, in the Mind of BdS (remember the Hebrew language) even the past participle suggested activity. Thus, we may come to see that *res extensa* could be translated "an extending thing." The choice of the *tense* of the participle used in the translating language may well be a matter of some prejudice. The translation of a verbal form, on the other hand, has more strictly to do with what is actually being translated. The name of the other attribute, that is, in the thinking of BdS, should be "extending." The two attributes, then, are thinking and extending.

This, it develops as we become better acquainted with BdS, is precisely the way that he thought of the second attribute. This thinking is accurately reflected in his definition of "God": "substance being established in infinite attributes, of which each expresses being eternally, & infinitely." A translation like Elwes', of course, does not reflect this: "of which each expresses eternal and infinite essentiality." Nor does it appear in the French translations: *dont chacun exprime une essence eternelle et infinie* ("of which each expresses an eternal and infinite essence"). BdS was saying that *Being* is expressed in infinite attributes, each of which *is* eternally and infinitely. The adverbs modify the way the attributes *are.* Both attributes are eternally and infinitely doing something: thinking and extending.

Sp's great insight requires this. Reality, he saw, may be seen as *Being,* rather than as a substance or substances doing things and having properties. However, in his letters BdS *says* this of extending, in particular in Letter 83. Tschirnhaus had asked him (Letter 82) whether motion and therefore the variety of things can be deduced from extension. Was Descartes not right that motion can only be accounted for by an appeal to God as its cause? In Descartes' thinking God really is the *Deux ex machina*, the God outside of the machine who makes it run. And when Tschirnhaus asked whether we can deduce motion from extension, he was asking the equivalent of can we understand motion in terms of extension?

Sp's reply is extraordinarily to the point, though he immediately admits that he has not been able to set these things out in order (in effect, that he has been unable to make them clear to others). Maybe even a lifetime does not suffice for this. The reply is that, as Descartes conceived extension, motion cannot be understood in terms of it. If, however, we define "extension" as "an attribute which expresses being eternally, & infinitely," the matter is quite otherwise. And, of course, it is. For with this definition of extending, so-called "extension" is seen as eternally and infinitely extending. Motion, then, is easily understood in terms of extending.

It is highly interesting that in his definition of extension (for which see, for example, *Principles* I, 53: "length, breadth, and depth") Descartes does not indicate that extension is inert. The implication, of course, that it is, is always there in his thinking. In the definition he attributes to Descartes, however, in *Descartes' Principles*, BdS caused the definition to read: "*Extension* is that which is established in three dimensions; we do not, however, understand by means of *extension* the act of extending, or something different from quantity." "Act of extending" should be emphasized. BdS made explicit what was only implicit in Descartes.

When the full extent of Sp's commitment to being is realized, as it better is with an understanding of the attribute of extending, the propositions in P. I after Prop. 14 become clearer and clearer. I have in mind particularly Prop. 16: "From the necessity of the divine nature countless things in countless modes (that is, all that can fall under an infinite understanding [or understanding infinitely]) are bound to follow." Why are they bound to follow? Because that is what the divine nature, or

Divine Nature, *is:* countless things flowing in countless modes.

We are in position for another glimpse of unity. It involves acceptance of *being*. Recalling that in the TTP BdS said that "God" was used by the ancient Hebrews as an adjective as well as a noun or name, so that God's wisdom is simply wisdom above the common, we can sense that to be in God's way would be being in a way above the common. What seems to count is living fully, not living in this or that way. This can be sensed when "being" is experienced verbally instead of nominally or substantivally.

We have still, however, to talk of that other way of knowing that preoccupied BdS before we can sense this at all well. Even then we shall realize that more than books are required for it. As BdS said, all these things can be demonstrated beyond chance of doubt, but this will not so affect the Mind as an experience of them can.

CHAPTER 6

Egolessness

Spinoza's reply to Tschirnhaus in Letter 83 was that "extension" should be defined by *attributum, quod aeternam, & infinitam essentiam exprimat*. In Elwes' and Wolf's translations this comes out: "an attribute, which expresses eternal and infinite essence." In this form, of course, it is not at all clear that BdS can understand motion by means of extension. When he wrote the letter, however, in which he asked his question, Tschirnhaus had Sp's ETHIC in manuscript, and therefore the definition of "God" from which the line comes (though Elwes did not see this when translating the letter; see his translation of the line in Def. 6 on p. 86 above). Thus even in the original Latin Tschirnhaus had not understood that the attributes are thinking and *extending*. More than books and words, then, are necessary for understanding Sp's insight. Before turning to one of the most important and novel consequences of this insight, another view of knowing, I want to discuss briefly an aspect of what more is needed. This will also give us some understanding of the empirical grounding of Sp's thinking.

The first notice, that I know, of a resemblance between BdS and Ch'an or Zen Buddhism occurs in the entry on Spinoza in Pierre Bayle's dictionary, where Bayle related Spinozism to "the theology of a sect of the Chinese." It is clear when you read his description that he was reporting on Jesuit accounts of Ch'an Buddhists or, as the Jesuits called them, the followers of Foe Kaio (No-man). In this notice Bayle said that there was nothing new in BdS, for "the theology of a sect of the Chinese" is also based on the incomprehensible notion of nothingness. Bayle had observed, you see, that BdS believed that there are no substances. For Bayle this meant that everything substantial was removed from reality. Aside from the reference to "theology" in Buddhism, Bayle's striking the resemblance was remarkably keen.

A central notion in Buddhism is that of the ego. In *The Three Pillars of Zen* Philip Kapleau defines the notion as follows: "ego: According to Buddhism the notion of an ego, that is, awareness of oneself as a discrete individuality, is a delusion. It arises because, misled by our bifurcating intellect (the sixth sense) into postulating the dualism of 'myself' and 'not-myself,' we are led to think and act as though we were a separated entity confronted by a world external to us. Thus in the unconscious the idea of 'I,' or self-hood, becomes fixed, and from this arise such thought-patterns as 'I hate this, I love that; this is mine, that is yours.' Nourished by this fodder, the ego-I comes to dominate the mind, attacking whatever threatens its domination and grasping at anything which will enlarge its power. Antagonism, greed, and alienation, culminating in suffering, are the inevitable consequences of this circular process."

Generally the Buddhist view of life is that it is characterized by suffering caused by the delusion of the ego. A second Buddhist tenet is that the suffering can be reduced and varying degrees of happiness induced by seeing through this delusion. We might also say, by understanding it. The gradual outcome of this understanding is called awakening or enlightenment. (The name "Buddha" derives from a Sanscrit verb meaning "to awaken" and a Buddha is an awakened one.) Over the centuries a practice for achieving this based on that used by Gautama, the Buddha, has developed. The practice is called "meditation" in English, a misleading translation of the Japanese word *zazen*.

I have described *zazen* in *The Matter of Zen*. For our purposes here the following account will suffice. *Zazen* is a practice which involves both the body and the mind; that is, the whole individual, which is why "meditation" is a misleading term for it. Until recently we have been inclined to think of meditation as

[90]

an intellectual affair (see pp. 32–3 above). In the practice the practitioner sits quietly in a cross-legged position called the "lotus," and endeavors by various means to achieve a state known sometimes as no-mind. That is to say, to use this imagery, the practitioner endeavors to empty the mind of all ideas, and this includes feelings. He or she endeavors to achieve nothingness, a description of which is probably the source of Bayle's account of the "theology" of that sect of the Chinese. Nothingness is otherwise known as egolessness.

According to the legend you read, the Buddha attained awakening after either nine or fifteen years of practicing *zazen,* and this was begun only after he had tried other means for wakening for several years. The point is that the practice is enormously difficult and requires unremitting effort and work. For this reason there has developed around it a number of aids for those who indulge in it. Places in which to do it have been built, *zendos* or meditation halls. Around these have clustered other buildings that comprise a temple: living and eating accommodations, halls for lectures, and halls for celebrations and certain rituals. These are all, down to the cushions on which the practitioner sits, part of the physical aspects of the process. Certain mental aids have also been developed: instructions by those in the temple who are furthest along the path of enlightenment. This instruction includes lectures, and the use of the koan in the strictest sect of Buddhism. The most important of these aids are the master or teacher and all the practitioner's fellow temple-members. (We are now at several lengths removed from the so-called "theology" of this sect of the Chinese.)

Not only is the practice of *zazen* long and arduous. It is also gradual and continuous. That is to say, it goes on over the months and years and with it steps in awakening are taken. The process is never completed. When a *roshi,* or old teacher, tells a pupil that he is now ready to go out on his own, and perhaps teach others, this does not mean that the pupil has achieved final enlightenment. It simply means that he has reached a rung on the ladder which is level with that on which the teacher stands. The pupil may go on to climb higher on his own, or he may be assisted in this by another teacher. But there is no end to the rungs. Hakuin, a great Japanese teacher of the eighteenth century, reported that he had had innumerable small *satori* (taken innumerable small steps) and seven great ones in his life. With the seventh he realized that all his previous steps had been illusory.

The process is long and gradual because it is like a mirror of life itself. This is also true because it is physical as well as mental. When Westerners first began to read about Zen Buddhism ("Ch'an" is its Chinese name which we heard only later), they came across numerous stories of sudden enlightenment. So and so heard a snowflake fall and was enlightened, this one heard a pebble strike a tile and awakened, and so on. What these stories did not relate was that in each of these cases the individual in question was practiçing *zazen,* perhaps had been for years, and would continue to do so. The stories also failed to relate the fact that the marks of awakening are in the body as well as in the mind, even as they are in ordinary awakening from sleep. He seeks in vain for egolessness who believes it will come simply from something he sees or hears.

At the end of Chapter 5 it was indicated that more than demonstrations are needed for understanding unity, or having knowledge of the union of the mind with total Nature. In Letter 37 BdS responds to a question whether there is a method by which we can attain understanding. Indeed there is, replies BdS. With it the first thing you have to do is to distinguish between understanding and imagination, or between true ideas and the rest "namely the fictitious, the false, the dubious, & absolutely all those which depend solely on memory." We will consider this in detail later and note the resemblance between Sp's notion of understanding and the Buddhists' notion of no-mind. I am concerned now with the advice that comes at the end of the letter. "It remains nevertheless to admonish you that for all these things assiduous meditation, & a very constant spirit and purpose are required; for which, that they be had, it is above all necessary to establish a certain mode, & fashion for living, & to prescribe some certain end. . . ." BdS, then, saw that virtually a way of life is needed beyond the demonstrations, and his description of that way is roughly similar to that of the Ch'an Buddhists.

There is, however a much deeper resemblance between BdS and the Buddhists. This lies in the comparison that can be made between his insight that there are not substances and the Buddhist notion of egolessness. Although many Buddhists do, the Ch'an Buddhist does not indulge in metaphysics. He describes the delusion of the ego and prescribes a means for reducing it. However, at the level of the human individual Sp's insight that there are no substances is the equivalent of the Buddhists' that the ego is a delusion. For in the language of the Buddhist the word "ego" corresponds to the word "substance" in the language of BdS. What the Buddhist calls the ego is the substance (the soul) that each of us thinks we have in us: the thing that gives us our identity as a person. (It may be recalled that on p. 25 I suggested that Descartes' idea of his soul was a fiction.) Furthermore, in what may seem a peculiarly round-about way BdS talked about this and gave two lengthy descriptions of egolessness. The first is in P. I of the ETHIC and the second in the last twenty-one propositions of P. V, where the subject is living or being eternally or freely in knowing intuitively.

In the EU BdS speaks of us conceiving a nature firmer than our own which we endeavor to strive for. In the Preface of P. IV of the ETHIC he says that "we desire to form an idea of a human being, as if an exemplar of human nature on which we may look" (p. 208; 189 in Elwes). In the TTP he several times refers to God as "the unique exemplar of true life" (notably Ch. 13, p. 171; 179 in Elwes; "true" was then more used as synonymous with "real" than it is today). This tends to confirm a view that one of the roles the account of God in P. I of the ETHIC plays is that of describing or setting forth the exemplar of human nature referred to in P. IV. It is, of course, also to provide the insight through substances; but I suppose that the account has complex functions.

I want now also to suggest that Sp's account of God in P. I is based on what he found as he came to understand himself. His own self-knowledge, in other words, provides the empirical grounding of his thinking or its grounding in his own experience. What he found with this knowledge, when "generalized," is that there are not substances. Particularly he saw through the idea of his own soul or identity. In a word, he was an egoless man. The more-than-demonstrations that is needed to impress the mind with unity is this experience.

The Appendix to P. I gives in essay or "analytic" form an essential part of the teaching of P. I. In the Appendix BdS describes and accounts for the anthropomorphic conception of God. This is the conception of God as *a* transcendent being who is like unto a perfect human being. Human beings have formed this conception of God in their imaginations from an inadequate understanding of themselves. This inadequate understanding has also given rise to the notion of free will. Human beings, says BdS, are conscious of their volitions and actions but unconscious of their causes. Thus they form the notion that the cause of their actions is something that is itself uncaused (i.e., self-caused) or free. BdS does not add this, but it is clear that the notion is formed from the idea we have of the soul or our substance, for the notion of the free will is precisely that of a substance (Corollary 2, Prop. 17: "solely God is a free cause").

Sp's conceiving of God, then, is also anthropomorphic. It is, however, with the difference that what is ordinarily called the anthropomorphic conception of God comes from conceiving God with an inadequate understanding of oneself. The God of the Hebrews, as BdS makes clear in the TTP, was a God conceived with imagination but not with understanding. In Chapter 2, when he discusses the prophets, BdS indicates that they were characterized by lively imaginations and limited understanding. Solomon seems to have been one of the few exceptions who, although admired for his sapience, was little thought of for prophetic powers, that is, for his proclaiming the Law. (BdS discounts the view that prophecy was prediction.) The characteristic of the prophets fitted with those of the people they had to instruct: a rude and childlike people who were long on imagination and short on understanding. It is little wonder, then, that the conception of God the Father developed. In the ETHIC, which may be called the Bible of the seventeenth century, the third in a series of Testaments, a much deeper and far more understanding idea of God appears. But in developing it BdS was only doing what all human beings do as they grapple their way toward understanding or being fully human: trusting his own experience.—One sees with this, by the way, why the TTP is so invaluable a companion to the ETHIC. Without it the ETHIC can seem abstract.

Lest this notion that human beings in the West have understood themselves by understanding God, or have formed the idea of themselves by forming the idea of God, seem strange, ask yourself, Whence-else could the idea of God have come? From God? For BdS that is to imagine rather than to understand.

We have related the Buddhist idea of the ego to that of substance, the notion of egolessness to the view that there are no substances, and the connection of these matters to the concept of identity. Before turning to examine the possibility that P. I of the ETHIC is in part a description of egolessness, we must now note something further about identity or the sense of identity.

To my knowledge neither the Buddhists nor BdS observed that developing an identity and a sense of identity is essential in the maturation process of a human being. BdS was certainly aware of the movement from childhood to adulthood. He sometimes compares children, fools, and the insane (for example, at the end of the scholium to Prop. 49, P. II). He speaks of the system of rewards and punishment in raising children (for example, in the Explication of Def. 27 of the Affections in P. III). And he speaks of maturing as an ever-increasing consciousness of ourselves, of God, and of things (Schol., Prop. 39. P. V). But nowhere does he discuss the role of identity, and therefore of the notion of substance, in this process.

It is the case, however, that the first thing parents set about

[95]

doing, aside from feeding, clothing, and loving a baby, is to give it both an identity and a sense of identity. In fact, the first frequently precedes the birth of the child, for it is often given its name then. Certainly it is as soon as it is born, except in very unusual cases. Eventually this makes possible identifying the child, and gradually it plays a vital role in the child's development of a sense of identity.

This being set off from other things or having an identity, which in turn develops the sense of identity in the young, makes possible a large number of distinctions which play a variety of roles. It leads to the distinction between I and thou and thus an awareness of both I and thou. In other words, it makes both consciousness of others and self-consciousness possible. That is to say, it is vital in becoming conscious of things, which is an important part of being conscious at all. Having an identity and a sense of identity also leads to the distinction between the subjective and the objective. As this becomes sharper, it in turn enables us to be objective. In a word, the development of science depends on it. In fact, a capsule history of philosophy in the West might run: the development of consciousness. The high mark of this has been taken to be rational knowledge, or science. In all this, then, do identity and the sense of identity play roles. Last, but not least, is the function of speech, or language, of which a central principle is the principle of identity: A = A.

Given this, it may seem that having Sp's insight, or developing egolessness must be extraordinarily difficult. For in a sense it requires going back on or going against one of the central things that has made us a human being. It involves departing from or at least seeing through our identities and our senses of identity. In getting Sp's insight or in coming to egolessness one must literally have the sensation that one is going out of one's mind, for in a way a mind is constituted by a sense of identity. Bayle saw the point, though he put it in another way, when he said that Prop. 5, P. I flies in the face of logic.

An illustration from science will not be amiss here. In the 1920s in atomic and quantum physics scientists discovered that they could not specify (or identify) the position and velocity of an electron at the same time. There has been a comparable situation in the theory of light since the days of Newton which helps to explain what is involved here. For some purposes physicists found that the hypothesis that light is composed of particles works. In other situations they found that it was better to think of light as made of waves. Nils Bohr resolved the difficulty in the 1920s with the idea of complementarity. With respect to the situation in the matter of light this amounted to the idea that the two hypotheses complement each other in practice. Therefore, let us assume that they do so in theory. This comes to the notion that we will never know *what* light is, that is, we will never know its identity. Theoretically this meant that physicists, when they accepted the idea of complementarity, abandoned the principle of identity in physics.

Little wonder that it took individual physicists some time to accept Bohr's idea. Yet the advances in atomic and quantum physics it made possible led to the splitting of the atom, which as far back as the Greeks was taken as the physical unit of identity. The atomic bomb was shocking in many ways. Probably the deepest was that in relation to what it meant for the notion of identity. And there seems little doubt that physicists had trouble accepting Bohr's idea of complementarity not only for what it means theoretically, but also because they sensed what abandonment of identity or the idea of it could or might do to the human psyche.

In Chapter 4 we saw that a way of looking at Prop. 5, that plural substances are not given, is to see that it gets through the traditional notion of identity. Because this involves making clear both the idea of substance and attribute the task requires fourteen propositions, the first fourteen of P. I. After these BdS expresses some things that can be properly said of God. He is not specifying God's properties, because, since God is uniquely, we cannot speak of his properties. We speak of properties when we can compare things and say that this is common to this group of them, or that this thing does not have that property of that. As with Prop. 5 so with the propositions after Prop. 14, there is more than one way of looking at them or more than one thing going on. Thus, having seen through the traditional or definitional notion of identity, there is the possibility that in these propositions about God BdS is dealing further with identity. (In Chapter 4 we got through P. I to Prop. 14. We now consider the rest of P. I, or most of it, in a particular way.)

There is another notion of identity than the one exposed in Prop. 5. It is as old, I suppose, as the latter but it can not be called "traditional" because it has so rarely occupied peoples' minds, at least philosophically. This is the notion of identifying with or becoming identical with something. It is almost paradoxical that we can hardly speak of it without thinking of the other notion of identity. For in a way becoming identical with something else requires that the two things that are becoming identical should be identifiable or have their own identities. Thus, a way of talking about identifying with something is to say that in identifying with something one loses one's own identity. *Pari passu* that something also loses its identity. The process is called "atonement," so that people in the West have thought about this kind of identity religiously. Many of the propositions after Prop. 14 can be read as laying bare this other notion of identity. These are the propositions having to do with egolessness, for in saying what can be properly said of God BdS says things that have remarkable psychological analogues.

The interplay of ideas, especially in P. I of the ETHIC, is so close that sectioning the part into groups of propositions is at best a dubious device for instructional purposes. Thus the propositions that have remarkable psychological analogues include Props. 12 and 13, which also have to do with making Prop. 14 clear, which is, so to speak, the last of the propositions making Prop. 5 clear. (Prop. 14 is: Besides God no substance can be nor be given. It has the corollaries we examined in Chapter 4: God is uniquely, and the thinking thing and the extended thing are affections of God or affections of his attributes. See p. 67.)

Prop. 12, in effect is: A substance cannot be divided (see the Appendix). Prop. 13, in effect, is: God is indivisibly. Psychologically speaking this may be said to characterize an egoless person. Such a person is a whole person in the sense that he or she is not torn, for example, by conflicting Affections.

Unfortunately I must interpose a terminological consideration here. In P. III BdS considers what he calls human Affections. The word he uses for these is *affectus,* the past participle of the verb *afficio* (affect in any way). In Latin this participle is used nominatively to mean something like "disposition." The verb is also the root for a noun *affectio* which is the word BdS employed in defining "mode" (a mode is an affection of a substance). Elwes translated *affectus* with "emotion," and for a long time people have spoken of Sp' theory of the emotions. The translation is not only inaccurate (the Latin for "emotion" is *commotio animi,* or "commotion of spirit"). It is also unfortunate and misleading, for it destroys the marvellous unity in Sp's thinking that was reflected in his writing by the use of basically the same word to speak of modes and to speak of the affective aspects of human behavior (in contrast to the cognitive). I, therefore, use the same word in English, capitalizing the initial letter in its one set of occurrences to distinguish it from its use in the other set. This difference corresponds roughly to the differences between *affectus* and *affectio* in the respect that it is a visual difference: "Affection" and "affection." Thus Affections are aspects of human behavior like Joy, Anger, etc. And affections are occurrences in God or *Being* which BdS calls the modes of being.

In P. III, to return to our subject, BdS discusses a kind of Affection which results from conflicting Affections. He calls these "Fluctuations of Spirit." An egoless person does not suffer from Fluctuations of Spirit. In this respect he or she might be said to be indivisibly. Such an Individual is also an indivisible whole in the sense that he or she is not made up of parts with different roles. She, for example, is not part housewife, part mother, and part career woman—with the different parts sometimes in confused relations. Each of these roles is a mode of her being and she is totally and clearly involved in each mode. She is literally each mode.

[99]

Prop. 15: "Whatever is, is in God, & nothing can be or be conceived without God." Psychologically speaking, the egoless person is self-contained. Prop. 16 and its corollaries (you can consult the Appendix for the full statement of a proposition where I paraphrase): God is the efficient cause of things; cause by means of himself, not by accident; and the first cause. The egoless Individual brings about his or her own behavior, is less and less dependent on fortune. Prop. 17: "God acts solely from laws of his own nature, & is constrained by no one." This proposition does not even need translation into psychological terms. It speaks for itself in relation to egolessness, even to its curious second half: he is constrained by no one. Why not "by no thing?" It is almost as though BdS had himself in mind as he wrote the proposition.

Prop. 18: "God is the immanent cause of things, not the transient." The egoless person *is* his or her behavior, not an agent like a little man within that causes that behavior. Prop. 19: "God, or all his attributes are eternally." The egoless person lives undisturbed by thoughts of the past and plans for the future. Prop. 20: "God's existing and his being are one, & the same." The egoless person is without illusions, is what he or she *is*.

As I have indicated, the propositions after Prop. 14 play various roles. I have been unable to find psychological roles for Props. 21 to 24. Props. 21 to 23 deal with modes which are infinitely (in the literature they are called "infinite modes"). Having ceased to be influenced by the notion of substance, BdS could think of, so to speak, huge "things" like all motions considered together as one "infinite mode" of motion; similarly for all cases of being at rest. He discusses these modes of being infinitely in Lemma VII in the long scholium to Prop. 13, P. II, which amounts to a small essay on bodies in the midst of the part on Minds (for, says BdS, we cannot understand the human Mind unless we also understand bodies).

Prop. 25: God is the efficient cause of things' existing as well as of their being. The egoless person is the adequate cause of his actions (see Appendix for Def. I, P. III of "adequate causes";

it is discussed in Chapter 8). They flow from him with necessity (Props. 26 and 27). His actions are all of a piece, clearly related to each other (Prop. 28), and necessarily so (Prop. 29). That is to say, they are firm, and understandable by himself as well as by others. Again (Prop. 30), the egoless person is without illusions.

I am increasingly not citing or paraphrasing the propositions. Those inclined may consult the Appendix for the propositions. For my purposes I am concerned with a sketch not a detailed map. To resume, rational thinking is a mode of thinking like other modes such as love and desire. It is not something absolute (Prop. 31). God does not act through freedom of will (Corol., Prop. 32). The egoless person sees through such notions as freedom of will, sees that all actions are an essential part of Nature; and that they, therefore, follow naturally the way that all things do. Our actions cannot be otherwise (Prop. 28). (In the first twenty propositions of P. V, where BdS discusses what he calls "remedies" for the passions, he indicates that an awareness of this necessity of all things is one of the best remedies. It helps us to accept life instead of struggling with it. But see also the discussion of necessity above.)

Prop. 34: "God's potency is his being itself." That is, the egoless tend more and more to act out of themselves. Increasingly whatever they see that they can do, they do (Prop. 35). And they understand that whatever they do has an effect: Prop. 36; "Nothing exists from whose nature an effect does not follow."

In the Appendix of P. I, which immediately follows Prop. 36, BdS says: "With these things I have explicated God's nature, and his properties [BdS is speaking loosely in the Appendix which is not in the geometric manner], as, that he exists necessarily [remember, that is equivalent to: there are not substances; see above p. 64]; that he is uniquely; that he is, & acts solely from his nature's necessity; that he is all things' free cause, & in what mode; that all things are in God, & so depend on him, that without him they can neither be nor be conceived; and finally that all things have been predetermined by God,

[101]

not, certainly, from freedom of will, or absolute good pleasure, but from God's absolute nature or infinite potency."

This, one thinks dualistically, is a description of the macrocosm or *Being*. But remember that BdS thought of God as that "exemplar of true life." With a wrench of your Mind you can see that we *also* have here a description of a human being when it has lost a sense of identity to find itself identified with Nature. This is a mode of human *being* which accepts the natural because it is natural.

BdS helps us to see this in the remainder of the Appendix which is a comment on supernaturalism. He indicates that wherever possible in P. I he has tried to remove prejudices which prevent us from seeing what he is getting at. Because, however, not a few prejudices may still remain, he calls them to an "examin of reason." The task is simplified because the prejudices all "depend on this one, that to wit human beings commonly suppose that all natural things, like themselves, act on account of an end." They then "state for certain that God himself directs all things toward some certain end: for they say that God has made all things on account of the human being, the human however that it may make a cult of him." Without going into detail about the nature of the human Mind, BdS continues, we may take as a foundation for the acquiescence of the majority in this prejudice the fact that "all human beings are born ignorant of things' causes, & that they all have an appetite for seeking what is useful to them, of which they are conscious."

The "examin" of this which follows proceeds easily and we need not repeat it. Conscious of their volitions and appetites, but ignorant of their causes, human beings come to think that they are free. They regard themselves, as BdS says in the Preface to P. III, "as dominions within a dominion." Thinking then that all things act for an end, they imagine God in the guise of a human being. Each makes a cult of God in his own way so that God will love him above the rest and direct nature for the use of his blind desire and insatiable avarice. "And thus this prejudice turned into a superstition, & drove roots deep in minds."

Things are judged good or ill absolutely, perfect or imperfect absolutely, and so beautiful and ugly, without any awareness that all these qualifications are made relatively to some purpose.

The driving force is the sense of oneself. (Think again of Descartes' idea of his soul as a fiction.) Ignorant of the causes working on us and conscious only of ourselves, of our actions, volitions, and appetites, we restrict what we are to ourselves. Unable in our ignorance to expand our boundaries, we sense ourselves as a unit in Nature but not an integral part of her.—"I am going to Osaka tomorrow." Questions: Have you ever thought how many people make this possible? Have you ever considered how many people made your trip to Japan possible? The shoemakers, the pantsmakers, the shirtmakers? Are you going to Osaka naked? How many people are there in the ninety generations of your family before you were born? Nor is it a question only of people. How are you going to Osaka? By train? What, then, is going to Osaka? *I* am going to Osaka, indeed!

"And this prejudice turned into a superstition, & drove roots deep in minds." More than demonstrations are needed. There is this deep superstition about identity. Understanding, since it is the form of the Body, requires more than words. Egolessness, as *zazen* shows, is as much of the Body as it is of the Mind. Both understanding and/or egolessness are also matters of degree.

CHAPTER 7

Understanding

Early in 1662 BdS wrote to Oldenburg that he had "composed an integral little work concerning this and also concerning the emendation of understanding," with the copying and emendation of which he had been occupied (Letter 6). "This" refers to a question from Oldenburg (Letter 5) about the nexus by which things depend on the first cause. That portion of the "little work" may have been the "Metaphysical Thoughts" which became the Appendix to *Descartes' Principles.*. The rest was what we know today as "A Treatise concerning the Emendation of Understanding." In it BdS frequently refers to another work he was writing, his "Philosophy." There is little doubt that this came to be called "ETHIC." Only the author of the ETHIC could have produced the work on the emendation of understanding.

The EU is short, only thirty-five pages, and unfinished. It is nevertheless probably the most important and revolutionary philosophical document of modern times. This is immediately apparent in an examination of its title: *Tractatus de Intellectus Emendatione.* If we follow its word order, and its grammar allows for this since *intellectus* is in the genitive case, it reads: "Treatise concerning Understanding's Emendation." A. Boyle rendered it: "Treatise on the Correction of the Understanding;" Elwes: "On the Improvement of the Understanding." We have: "A Treatise concerning the Emendation of Understanding." The little work's revolutionary character hinges here on the small matter of the definite article: "the." When we understand BdS it is understanding that is to be emended, not the understanding or some faculty of the mind. Schol., Prop. 48, P. II in the ETHIC: "In this same mode it is demonstrated that in a Mind there is given no absolute faculty of understanding, desiring, loving, &c." The notion that there are faculties in the mind corresponds to the notion that there are substances. Given Sp's insight into unity, it follows that there is understanding, but no thing that understands.

I interject here another admonition about reading BdS in existing translations. Great care must be taken with the articles: *a, an,* and *the.* BdS was a complete and thoroughgoing nominalist. That is, he believed that there are only Individuals, or singular things. Universals or universal things are only words, or if you like, names. For his account of this see Schol. 1, Prop. 40, P. II, where he calls them "universal notions." If care is not taken with the articles, we easily miss Sp's nominalism, or what comes to the same thing: his complete reliance on observation and experience for what he believes. Since there are no articles in Latin, those you read in translations have been provided by the translators. This means that all translations from the Latin have been influenced philosophically by the translators. For there is an enormous philosophical difference between referring, say, to the human mind, and referring to a human mind.

A further step must be taken with "understanding." The Latin word in the title of the EU is *intellectus.* This is the past participle of the verb *intelligere* (to understand), which is also used as a noun. In the line quoted above from Schol., Prop. 48 the word in the Latin is *intelligendi* which is a gerund of *intelligere,* that is, another verbal form. Possibly for this reason Boyle, Elwes, and others often translate *intellectus* with "intellect," though neither of the first two did in the title of the EU. In omitting the definite article, "the," before "understanding," I make the word even more strongly verbal than it is in the phrase "the understanding." It may be urged that, when it occurs as a noun, *intellectus* must be preceded by an article. That, however, is to be a slave to grammar and to ignore the fact that becomes increasingly clear in reading BdS; his thinking requires basic changes in the grammar we inherited from Aristotle. He himself wrote Oldenburg that he misunderstood a passage in the Gospel of John because he measured "the phrases of oriental languages by European modes of speaking" (Letter 75, toward the end), which makes it apparent that Sp's thinking not only required a different grammar, but that it was based on a different one.

I apologize for these details, but BdS is not to be understood without attention to them. The last line of the ETHIC reads: "But all very clear things are both difficult and rare."

The revolutionary nature of the EU may be more easily seen by reflecting on a common misunderstanding of the work. In 1620 Bacon's *Novum Organum* appeared and in 1637 Descartes' *Discourse on Method*. Both works were parts of the "new philosophy," and in Letter 1 Oldenburg asks BdS what he thinks "of the Principles of the Cartesian and Baconian Philosophy." Impressed with the development of science, both men were concerned with its method: to understand it, and to extend it to other spheres than anatomy, astronomy, and physics. Oldenburg may have sensed that BdS differed from Bacon and Descartes. He had visited and spoken with BdS, but ever since 1662 people have seen the EU as an early work and as part of the new philosophy in the respect that it represented a concern with science.

This is a mistake. The EU is not concerned with science or the method of science. It is concerned with an entirely different way of knowing, the way that BdS alternatively called "the fourth mode of perceiving," "knowing intuitively" (*scientia intuitiva*), and "understanding." The mistake has been due to a failure to understand the departure of Sp's thinking from the traditional Aristotelian thinking. It has also been due to the fact that some of the phrasing in the EU can be traced to the *Novum Organum;* a fact of which Carl Gebhardt, Sp's indefatigable editor, made much. (Gebhardt not only produced the Heidelberg edition of the *Opera Omnia* in 1925. He made all but two of the standard German translations of BdS in the *Philosophische*

Bibliotek. Those of the ETHIC and *Descartes' Principles* are not his.)

Sp's capital insight was that of unity. We have seen that it involves various expressions: God or *Being* is uniquely, there are not substances, thinking and extending are attributes, and thus the subjective is not really distinct from the objective. The distinction between them is either the attributive distinction or it is one of reason, a distinction that we make. From this insight it follows that there is a way of knowing in which the distinction plays no part. This way of knowing is the subject of the EU. BdS called it by the names I have indicated. It might also be called "mystical knowing." In the EU and the ETHIC BdS gave the only rational account of this way of knowing that I know in Western philosophy. The account in the ETHIC is in Schol. 2, Prop. 40; in Props. 26 through 46, P. IV; and in Props. 21 through 42, the last in P. V. There BdS also refers to this way of knowing as "a Mind being eternally."

Ever since Plato's *Phaedo* we have experienced great difficulty in talking and thinking about thinking and knowing. Thinking has always seemed so mysterious, dealing as it apparently does with things that we do not experience with the senses. We have thought of it as incorporeal and hence as ghostly or diaphanous. Further, it seems to require the distinction between the subjective and the objective, and the latter are so easy to confuse. We facilely mistake word for thing and vice versa. Shakespeare warned about this when he said that a rose by any other name would smell as sweet.

Thus it is to be expected that terminology for things mental, or having to do with thinking and knowing, should be confused and confusing. This may be expected to become all the more true when BdS attempted to discuss a way of knowing in which the distinctions between subject and object and mind and body disappear. And it is the case that the only terminological looseness anywhere in the writings of BdS occurs when he is discussing the ways of knowing. Indeed, a prime cause for the fact that the EU remained unfinished is a failure in its terminology. At its very abrupt end BdS was using "perceiving," "thinking," and

[107]

"understanding" interchangeably. He did not stop writing it. It ground to a halt.

These terminological difficulties affect what is probably the most important distinction that BdS employs throughout his writings: that between imagining and understanding. The distinction appears implicitly in Letters 2 and 4, explicitly in Letter 12, and then throughout the correspondence, but especially in Letter 37. It is discussed in the EU from pp. 32–34. In the ETHIC it first appears in Schol. 2, Prop. 8, P. I and then is used throughout. It helps with the distinction to know that both Descartes and BdS called imagination "the common sense" (Descartes' terminology was not as precise as Sp's, but when he spoke of what we call imagination he often used "phantasy;" BdS always used "feigning").

In the EU the distinction is described as follows: "And so we have thus distinguished between the true idea, & other perceptions, & we have shown that ideas feigned, false, & other have their origin from imagination, that is from certain fortuitous, and (to speak so) unconnected sensations, which do not originate from a mind's potency itself, but from external causes, accordingly as the body while sleeping or awake receives certain motions" (p. 32, also in Elwes). In Letter 37 the distinction is made thus: "It is necessary before all things to distinguish between understanding, & imagination, or between true ideas, & the rest, namely the fictitious, the false, the dubious, & absolutely all those which depend solely on memory" (p. 189; 228 in Wolf, who mistakenly translates *perceptio* with "conception" in this letter). Later in the EU BdS adds the use of words to imagination: "since words are part of imagination" (p. 33). Finally, although in the ETHIC he defines reason as a genus of knowledge (Schol. 2, Prop. 40, P. II), we can infer from Letter 12 that reasoning is a function of imagination *in Sp's sense of that term.* (Letter 12 is on the infinite. In it it is clear that most common thinking about the infinite is the result of imagination, again in Sp's usage.) What we call science, in other words, was for BdS a function of imagination.

It is apparent from the manner in which the distinction between understanding and imagination is made that the term "idea" may prove confusing in BdS. For this reason great care must be had with it *unless* it appears in the phrase "true idea." Usually BdS is clear even with "idea," provided that one pays close attention to the context. However, the latter is made extremely difficult by our own preconceptions and prejudices. Furthermore, the inherent difficulties with terminology about the mental seem often to have confused even BdS. One takes this as a sign of the unfinished character of the ETHIC, until it is realized that the work was intended to convey an insight and not to give us a detailed metaphysic and epistemology. In the case of the notion of idea the insight comes in the form of realizing that a *true idea* is not an idea in the ordinary sense at all. It is a state of being. It is not something that we have, as when I say that I have the idea of going downtown. A true idea is something we are. In the case of the idea of God the true idea becomes God's idea, i.e., the highest or clearest form of *any* idea.

(In view of these things it is small wonder that in P. III of the ETHIC Elwes translated the Latin noun and verb for "imagination" and "imagine" with "conception" and "conceive." However, the amount of confusion this engenders is vast.)

Thus, the insight into unity is carried over into the area of the mental makeup of a human being by distinguishing imagination and understanding, and by seeing true ideas as ways of being or states of the whole person rather than as individual psychological units. BdS adopted various ways of further explicating the way of knowing which his predecessors and contemporaries had not seen. One of these occurs in both the EU and the ETHIC. It consists in distinguishing "four modes of perceiving," as they are called in the EU (p. 10, 8 in Elwes); or four kinds of "knowledge," as they are called in the ETHIC. The fact that this occurs in the ETHIC in a scholium (i.e., in a note) indicates that it is important only as a means for explicating something far more important. Otherwise it would have occurred in a definition or in a proposition. The scholium is number 2, Prop. 40, P. II. In the EU the first mode of perceiving is the second kind of knowledge, and the second mode of perceiving the first kind of knowledge in the ETHIC.

The four modes of perceiving or knowing are (remember, their order differs in the EU and the ETHIC): by vague experience; by signs (reading and conversation); and by means of universal notions (Human Being, Horse, Dog, etc., see Schol. 1 of Prop. 40 for these) and common notions (or axioms such as, that bodies move or are at rest). *"Besides these,"* BdS then says in Schol. 2 (emphasis added), "there is given . . . another" way of knowing, "which we shall call *knowing intuitively.*" It proceeds from an adequate idea of God's attributes to a knowledge of the being of things. In the EU this mode of perceiving things is said to occur "when a thing is perceived solely by means of its being, or by means of knowledge of its proximate cause" (p. 10, 8 in Elwes). In both the EU and the ETHIC BdS then illustrates the four ways of perceiving or knowing things. Before turning to this we have again to note some matters of terminology.

In Schol. 2, Prop. 40 BdS also introduces some terminology. Knowledge by vague experience *and* by signs he calls "knowledge of the first genus," "opinion," or "imagination." Knowledge by means of universal and common notions he calls "knowledge of the second genus," or "reason." Knowing intuitively is thereafter referred to as "the third genus of knowledge." In view of the distinction between imagination and understanding the use of "imagination" for the first genus is unfortunate. We have simply to regard it as a mistake, although it occurs in both the Latin and the Dutch first editions. It should also be noted that the distinction between the four ways of knowing is one of reason, that is, one we make, and not a real one. In any one of us any given thing may be perceived or known by any one of the four ways, or by some combination of them. In the ETHIC, too, BdS makes it clear that the third way leads to the fourth, or that the fourth arises out of the third rather than out of the other two (vague experience and signs).—This is a respect in which what he calls "knowing intuitively" differs from so-called "mystical knowing," which is commonly thought of as occurring without the use of reason.

In illustrating the ways of knowing or perceiving BdS relies on another distinction which he defines in P. I, Ch. 1 of the *CM:* the distinction between *beings* of reason and real *beings.* Generally *beings* of reason are things in or of the mind. The objects of mathematics are included here. Real *beings* are things outside the mind: trees, people, etc. BdS points out that the distinction, current in his day, is a poor one, since *beings* of reason are also real. This point marks him off sharply from his contemporaries, who alloted some kind of quasi reality to *beings* of reason (think of the Platonic Forms, the meaning of a word, etc.). Nevertheless, BdS employed the distinction and often used *beings* of reason to illustrate a point because he thought that they are simpler than real *beings.* (He remarks about this in Letter 83.) This has misled readers of BdS into thinking that the fourth way of knowing or perceiving is specially related to mathematics. In both the EU and the ETHIC, for example, he illustrates the four ways of knowing or perceiving with the example of the proportional: Given three numbers, find a fourth that is to the third as the second is to the first (*2 : 4 and 3 : 6*). Nothing could be farther from the truth. All four ways of knowing or perceiving are ways of being aware of particular or singular things, whether of a *being* of reason or of a real *being.*

Illustrations of each of the four ways are the following. My birthday is known from signs (conversation, what I have read). That I shall die is known from vague experience. That is to say, my death is known thus. I have seen others die and expect that I will. By means of vague experience I also know that oil nourishes fire and water quenches it, that a dog is a barking animal, etc. In fact, by vague experience, that is, experience not determined by understanding, "I have known almost all the things, which make for the use of life" (EU, p. 11).

The third way of perceiving gives us such knowledge as that the sun is larger than it appears. Thus, as soon as we have known the nature of vision and therefore that it has this property, that we see one and the same thing smaller at a great distance than if we look at it close at hand, we infer that the sun is larger than it appears. This kind of knowledge always involves some general proposition or propositions.

The descriptions of this third way of knowing in the EU and the ETHIC differ. That in the ETHIC is on p. 110 above. The one in the EU runs: "Perception, where the being of a thing is concluded from another, but not adequately; which happens either when we gather a cause from some effect, or when it is concluded from some universal, with which some property is always concomitant." From the things that BdS says about what he calls "reason" in the ETHIC from Props. 41 to 47 in P. II I infer that he came to regard the third way of knowing as transitional between imagination and understanding. It is both what we ordinarily call "reason" *and* the action of developing clear and distinct ideas. It might even be the sort of thing that Wittgenstein came to call "philosophy" as distinct from old-style metaphysics, namely "a battle of the bewitchment of our understanding through the means of our language" (*Philosophical Investigations,* #109).

In any case we have to be careful with the term "reason" as BdS used it. Thus, in Parts IV and V of the ETHIC a crucial phrase makes its appearance: "the dictate of reason." In Prop. 26, P. IV "reason" is even employed to define understanding in so far as the latter is thought of as affective as well as cognitive: To understand is whatever we endeavor according to reason. And in the Preface to P. V "reason" is alternated with "understanding" as BdS refers to the potency of reason, or understanding among the Affections. Thus, I regard the use of the term "reason" and its definition in Schol. 2, Prop. 40, P. II as being associated with the terminological difficulties we experience in thinking and talking about the so-called "mental" aspect of our makeup, especially when we come to consider the kind of knowing BdS described as a result of his insight into unity.

Besides these ways of knowing, i.e., the first three, however, there is the other, knowing intuitively, and in endeavoring to give an example of it we come to the crux of the matter. For we have to give an example of a way of knowing an individual thing which does not make a distinction between the body and the mind. It

[112]

is a way of knowing of which BdS became aware after he had penetrated the notion of unity. Or, *the other way around,* he was knowing or perceiving in this way when he penetrated the notion of unity and had it become a *true idea* or a state or way of being.

To get at this way of knowing it is helpful to notice, first, that awareness (or consciousness) of some individual thing is involved in all four ways: my birthday, or a property of fire, or the sun's distance from me. Notice, secondly that, although we are aware of an individual thing in each case, a given individual thing may or may not be known by all of the ways. Thirdly, it is important to see that the first three ways of knowing a thing are marked by different degrees of certitude and precision. My knowledge of my birthday is quite uncertain. Even my knowledge of the sun's distance, though precise (I even know the measure of it), is not like being directly acquainted with the distance.

This is related to another characteristic of these three ways of knowing and possibly gave rise to the name of the fourth way used in its definition in the ETHIC. This is that each of these ways of knowing a thing is *indirect.* It occurs through the medium of signs, vague experience, or general propositions *about* things. A characteristic of the fourth way is that it is direct. Hence, perhaps, BdS called it "knowing intuitively" (*scientia intuitiva*). The Latin verb *intueor* (past participle: *intuitiva*) means to look directly into or at. (I translate the adjective as an adverb because of the effects of Sp's thinking on grammar.)

Now consider the illustrations BdS gives in the EU (p. 11), where he is far more helpful with illustrations than he is in the ETHIC. He says that the fourth way of knowing occurs when a thing is perceived solely by its being, that is to say, when solely *it* is perceived, without relation to anything else. (He allows on p. 10 that this way occurs either when we perceive the thing itself or its "proximate cause," that is, roughly, what immediately precedes it and seems to bring it about.) For example, when I have known something, I know that particular knowing (so to speak what *it* is). Here the thing known is an act of knowing

[113]

something, and the knowing of that knowing something is direct. Having known knowing something I know directly what the latter is. Observe that there can be no doubt about this. We are not saying that we know thereby what *knowing* is. We are simply concerned with a particular act of knowing. By this same sort of knowing, says BdS, we know that two and three equal five. We must recall here that this, 2 + 3 = 5, is a *being* of reason. Both examples show that a characteristic of this way of knowing is certainty.

Fortunately BdS also gives an example of knowing a real *being* by this way of knowing in the EU (he does not in the ETHIC, the only example there being the proportional). It is that, when I have known my soul (an alternate word for "mind" in the EU), I know it *to be* united to the body; that is, this is its mode of being: united. He *also* uses this thing, the soul or its union with the body (for knowing the soul is also knowing the union), to illustrate the third way of knowing. In knowing it by this way, however, BdS explains in an extraordinary footnote ("h," see above p. 77) that people must be "maximally on their guard." Otherwise "they fall at once into errors." For in this way of knowing the mind and its union with the body they conceive things "abstractly" and "are at once confounded by imagination. For that which is in itself one, human beings imagine to be multiple." They do this in thinking abstractly, that is, imaginatively, about things and by using names or words improperly. (Here is one explanation of dualism.)

At the end of the paragraph in which these examples of the fourth way of knowing occur, BdS makes a statement which has puzzled readers: "Nevertheless the things which I have thus far been able to understand by such knowledge have been very few." The puzzlement arises from failure to keep the distinction between *beings* of reason (relatively simple things) and real *beings* in mind. The things that he has been able to understand that are few are real *beings:* his soul, another person; all very complicated things (we learn in the ETHIC that the Mind is all the ideas we are, mentally speaking: Props. 1–13, P. II).

Although BdS is more helpful with examples in the EU than

in the ETHIC, he tells us other things about knowing intuitively in the latter which add to our understanding of it. Thus in Schol. 2, Prop. 40 knowing intuitively is said to proceed from an adequate (i.e., true) idea of God's attributes to adequate knowledge of things. In other words, it seems to involve a true idea of unity (which involves seeing mind and body as attributes, not as substances). As long as you are stuck with Cartesian dualism, knowing intuitively will be either difficult or impossible, at least such knowing of real *beings* as opposed to that of simple *beings* of reason will be.

However, in the last half of P. V, in which BdS again discusses knowing intuitively, he does not use the point that it proceeds from an adequate idea of God's attributes. He simply distinguishes it as the knowing of singular things and opposes it to universal knowledge or reason (Schol., Prop. 36). And this seems to be its essential characteristic: That it is directly of a thing and unmediated by words, notions, and images of things. Thus it may be that the definition of knowing intuitively in Schol. 2 should not bind us in our thinking about it. Its definition in the EU, that is, of the fourth mode of perceiving, simply specifies that it is an awareness of a thing's being, that is, of a thing.

Another aid that BdS provides in the ETHIC comes early in the long scholium for Prop. 49 of P. II, a scholium so lengthy that it is virtually an appendix to the part. It is in this proposition and its corollary that BdS makes it clear that will and understanding are the same. In the scholium he grants with Descartes that perhaps at the level of rational knowing the will can be distinguished from simply knowing. With knowing intuitively, however, this is not the case (notice that when he says will and understanding are the same he uses "understanding" instead of "knowing intuitively"). That this should turn out to be so should not surprise us when we reflect on the attribute of thinking. It is a way of being eternally and infinitely; that is, it is an activity.

Also in the scholium BdS admonishes readers to "distinguish accurately between an idea, or a conceiving of a Mind, & images

[115]

of the things which we imagine." "It is next necessary," he continues, "that they distinguish between ideas, & the words by which we signify things." For when these three are confused it is impossible to be clear about this fourth way of knowing. When, for example, we confuse ideas with images, we "look upon ideas, then, as mute pictures on a tablet." We do not see that they are actions, that is, involve willing. (BdS could not have known of Locke's claim that experiences writes ideas on the mind which is at first like a *tabula rasa,* or white tablet. However the imagery here is the same, and it brings out the fact that for BdS imagination included perceiving by the senses.)

The insistence that ideas not be confused with words and images helps to make clear a reason for BdS's distinction between understanding and imagination *and* his inclusion of the first three ways of knowing or perceiving in what he calls "imagination." Basically an image is a copy, likeness, or representation of a thing. In this sense, then, words are images. All of the first three ways of knowing involve images either as words or in mental pictures of things. By their means we see or perceive the thing we are knowing "as if through a cloud," to use a metaphor BdS employs in Schol., Prop. 7, P. II. Our awareness of it is indirect, as we have said. It is as though we dream of it with our eyes open, another metaphor that occurs at the end of Schol., Prop. 2, P. III. In terms of these metaphors knowing intuitively may be described as awareness of a thing with the cloud of words and other images removed, or awareness of it when we are awake and not dreaming.—I have already observed the resemblance of this to Buddhism. One who knows intuitively may be likened to a Buddha.

The metaphor of dreaming with eyes open is more powerful than that of the cloud. For in the first three ways of knowing the media by which things are known (words and images) come to be regarded as the objects of knowledge. This is particularly true of the third way, reason. The propositions of science, the prime example of this way, can be stored in books. We then take this for knowledge and forget that it is only the means by which we have been attempting to get acquainted with individual things. In this manner universals instead of particulars come to seem to be the objects of knowledge. Possibly for this reason BdS was particularly happy with the example of the proportionals. It enabled him to show how the same thing comes to be known in the four different ways. Given three numbers, find a fourth which is to the third as the second is to the first: 2, 4, 3, ?. Merchants, using the first and second ways of knowing, that is, from what they have been told by teachers and from vague experience with proportionals, get the answer by a rule of thumb. Mathematicians know it from the demonstration of Prop. 19, Bk. 7 of Euclid, that is, rationally. It is, however possible to know it intuitively without making any operations. The illustration makes it clear that the same thing can be known or perceived in four different ways, and thus that we must not confuse what is known with the means of knowing it.

The enormous difference between the kind of knowing that Bacon and Descartes had in mind when they talked of method and that which BdS had when he spoke of the method for emending understanding is dramatically indicated by what Descartes did in his *Principles* after the philosophical P. I, as compared with what BdS did after Parts I and II of the ETHIC. Descartes attempted to apply what he had come to see about the human mind to physics. Look at the latter half of *Principles* II, and III and IV, which have not been translated into English because they are now of such small import. In the ETHIC BdS turns to human conduct, human servitude, and human freedom; *but largely because,* as we shall see, the fourth way of knowing could only be thereby clarified. It is not simply something that goes on in the head, so to speak. It involves the whole person and with him or her the society in which human beings live. Descartes went on to science, Spinoza to what he called "ethic." With dualism we think that P. II ends the discussion of knowing. With non-dualism we find that the rest of the ETHIC is also required for understanding the fourth way of knowing. This is another facet of the notion of unity. Sp's thinking is indeed abound with paradoxes.

This observation prepares us for the next thing that has to be said about the fourth mode of perceiving or knowing intuitively, which even more clearly than all the foregoing distinguishes it from the other three—to such an extent that in approaching it in the ETHIC BdS said: "Besides these there is another," as though clearly there are two kinds of knowing: imagination and understanding. Discussion of this next characteristic of this knowing can only be begun in this chapter, for, as I have just observed, we must talk of Parts III, IV, and V of the ETHIC before it can be made very clear. Indeed, BdS does not finally discuss it till Prop. 22 to the end of Part V. The EU may well also have remained unfinished because of this characteristic as well as because of terminological difficulties.

It is a mark of this kind of perceiving or knowing, the knowing of particular things, that it turns into, or develops into, or becomes, or is indistinguishable from loving. We have been minimally prepared for this by the recognition that the Hebrew verb *Jadah* can be translated either with "to know" or with "to love." This, however, is not simply true for that Hebrew verb. It is also true in other languages. We have it in English when we say of Abraham that he knew Sarah and she was with child. Of course, this is now called "carnal knowledge" and is not rated as a form of *knowing*. Still, there it is. The word "conceive" also has a meaning in this connection. We conceive ideas (see Def. 3, P. II: "By means of *idea* I understand a Mind's conceiving"). Men and women conceive children in an act of loving.

Knowing intuitively, in other words, either becomes or is an Affection. I probably say "either becomes or is" because we seem to be dealing with a way of *knowing*, that is, with something of the mind. This is a clear sign that the notion of unity is extremely difficult to get into. However, as we get somewhat clear on it, we realize that there is a way of knowing which is of both the mind and the body. The attributes of thinking and extending are attributes of the same thing. Paradoxically in Schol., Prop. 49, P. II and elsewhere BdS describes imagination as primarily a physical or bodily function. That is to say, with knowing intuitively we come to a way of knowing in which the potency of the Mind is stressed over that of the Body, though it is still a way of knowing in which the Body is involved. Of course, when you come to reflect on it, all the ways of knowing involve the physical: the eyes, ears, fingers, etc., and words, the mouth, and so ad infinitum. In other words, in thinking about thinking and knowing we are usually involved with a chimera.

Thus, having pointed out that knowing intuitively involves the Body and seen it as a truism, it is better to return to the point that it is an Affection or a way of behaving affectively. It is not simply cognitive, as imagination distinctively is. It is an Affection, that is, an affection of the Body (see Def. 3, P. III) which increases our potency for living. That is to say, it is Love. In its highest manifestations BdS calls it "God's understanding Love." It arises with or is the intuitive knowing of singular things, the knowing which is not like seeing through a cloud or dreaming with eyes open. The phrase "understanding Love" strikes the keynote by bringing the cognitive and affective terms together. Further, since God is the singular things, or *Being*, this Love is a Love of God as well as God's Love. With it the image of God no longer stands between us and the things.

In Letter 37, talking about the method for emending understanding, BdS says that first you have to distinguish between understanding and imagination, that is, between the true idea and all the rest, namely the fictitious, the false, the dubious, and absolutely all those of memory. Then, presumably, attempt to have true ideas. This is arduous work and requires a firm purpose and a particular mode of living.

This description of the fourth way of knowing or perceiving enables us to recognize that it has been described by others, though they are not commonly referred to as philosophers. Thus, the anonymous author of *The Cloud of Unknowing*, St. John of the Cross, both Christian mystics, and Buddhists offer similar advice in the matter of coming to what they respectively call union and awakening. Enter the clouds of unknowing and forgetfulness, says the first; empty the memory of all natural apprehensions, remarks St. John; attain no-mind, advises the Buddhist. All are agreed that this requires work, a firm purpose, and a particular mode of living.

The superstition that often surrounds religion and the fact that this way of knowing is affective as well as cognitive have tended to render it obscure as a way of knowing. Sp's rational account of it reduces this obscurity. We find then that he has not only brought religion and philosophy together in identifying God with the natural. He has also done this by describing as a mode of awareness or consciousness a phenomenon of human being that has till his time and usually since been regarded as having to do with the supernatural or religious. His insistence in the ETHIC that this awareness is a knowledge of singular things is the key to his clarity in this matter.

A further word of clarification will not be amiss. When BdS and the others say that attaining to this way of knowing requires work, a firm purpose, and a particular mode of living, we are inclined to ask: Why lead such a disciplined and strict life, a life that sounds monastic? Why not relax and enjoy life? The answer is that the discipline and strict measures are preliminary to coming to understand. We must not, as Wittgenstein pointed out about language, confuse learning to do something with doing it. Discipline is required for the learning of any skill. After you have the skill you enjoy it. Indeed, the joy can commence in learning the skill (recall your formal education which trained you in imagination). Of course, you may have to continue with some training even after the skill is acquired. But the joy of exercising it compensates for that. Furthermore, all these things are matters of degree. Just because you may never run a four-minute mile is no reason not to learn to walk.

Thinking of the other way of knowing as something esoteric or extraordinary, surrounding it, so to speak, with a halo, can and has blinded us to these matters of fact. It is important for understanding the other way to see that it is quite as practical and down-to-earth as knowing in the imaginative way. It is, if you will, simply another skill. That it has been less common than the other way should not lead us to think that it is uncommon. Indeed, in the context of BdS it should appear, as it is, thoroughly natural.

CHAPTER 8

Human Servitude

I

Correspondents questioned BdS about *Descartes' Principles;* about the TTP; about Parts I and II of the ETHIC; about chemistry, optics, and games of chance. They never, at least in the letters we have, asked him about Parts III, IV, and V of the ETHIC, which concern respectively human Affections, Servitude, and Freedom. That is to say, except in the context of religion, they never asked him about his views on human nature and conduct. Yet the things he saw in these regards were and are as novel as his insights into unity and understanding. Indeed, they re-present these visions in somewhat more concrete form.

"The majority," says BdS (Preface, P. III), "who have written concerning Affections, & human beings' fashion of living, seem to treat, not concerning natural things which follow Nature's common laws, but concerning things which are outside Nature. Indeed they seem to conceive a human being in nature as a dominion within a dominion" (the mixed capitalizing of "nature" is deliberate). They believe that a human being is more at odds with nature than in accord with her, and they attribute an absolute potency to it in its actions; as though it were not otherwise determined than by itself. They find the cause of human impotence in some defect in human nature and ignore the common potency of Nature.

BdS, in contrast, will endeavor to determine the nature of the Affections and their forces, and what a Mind is capable of in their moderation. He will "consider human actions and appetites as if it were a question concerning lines, planes, or bodies;" that is, dispassionately and objectively.

The dominant themes of Parts I and II are in this declaration of intention. A human being is at one with Nature. Since there are not substances, it does not have a free will nor is it the cause of its own actions. Finally, we will look at it with as much understanding as possible. For this reason, because the phrase "he or she" is cumbersome, and because Sp's word for human being was the Latin *homo* which is basically of common gender, I will refer to a human being by "it."

The central conception in Sp's view of human nature is that of the Affection (for the capitalization of this term see above). It is formally defined at the beginning of P. III (Def. 3) and again at the end of the part, a treatment accorded no other term in the ETHIC. In fact the whole part is a third definition. The concept is thus manifoldly complex. It becomes apparent with "Affection" that the same is true of all Sp's other terms. They may be formally defined at the beginning of a part, but they get their uses in contexts, which means that they have no one or definite meaning.

BdS, of course, sees a human as a mode of being, or an affection of *Being*. Modes of being endeavor to be, or, as BdS puts it, endeavor to persevere in their be-ing (*esse;* see Appendix p. 174) or to conserve it; this endeavor is an aspect of being. BdS calls it "conatus." In a human being when it is related to the Mind he calls it "Will," and when simultaneously to the Mind and to the Body "Appetite." (These words are being capitalized because they have in BdS a usage quite different and only derivative from the common: a non-dualistic usage.) When human beings are conscious of their Appetites he calls them "Desires." "By means of *Affection* I understand a Body's affections, by which this Body's potency for acting is augmented or diminished, helped or coerced, & simultaneously these affections' ideas."

We pause to note something of extraordinary importance. One sees it by reflecting on Sp's insight into unity. It is that, although (as the terms "Mind" and "Body" indicate) BdS has defined Affections in relation to human beings, there is nothing in the definition that precludes the possibility that other modes of being should have Affections; or *emotions* as Sp's Latin word *affectus* has been most commonly translated. We have found that all modes of being are established or exist in the attribute of thinking. Hence all things "think." We are now to find that they also have Affections.

BdS explicitly refers to the Affections of animals in Schol., Prop. 57, P. III ("for we can by no means doubt that brutes sense, as soon as we have come to know a Mind's origin." The Latin for "sense" is *sentio* which means "think", "feel"). However, it becomes apparent by the same token that so-called "inanimate" things can have Affections, or be affectively. It is only our prejudices reflected in a narrow notion of "idea" in Def. 3 that keeps us from seeing this. Part III of the ETHIC as well as Parts I and II expand the limits of our understanding.—The notion of the pet rock was recently seized on to what some regard as an alarming extent. Because of its ludicrousness? Or also because of a deep recognition of something profound. As BdS says in Schol., Prop. 34, P. V, we are all conscious of the eternity of our Minds, but we confuse it with duration and think of immortality. We sometimes see deeply into ourselves, but are not clear about what we see.

A few more definitions are needed. Thus in P. II BdS indicates that he understands the same by "reality" and "perfection" (Def. 6), and he has the latter word in mind in the sense of "completion." In P. III he says that by "adequate cause" he means that whose effect can be clearly perceived by means of it (Def. 1). Thus a woman, for example, can be said to be the adequate cause of a kind act if she is a kind person. One can understand the act by knowing her. We are surprised by a kind act from one not known for her kindness. Finally, BdS specifies that he will call an Affection an *action* if we are its adequate cause, otherwise a *passion*. The notion of adequate cause proves important. Descartes wrote a book on the Affections or emotions called *The Passions of the Soul*. For him the human being is always passive in its affective behavior. There is no notion of an action in *The Passions of the Soul*.

[123]

BdS then defines two Affections: Joy, a passion by which the Mind passes to greater perfection; and Sadness, a passion by which it passes to less perfection. As he uses "perfection," the definition of *Joy* means that it is a passion by which a Mind (i.e., a person mentally considered) passes to fuller reality, that is, more being. The reverse, of course, is true for Sadness. BdS then says that he takes Desire, Joy, and Sadness to be the three primary or primitive Affections from which originate all other passive Affections. He proceeds in the rest of P. III to demonstrate this by deriving some forty-eight passions from these. Thus, Love is Joy concomitant with an idea of an external cause. Hate is Sadness concomitant with an idea of an external cause (Schol., Prop. 11).

I say "some forty-eight passions" because a list of the passions in the ETHIC depends on the part of the ETHIC in which you count them (i.e, in the propositions and scholia of P. III or in a section called "Definitions of Affections" which follows the propositions). Actually there are forty-eight or so sketches of passions, for it is characteristic of Sp's thinking that Affections as he regards them "can be defined by no number" (Schol., Prop. 59). There are as many as there can be objects of Affections. Thus, the Love of a mother for her first child is one, for her second another, and for her spouse a third. But also, her Love for child #1 on this occasion is one, her love for it on that occasion another, and so ad infinitum.

We said that the notion of Affection is complex. In the formal definition it is said to be an affection of the Body together with the idea of that affection. When the primary Affections are specified, it is found that Desire is one of them. However, a Desire is an Appetite of which we are conscious. (Note that we do not want to speak of Desire, but of *a* Desire and *an* Appetite. There is nothing like universals outside the Mind for BdS, nothing like substances.) An Appetite in turn is a conatus for persevering in be-ing. There is, finally, Sp's distinction between an action and a passion, or between an active Affection and a passive one. As these complexities become apparent, so does the inadvisability of the use of the word "emotion" for what is

being discussed. This inadvisability amounts to extreme unde-
sirability when we consider the role of the ideas of the Body's
affections in Affections.

BdS does this in Props. 58 and 59 of P. III, the only two in
that part in which actions instead of passions are considered.
When the ideas of the Body's affections are confused and mutilated, the Affection in question is a passion. When these ideas
are clear and distinct, the Affection is an action. In the first case
the Mind is said to be passively, in the second actively. In the
first case a person's behavior is confused or, we might say, irra-
tional; in the second it is straightforward or rational. The distinction between the two is comparable to that between imagination and understanding. Indeed, it is Sp's insight into the
fourth way of knowing that leads him to distinguish, as Descartes did not, between passions and active Affections.

This fact is related to another factor in defining active Affections: The primary or primitive Affections from which these
Affections originate are Love and Desire (in existing translations of Props. 58 and 59 "pain" or "sadness" are listed instead
of "Desire," making the rest of the ETHIC incomprehensible).
Unlike the passions there is never an element of Sadness in
them. The reason for this is apparent from the characteristic of
the intuitive way of knowing discussed at the end of Chapter 7.
It is a way of knowing which is Loving. People wonder why
Sadness is not in the makeup of active Affections. That it is not
seems quite arbitrary until it is seen that a different kind of
knowing is involved in active Affections. Thus does Sp's insight
into unity enter into his view of human Affections and the latter
become important for an understanding of knowing intuitively.
Let us consider an active Affection.

"All actions, which follow from Affections which are related
to a Mind in so far as it understands, I refer to Fortitude, which
I distinguish into High-spiritedness, & Generosity. For by
means of *High-spiritedness* I understand *a Desire by which each
endeavors to conserve his be-ing solely according to reason's dictate.* By
means of *Generosity*, however, I understand *a Desire by which each
solely according to reason's dictate endeavors to help the remaining*

human beings, & to join them to him in friendship" (Schol., Prop. 59).

(Descartes listed friendship as a passion. It may be considered an Affection in BdS, though he never discusses it as such. The word is an interesting one. "Friend" comes from a participle of a verb, Anglo-Saxon *freon,* meaning "to love." The Latin word for friendship also reflects this: *amicitia,* from *amo* or "I love." The Anglo-Saxon word also gives English "free" and German *Friede,* peace, and *Freude,* joy.)

Sp's example of an active Affection bears considerable reflective scrutiny aside from that in the parenthesis. "Understands" (in "a Mind in so far as it understands"), for example, is used instead of "knowing intuitively;" and "reason's dictate" appears on our scene. In Prop. 26, P. IV the phrase is used to give still another definition of understanding" (others being those of "knowing intuitively"). Understanding is *whatever we endeavor* according to reason's dictate. In other words, it is a kind of behavior. This usage of the word "understanding" appears in common parlance when we speak of an understanding person. Because of these complexities I can only urge the reader to reflect, as I say, on Sp's example.

It is clear, for instance, that the word "reason" in "reason's dictate" or in "the dictate of reason," as BdS sometimes has it, does not have the same use as it does when BdS styles a genus of knowledge as "reason." However, knowing intuitively does grow out of reason. We do not have what BdS calls knowing intuitively until we are rational, for example, until we can speak. Think of the baby growing from infancy through learning to talk, through school and into adulthood. Thus the dictate of reason is what we follow with ever-increasingly adequate ideas. One has, I repeat, to reflect on these things and realize that what BdS calls "reason" in P. II is not *precisely* what we call "science," though the latter is an advanced form of the former. Nor is the distinction between reasoning and understanding a real one. It is one BdS made for purposes of conveying his insight—here in the area of human conduct.

Before turning to what BdS calls "human Servitude," it may

be of some assistance to observe that passions can turn into actions (in Sp's sense of the term). In noticing this the relation of Sp's view of Affections to his insight into unity is seen even more sharply. For example, the Love between a man and a woman that may lead to marriage is initially usually a passion. Commonly they are young and the relation between them is one of dependency. Each needs the other for further maturing. Each passes to greater perfection with this Love, but that it is often marked with Sadness (in Jealousy, say) is a sign that it is a passion. As understanding of each other and themselves increases, their Love turns into an active Affection. This also happens as each becomes more mature, that is, dependent on self rather than on the other. This growing independence is the mark that the Individual is approaching that exemplar of human nature which we call "God"; which, remember, is *causa sui* (cause of itself).

The reader is finally urged to take up P. III on his or her own. Aside from anything else it is a marvellous and fascinating analysis of Affections. I know of none other in philosophic literature which is its equal. I think, for example, of Self-love which can turn either into the passion of Pride (one of the worst) or into the action of Acquiescence in oneself. In the first the Love is thinking more than justly of oneself. In the second it is understanding oneself. However, through it all in uncounted ways, as in this example, the basic notions of unity and understanding are repeatedly at work, being thus illuminated by concrete examples. This should also be kept in mind as I turn to P. IV. We should not allow dualistic thinking to prevent us from seeing that Sp's account of Servitude is also further explication of knowing intuitively and hence of unity.

II

BdS defines *Servitude* in the Preface of P. IV, in which he also refers to that examplar of human nature. Servitude is human impotence in moderating Affections; "for a human being subject to Affections is not dependent on itself but on fortune, in whose power it is such that it is often constrained, although it sees the better for it, to follow nevertheless the worse." His purpose in P. IV is to demonstrate the causes of our impotence, and to show what Affections have of good or ill.

BdS continues in the Preface by amplifying what he says in the EU (p. 8) and the Appendix, P. I about *perfect* and *imperfect*, and *good* and *ill*. "Perfect" is a relative term and indicates completion. "Good" and "ill" "also indicate nothing positive in things, considered to wit in themselves, and are not other than modes of thinking or notions, which we form from this, that we compare things to each other." Nevertheless they are all useful terms, once this is understood.—"By means of *good* I understand that which we know for certain to be useful to us. By means of *ill*, however, that which we know for certain to be an impediment to our sharing some good" (Defs. 1 and 2).

A common notion or axiom introduced in P. IV enables BdS to explicate the first of the two causes he finds for human impotence. This is the notion that in the nature of things no singular thing is given than which another more potent and stronger is not given. From this it clearly follows that our impotence is due in part to the fact that Nature is more potent and stronger than any one of us. We can and do act on Nature. Witness our dams, highways, levelling of hills, and forming governments. But it is obvious that Nature acts more on us than we do on her and that we are, relative to her, passive.

The second cause of human impotence in moderating Affections can by no means be deduced from any commonly held notion, though, paradoxically, it has long been in our ken. However, awareness of it is clearly related to the view of human knowledge and knowing which Sp's insight into unity provides. This awareness is expressed in a quotation from Ovid's *Metamorphoses* which BdS cites in the scholium for Prop. 17: "I see the better and approve; the worse I follow."

The quotation was a favorite and BdS either recites or paraphrases it some ten times throughout his writings. It puts the finger on a very important aspect of his thinking with remarkable aptness. He also quotes Ecclesiastes in this scholium: "He who augments knowing, augments sorrow." This does not do the job as well as Ovid's lines. However, the Old Testament was never far from Sp's Mind, and several sections of the scholia from propositions after Prop. 17 are either repeated or amplified in the TTP. It becomes evident that Sp's insight in Part I of the ETHIC turned the moral commandments of the Old Testament into "eternal verities" (see Annotation 34 in the TTP; it is Note 28 for Chapter 16 in Elwes' translation). That is, the "justification" of moral laws (Why must or should I do this?) is not a matter of reason but of understanding.

Ovid's remark concerns a fact with which we are all familiar. We can know or recognize what is the good or right thing to do on an occasion, and not do it. Instead we find ourselves doing what we "wanted" in place of what we knew we "ought" to do. Sp's explication of this occurs in Prop. 14: True knowledge of good and ill can moderate no Affection, in so far as it is true, but only in so far as it is itself an Affection. That is, there is, as we say today, a kind of knowledge that is off the tops of our heads, and it is of no avail as compared with gut knowledge. And this fact, that there is a kind of knowledge, some of which we venerate by calling it "science," but which is of no avail in human conduct, deceives us. It lulls us into a false sense of security and prevents us from turning it into something which is of avail. As such it is the second prime cause of human impotence in moderating Affections.

I have remarked that there is little wonder that BdS never finished the EU. The fourth mode of perceiving, knowing intuitively or understanding, turns out to have a surprising property: It *is* some activity as opposed or perhaps in addition to knowledge *about* that activity. At the end of the EU (p. 38) BdS lists the properties of understanding: It involves certitude, it forms ideas absolutely, it forms positive prior to negative ideas, etc. The EU then terminates abruptly. BdS was talking about understanding as though it were another, more excellent, kind of reasoning or thinking. It is not. It is a way of behaving, or affective as well as cognitive. This is made clear in Parts IV and V of the ETHIC. The EU could not be finished because it had been couched in all the standard terms for things cognitive: "perceiving," "knowing," "understanding," "idea," etc.; whereas effective explication of understanding (as BdS came to employ the term) requires the use of words that apply to the affective or emotive aspect of human behavior: "will," "Affection," "passion," "action," and "Joy."

Consider an example. We can know *about* swimming by seeing people swim, by reading about it, and by thinking and reasoning about it; but we will only understand swimming by first learning to swim and then swimming. (Wang Yang-ming, the sixteenth-century Chinese sage, was on to this with his dictum that knowledge and action are one and the same.) Then contrast the swimming person with a person laid low by a blow. You would not say that the former was unconscious. You would properly say this of the latter. No, the swimming person is consciously swimming, though he is not conscious *of* his swimming or *that* he is swimming. In fact, if either of the latter happen, he will swim less well than he was. We have long associated consciousness and awareness with thinking *of* something. BdS perceived that there is another kind of being consciously. It is the subject of the last twenty propositions of P. V.

We will only note here that, in this way of being, objects of consciousness no longer play a role in being conscious. In the case of one object of consciousness, the idea of God, this fact has a curious consequence: One is left with an experience that has no object. Knowing God intuitively is a way of behaving. Theology is a study in imagination, or a study of the grammar of speech in which "God" occurs. (We noted the peculiarity of the idea of God in the chapter on Descartes.)

It is small wonder that P. IV is curious. In its Preface BdS tells us that he will examine the causes of our impotence, and what is good or ill in Affections. In the scholium to Prop. 17 he announces that, having done this, that is, shown why we do not observe reason's precepts, he will now examine what reason prescribes for us. There is no mention of the good or ill in Affections. Finally the Part concludes with a lengthy Appendix which, BdS tells us, redoes in another form what he has just done. In fact the Appendix amounts to a series of maxims on practical living, and toward the end of the propositions of P. IV there are several on what is good or ill in the Affections.

There is only apparent confusion in this part which seems to have a title that applies only to the subject of the first eighteen propositions, that seems to have a different purpose after Prop. 18 than the announced purpose, and that has an Appendix different in tone from the part though its author says that the subject is the same. As his understanding of understanding unfolded, BdS found himself immersed in the practical. Penetration into unity was not an upward movement to loftier realms of thought than the rational. It was a downward movement into the concrete elements of everyday life. As we have just seen, the understanding of the spiritual element in a human being, which in the Middle Ages seemed to have become only flights of theological phantasy, came down to earth in the here and now. The spiritual life was seen not to be one in another realm, but a way of being in this. Augustine's City of God was found to be an imaginative projection of the cities human beings may develop according to the conduct of reason. The spiritual (as the word suggests) was seen to be a life according to another way of knowing, knowing intuitively or understanding. (And the original Christian message was one of Love before it came to be thought of abstractly or imaginatively.)

BdS summarizes what reason prescribes in the scholium to Prop. 18. Reason postulates that "each love himself, seek what is useful to him, what is really useful [i.e., not imagined so], & have an appetite for all that which really conducts a human being to greater perfection, & absolutely that each endeavor, as far as it is in him, to conserve his be-ing." Next, since virtue is nothing other than to act according to the laws of our own nature, "it follows *firstly* that virtue's foundation is the conatus itself for conserving one's own be-ing, & that felicity consists in this, that a human being is able to conserve its be-ing." It follows, secondly, that one is to have an appetite for virtue on account of itself (BdS is using "virtue" in its original sense of "strength"), and, thirdly, that those who kill themselves are impotent in spirit.

BdS then adds that it is obvious that we need many things outside us for conserving our be-ing, of which none "is more useful to a human being than a human being." (He takes the first part of this to be obvious from Postulate 4, P. II, which occurs at the end of the section on bodies after Prop. 13: A human Body, that it be conserved, needs a great many other bodies. The unity or non-dualistic character of Sp's thinking throughout Parts III, IV, and V is present in his constant reference to the Body. Think only, for example, of the definition of an Affection: an affection of the Body, together with that affection's idea.) Since two Individuals of the same nature joined together compose an Individual doubly more potent than a singular Individual, "nothing, I say, more outstanding can human beings opt for conserving their be-ing than that all so agree in all things, that the Minds and Bodies of all compose as it were one Mind, & one Body." From which it follows that human beings governed by reason, that is, who seek what is useful to them according to the conduct of reason, have an appetite for nothing for themselves which they do not desire for the remaining human beings.

The scholium concludes with the observation that there are those who believe the contrary: "that this beginning, to wit that each is held to seek what is useful to him, is the foundation of Impiety, *not* the foundation of virtue, & Piety." The penultimate scholium of the ETHIC strikes the same note: "The common persuasion of the vulgar seems to be other." The majority seem to believe that they are free to the extent that they are permitted to yield to every impulse. Piety, Religion, and all things relating to Fortitude of spirit they take to be onerous things, "which they hope to put aside after death, & to receive the wages of servitude, namely of Piety, & Religion." The effect of the insight into unity is that of turning things on their head. There are not substances. True or real knowing is not of universals but of particulars. "Beatitude is not virtue's reward, but virtue itself" (Prop. 42, P. V). The rest of P. IV consists in demonstrating that virtue's foundation is interest in self because interest in self is interest in others. We are all modes of the same thing. With this insight the distinction between selfishness and altruism either dissolves or is seen for what it is, a distinction of reason.

You can follow the demonstration of the prescriptions of reason for yourself by turning to the propositions of P. IV from Prop. 18 on (see Appendix). As you do, it becomes apparent that human Servitude consists in living according to imagination in Sp's broad sense of that term, that is, according to the first three ways of knowing or perceiving. "Take here by means of *imagination* whatever you will," says BdS in the EU (p. 32), "provided it be something diverse from understanding, & whence the soul has the condition of being passive; for it is quite the same, however you take it, as soon as we know it to be something vague, & in relation to which the soul is passive, & also simultaneously know the mode in which we are freed from it with the help of understanding" and when our ideas "originate from the Mind's potency itself."

As BdS explicates the prescriptions of reason, he observes that suicide occurs only when a human being is constrained by external causes, never from the necessity of its nature (Schol., Prop. 20). Its nature is to persevere in its be-ing. He defines "Religion:" "whatever we desire, & act, of which we are cause, in so far as we have an idea of God, or in so far as we know God, I relate to Religion" (Schol. 1, Prop. 37). (Remember, we can know God imaginatively, or with understanding.) In Schol. 2 of that proposition he discusses merit, wrongdoing, justice and injustice; relating them all to the nature of the civil state (they have no place in the natural state). This discussion is taken from Chapter 16 of the *TTP*: "Concerning a Republic's Foundations; concerning the natural and civil right of each individual, and concerning the right of the Highest Powers."

(Sp's views on the origins of a civic body or state resemble Hobbes' with two important exceptions, one of which BdS notes in Letter 50. He preserves the natural right intact so that the Highest Powers, whatever the form of government, have no more right among subjects than is proportionate to the power by which the government is superior to the subjects. The second exception is that BdS did not believe with Hobbes that the end of government is security for the citizens. The end of government is to help people compose as it were one Mind and one Body so that they attain the fullest possible development of their natures.)

As BdS proceeds he also notes that a person can die without becoming a cadaver, namely when his Body is so mutated that he is a different person (Schol., Prop. 39; an observation related both to Sp's insight into identity and to his view that the Body is not the vehicle of the soul or mind). He observes that Loves and Desires can be excessive, but not Hilarity (Props. 43 and 44). In the vein of Schol., Prop. 39, that is, with attention to our physical aspect, he notes that the sapient or wise "remake, & recreate [themselves], moderately, with pleasant food, & drink, as well as with pleasant odors, the amenities of green plants, ornaments, music, sports, theatres, & other things of this mode, which each can use without any damage to another" (Schol., Corol. 2, Prop. 45).

In a different vein BdS observes that Commiseration in one who lives according to the conduct of reason is *per se* ill and useless (Prop. 50). However, he notes that "he who is moved neither by reason, nor by Commiseration to be of assistance to others, is rightly named *inhuman*. For he seems to be dissimilar to a human being" (Schol., Prop. 50; the ETHIC is among other things concerned with specifying what it is to be humanly—"that exemplar of human nature"). That is to say, when we live at the level of imagination only, Commiseration, though not a virtue or a strength, is useful. In the scholium to Prop. 54 BdS notes the same for Humility, Penitence, and Reverence. Though not virtues, these are of great utility to a state. It is no wonder that the Prophets, who consulted the common utility and not that of a few, so greatly recommended them. (We are in the TTP again which deals with living according to the knowledge of God as that is in imagination.)

Props. 67 to 73 are transitional to P. V; they concern a free human being. BdS moves from observing that a free human being's sapience is a meditation not on death but on life to observing that a human being is freer in a civic body than in solitude. There is the theme of be-ing and the theme of unity which is identification with others.

In the final scholium (to Prop. 73) he notes that these observations about true freedom are related to Fortitude, that is, to High-spiritedness and Generosity. The fortitudinous human being "hates no one, is angry with, envious of, indignant with no one, despises no one, and is minimally proud" (the qualities listed are like those mentioned in the third of the advantages of his teaching which BdS lists at the end of P. II). All the things, says BdS, that look to true life, & Religion are set forth in Props. 37 and 46 of P. IV: "namely that Hate is to be overcome with Love in return, & that each who is conducted by reason desires that a good, for which he has an appetite for himself, also be a good for the rest." A fortitudinous person "considers this above all, namely that all things follow from the necessity of the divine nature [Note that this could be read "necessity of Divine Nature"], and accordingly that whatever he thinks is molesting, & an ill, & whatever further seems impious, horrifying, unjust, & dishonorable originates from this, that *he* conceives the things themselves disturbedly, mutilatedly, & confusedly; & for this cause he above all endeavors to remove impediments to true knowledge, such as Hate, Anger, Envy, Dirision, Pride, & the remaining things of this mode. . . . He endeavors, as much as he is able, as we have said, to act well, & to rejoice. How far however human virtue extends itself to attaining these things, & of what it is capable, I shall demonstrate in the following Part."

(Notice that in describing a virtuous person BdS is *at the same time* indicating a means for coming to "true knowledge," that is, understanding: the removal from our lives of Hate, etc., in a word, the moderation of passions. Understanding is emended not only by distinguishing true ideas from all the rest. It is also emended by reducing the passions.)

The dictates of reason are familiar. They are the moral precepts taught in the great religions. In the early Hebrew and the

Christian religions their justification lay in faith and revelation (see the TTP). This is Servitude. In the ETHIC their justification lies in understanding or knowing them intuitively. This, we are now aware, consists in having clear and distinct, or true ideas of them; *which also means living them.* True ideas are Affections or ways of behaving. Understanding is "whatever we endeavor according to reason" (Prop. 26, P. IV).

I will only add, that as the third way of knowing, reason is midway between imagination and understanding (see above). In so far as it issues in general propositions, it is part of imagination. In so far as it renders ideas clear and distinct (see the quotation from Schol., Prop. 73 above), or forms them truly, it is part of understanding. In either case, until the propositions or ideas are embodied in particular behavioral acts, that is, are Affections, they are not being understood. To know them merely rationally is to be in Servitude. This is another reason why the EU had to remain unfinished, and did so remain. We can talk about a method for emending understanding. Only practice will emend it.

CHAPTER 9

Human Freedom

BdS commences his discussion of human Freedom in the ETHIC with a Preface to Part V. He is, he tells us, going to show "what reason itself is capable of in Affections," and "what a Mind's Freedom or beatitude is." He is not concerned with details. The actual perfection of the Mind looks to Logic and the care of the Body to Medicine, which observation gives us another reason why the EU remained unfinished. BdS had insights to convey, not a philosophic system.

He then examines the view that a human being is "a dominion within a dominion," as he put it in P. III. He traces it as far back as the Stoics, who thought that our Affections (that is, our behavior) depend absolutely on our will. He next analyzes the most recent expression of this view: Descartes' claim that the mind and the body are substances and that the union we observe between them takes place by means of the pineal gland in the brain. BdS emerges from the incredibility of this in wonder: "this is the sentiment of this celebrated Man . . . which I could scarcely believe to have been brought forth by such a man, were it less acute." How can one understand the union of mind and body in terms of a material thing, that little gland?

The exposition of the poverty of Cartesianism in this regard, of course, rests on the proposition, 5 of P. I, that there are no substances. A human being is not a dominion within the dominion of Nature. And thus, too, Descartes' notion that the will is free (i.e., self-caused or a substance) is to be abandoned, as BdS has in Parts I and II. This insight, however, has brought us to

[137]

an appreciation of a Mind's potency, namely understanding or intuitively knowing. Awareness of this enables us to determine the things by which Affections can be moderated or coerced (BdS is referring to Affections which are passions). BdS calls these things "remedies" for Affections, "which I believe *all certainly experience, but do not accurately observe, nor distinctly see* (emphasis added). Finally, from this knowledge of Mind, that it is understanding, "we shall deduce all those things which look to its beatitude," or well-being. In other terms, this is our being well, considered as thinking modes of being.

It is of the utmost importance in following BdS here that we keep in mind the fourth mode of perceiving or knowing; that it is of singular things, not universals; and that it is an Affection or an affective way of behaving. BdS reminds us of this in the first proposition of P. V (see Appendix). He then states the first "remedy" for passions: Think of other things than the object of a passion and the passion will gradually be destroyed (Prop. 2). As BdS has said, we all experience this phenomenon, though we may not be sufficiently aware of it. When we think of other things than the causes of our woes, our passionate responses to these causes subside.

A second remedy is associated with the fact that a passion ceases to be a passion as we form a clear idea of it, that is, understand it (Prop. 3). As I come to understand my Anger for someone, which involves understanding both myself and that person, I become less angry with that person. "Than this remedy for Affections, which consists to wit in true knowledge of them, no other more outstanding can be thought of, which depends on our power, since no other potency of a Mind is given than that for thinking, & forming adequate ideas" (Schol., Prop. 4). In this scholium BdS indicates that this remedy can also transform a passion into an action, that is, an active Affection. This is a further reason for its outstandingness. For example, Ambition, or a Desire to have others live according to our lights, and which is not much different from Pride (thinking too highly of oneself), can with understanding it be turned into Piety, or a Desire for benefitting others (see Schol. 1, Prop. 37, P. IV).

Another remedy for passions is the knowledge that all things happen of necessity (BdS also lists this at the end of P. II as the second advantage of the teaching that the will is not free). The more this knowledge is about particular things the greater is the potency of the Mind in Affections. Thus, Sadness over some good which perishes is mitigated by considering that it could in no way have been preserved. So also no one commiserates with an infant because it cannot walk. Yet, if the majority were born adults and only one or two infants, the majority would commiserate with the latter (Schol., Prop. 6). To take another example, if my watch is stolen, it helps to reflect that one of the watch's properties was that it should be with me for only a certain period of time. As I understand the watch I know this, and bemoan the theft the less. (See above p. 66: The necessity of which BdS is speaking is that *all* a thing's properties are necessary for it to be what it is. This is not ordinary "determinism." It is a consequence of the insight into unity.)

BdS continues to describe remedies for Affections in P. V, so that we need not be concerned with reproducing the list here (sometimes two or more propositions are required for one remedy). He explains, for example, that we can, by repeatedly reflecting on certain maxims "for a right fashion of living," and committing them to memory, prepare ourselves to some extent for emergencies which may arise. Thus, if we have convinced ourselves that Hate is overcome by Love, or Generosity, and not compensated for with reciprocal Hate, we will less easily turn on one who hates us (Schol., Prop. 10) (Benjamin Franklin wrote highly of a version of this remedy in his *Autobiography;* see under "Franklin's Plan of Life").

I must interject something here. I have said that BdS is not concerned with details. Why, then, this attention to the remedies? An answer is to consider what it reveals. Thinking dualistically, we are inclined to reckon knowing intuitively as really distinct from the other modes of knowing. But the distinctions

[139]

between the ways are only rational ones that BdS made for purposes of sharing his vision. He himself tells us that understanding grows out of reason, though not out of vague experience and from signs. He excludes the latter when he says this (Props. 41 and 42, for example, in P. II), because the adequate ideas of understanding come from the clear ideas which it is one of the functions of reasoning to provide. But it must also be clear that reasoning depends on experience, and on reading and conversation. So too in the third remedy we see that a proposition of reason, that all things happen of necessity, is involved in an intuitive knowing or the understanding which reduces a passion. And in the fourth remedy we find a reliance on memory, which was excluded in *making* the distinction between imagination and understanding and in *preparing* to understand, but is now seen to play a role in *understanding*. This is confusing until it is realized that knowing intuitively is not *really* distinct from reason, and imagination not really distinct from understanding. Thus, the discussion of the remedies illuminates understanding.

To resume, BdS reminds us (Prop. 15) that he who understands himself and his Affections loves God, and the more so the more he understands. When it is remembered that for BdS God is *Being*, everyone will recognize that he or she has had this experience, for an understanding of ourselves increases our Joy in being, more strictly, in be-ing. BdS then discusses this experience. It impresses us enormously (Prop. 16). Well-being or being well is exempt from passions (Prop. 17). No one can hate be-ing (Prop. 18), at least no one who is being well. No one expects a reward for this (Prop. 19, another version of which closes the ETHIC: Beatitude is not virtue's reward, but virtue itself). This Love of be-ing cannot be defiled with Envy, nor with Jealousy, but it is increased as we think of plural human beings joined with *being* in the same Love (Prop. 20). We need not imagine a multitude of human beings so joined; even thinking of more than one increases this Love.

Once again experience testifies to this, though we will "not accurately observe, nor distinctly see" what it teaches if we do not understand God, that is, *Being*. For in that mode of being the *image* of God plays no part. We no longer think of him. We simply are. "Thou shalt have no other Gods before me. Thou shalt not make unto thee graven images" (Exodus 20 vs. 3 and 4). There are not substances. Distinguish imagination from understanding. See Schol., Prop. 68, P. IV where BdS refers to the story of the first human by Moses, saying that this and other things seem to have been signified by that story. BdS has not departed from the Old Testament. He has deepened his understanding of the religion of his fathers.

BdS is now ready to discuss human Freedom (Props. 21 to 42). Having done with the mode of living in which we are passive, he moves on to that in which we are active. Before we follow him there, it will be well to answer a question which occurs to those who read about the remedies for the passions, or the potency of reason or understanding among the Affections. Note first that BdS alternates "reason" with "understanding" in the Preface to P. V. Try not to get hung up on either of these terms. Note second that "reason" or understanding is itself an Affection and we have been considering its power *among* the Affections, not *over* them. The question, then, is: BdS says, think of some thing other than the object of a passion, think of maxims for living, etc., but who does this or how is such thinking initiated?

If we do not have free wills, if we do not have some absolute power for doing these things, how do they come about? Answer: Before you try to explain them, recognize, as BdS urges, that they do happen. He has simply called attention to matters of everyday experience. Then you may notice that you have introduced the notion of free will to explain them, or the notion that you are an independent agent. Why? As BdS says in the Appendix, P. I and the scholium of Prop. 2, P. III, we are conscious of our actions, but ignorant of their causes. In that ignorance we postulate or assume a cause: ourselves, that is, our free wills. Why? The notion of substance, or the self-caused (the notion that we are discrete units). This in turn blinds you to the fact that you are not a separate entity, really distinct from other modes of being. In fact, the causes of such thinkings as those in the remedies are other human beings. They, so to speak, at first do your thinking for you. Then the thinkings they have caused in you cause other thinkings in you. We are all as one Mind and one Body. Nothing is more useful to a human being than another human being.

Let me repeat this for emphasis. Why do we make the assumption that we have free wills? The answer is the thinking that we are separate entities, really distinct from other people. What else, then, could cause me to do the things I do, *at least initially*. In this thinking, this vast subjectivity, we are blind to our real union with other beings. We do not see that it is other human beings who initiate our thinking, who, so to speak, at first do our thinking for us. Then our own thinkings cause other thinkings in us. We are all, as BdS says, as one Mind and one Body.

That our thinking is at first initiated by others, or that we are not its first cause, so to speak, is a variation of the notion of unity. The proposition, of course, is confirmed by experience. Just watch infants growing to childhood, children to adolescence, and so on. However, something blinds us to this obvious fact. It appears in another form of the question just answered. If we do not have free wills or some absolute power over our actions, how can we be held morally responsible for anything we do? If everything we do is the result of the influence of environment or heredity on us, then we are not free to do what we do and thus not responsible for what we do. But we do hold each other responsible and we do praise and blame.

Sp's answer to this form of the question is given in Schol., Prop. 29, P. III; the Explication of Def. 27, P. III; and Schol. 2, Prop. 37, P. IV. It also lies in the whole of the TTP, and finally in his notion of understanding or knowing intuitively. Briefly, we praise when people do something that pleases us, and blame when they do the reverse. The education of children consists in a system of rewards and punishment, which are forms of praise and blame. In order to live together and attain the benefits thereof, human beings form civic bodies or states to which each transfers some of his right and power for living. Our notions of merit and wrongdoing, and justice and injustice develop in this connection. In a natural state there is no place for such notions. We also praise and blame, *and* hold people responsible for what they do in this civil context. We hold them responsible to make them responsible, that is, good citizens. Reward and punishment, then, are educative and civilizing.

But this natural answer to the question about moral responsibility does not suffice for most of us. It seems to suck the meaning out of the word "moral." There *is* a difference between that we want to do, and what we *ought* to do. Sp's naturalism seems to concern the former, but not the latter. We all have a conatus for be-ing. With reason we find that we accomplish that conatus best, generally, by having societies and governments. That is reasonable. But what about the notion of the ought?

If you return to the first question: What initiates the thinking that remedies passions? and its answer: The thinking of others, you find the dissatisfaction with the answer to the question about moral responsibility looming in a simple form. But what causes the thinking of others? The thinking of still others. But . . . and so ad infinitum, till you seem driven to what BdS called "the asylum of ignorance": God's will (see Appendix, P. I; BdS points out again in the Preface to P. V that Descartes finally had to turn to God for the cause of the union of mind and body).

This simple form of the dissatisfaction with the natural answer to the moral question provides a clue for understanding the means for the dissolution of that dissatisfaction. The clue is the reference to ignorance. When we are children we have, in our ignorance or innocence, to accept parental authority. We do not know how to live. Parents teach us how. Because we cannot understand the reasons for doing this or that, we have to be ordered to do this or that—and are punished if we do not, praised in some way if we do. Here it is clear that the source so to speak, of the "ought" is authority. And authority's reason is ignorance or innocence. We need authority when we do not understand. The meaning of "moral" lies in that need buried in innocence.

Being childish is not entirely a matter of age. We can be as children when we are chronologically adult. Several times in the TTP BdS remarks that the ancient Hebrews were as children and that the prophets had to deal with them as such. The moral laws, the Law, appeared in the form of commandments and the prophets had to construct a whole parable to make the commands palatable or "reasonable" (see Letter 21, indeed the whole correspondence with Blyenbergh is helpful). Our childishness as adults, that is, our ignorance or inability to understand, invests the "ought" with mystery. We can appreciate hypothetical imperatives (if you want to get well, you ought to take these pills). The categorical or moral imperative is another matter.

Kant and others have tried to justify such imperatives, that is, to make them reasonable. In their very nature they cannot be. The *raison d'être* for such imperatives is ignorance. When we cannot understand how to behave, we have to be told how to behave. With understanding, as BdS points out in Annot. 34 in the TTP (see above), the commandments turn out to be "eternal verities," by which he simply means truths that are manifest to all who understand. We now know, however, that by "understand" he does not mean only a rational grasp of some proposition. We may have this in the first three ways of knowing, especially in the third. BdS means something in addition: An Affection, or a manner of behaving. This, of course, cannot be conveyed by words. So that, although these things can be shown beyond chance of doubt, this will not so impress the Mind as an experience of them (Schol., Prop. 35, P. V). Thus, all who *honor* their parents understand "Honor thy father and thy mother."

With non-dualistic thinking the vexing moral problem dissolves. So-called "moral philosophy" is seen to be either a mistake or blind reasoning about the language of raising children.

As BdS turns from his account of the mode of living in which we are passive to an account of that in which we are active, he makes two statements which have ever confused readers despite all that has gone before. "And with these I have finished all the things that look to this present life." "It is now time, then, that I pass to those things which pertain to a Mind's duration without relation to the Body" (Schol., Prop. 20). The reference to the present life seems to those strong in imagination to imply a future life. The reference to a Mind's duration without relation to the Body seems to confirm the implication that the soul or mind is immortal (in the earliest English translation of the ETHIC, see Bibliography, the translator substituted "soul" for "mind" in rendering *Mens* in P. V).

The wrongheadedness of seeing this implication and its confirmation is easily observed. A future life would occur in another realm of Being. But plural realms of Being are not given (Prop. 5, P. I). Existence of a mind without a body may be conceivable, but that of a Mind without a Body is impossible. Mind and Body are attributes of the same thing. So conceived, one without the other is impossible. (BdS demonstrates this in Prop. 8, P. II, one of the most difficult in the ETHIC. In its scholium he says that strictly speaking the matter cannot be illustrated because it is unique. However, he nonetheless attempts to illustrate it. See above.)

Actually, the possible implication of the reference to the present life, that there is a future life, may be strangely prophetic. If we take "present life" to mean other than "the life under consideration," and so think of a future life, it could be the life BdS envisaged when human beings more and more lived with understanding and thus less and less subject to their passions. There is, speaking speculatively, a respect in which human history can be viewed as a development from relative unconsciousness, to some consciousness, to imaginative living (Sp's sense of "imagine"), toward a future of more and more understanding. This future, of course, will be in this life.

BdS prepared for his account of the active life in a definition of freedom in P. I: A thing is to be called "free" which exists solely from its nature's necessity. It acts necessarily or is constrained when its existing is determined by another. The ground work is further laid in many ways. Thus in the scholium to Prop. 30, P. I BdS speaks of the difference between *Natura naturans* (Nature naturing) and *Natura naturata* (Nature natured), that is, between God or *Being* and the modes of being. Then there is the distinction between understanding and imagination (I do not care what you call the latter, says BdS in effect, so long as you recognize in it that the soul is passive; see above p. 133).

In the active life, considered with respect to the Mind (that is, without relation to the Body), we are concerned with a Mind's potency or power in so far as it is considered solely mentally, or not determined by another. Being actively rather than passively is human Freedom. We are so being to the extent that our Minds are forming our ideas, that is, to the extent that we are knowing intuitively. The last half of P. V contains Sp's prime account of this way of knowing. Another way of speaking about it appears here: When we know in this mode, our Mind is said to be eternally. This is a way of speaking about it which is obscured by saying instead that in this mode of knowing the mind is eternal; which is how, for example, the end of Prop. 31 is commonly translated (see Prop. 31 in the Appendix).

If you, Reader, will now compare the statement of Props. 16 through 20 on p. 140 above with Sp's statement of these propositions in our Appendix, you will find that the comparison helps with understanding Sp's account of knowing intuitively from Props. 21 to 42. The statement of Props. 16 to 20 relies on using God's other name, *"Being"* as a verb. Thus, Sp's statement of Prop. 18 is: "No one is able to hate God." Ours is: No one can hate be-ing. In effect this is to say that no one can hate living— provided, of course, that one is living well.

With this device in mind and remembering the account of the fourth mode of perceiving or knowing intuitively in Chapter 7, that is, that it is a quite different kind of knowing from what is usually called "knowing," let us now see how BdS describes its characteristics in Props. 21 to 42. First, our Minds imagine (his sense) and remember things only while the Body endures (Prop. 21). That is to say, imagining and remembering depend

on the Body in a particular way, for they involve mental pictures of things like "mute pictures on a tablet" (Schol., Prop. 49,
P. II, see above). Recall in this, that words are among the images
in this way of being aware of things. Imagining and remembering also involve the Body's actually existing.

Nevertheless, in be-ing we can also form an idea of our Body
which expresses it under a species of eternity (Prop. 22). Here
we have to rely on Sp's definition of eternity in P. I, Def. 8
(which see). Eternity is a thing's existing without regard to time.
In the definition Sp uses the phrase "eternal thing," which is
made clear on pp. 35 ff. in the EU (same pages in Elwes). There
BdS also calls them "uncreated things," and it is reasonably
clear that an uncreated thing is *any* thing regarded
a-temporally. Any thing is said to be eternally or is uncreated
when we regard it without reference to past, present, or future.
This turns out to be, when you reflect on it, when it is regarded
without relation to any other thing. An example of so regarding
a thing is the regard for a thing which we have in moments of
ecstasy: thus, during intercourse at the time of orgasm, when
we are intensely conscious, but not conscious *of* anything. At
that time the partners "regard" each other as being eternally.

It is absolutely vital in understanding this way of knowing
that we note well that BdS discusses it in terms of the Body (as
the foregoing example and Prop. 39 brings out. See also "motion" in the Index.). For otherwise Prop. 23 throws us completely. It says that the Mind cannot be absolutely destroyed
with the Body, but something of it remains which is eternally.
With our ingrained and natural dualism we immediately think
here of a part of the mind which cannot be destroyed with the
body. We forget that Thinking and Extending are attributes of
the same thing. Therefore, what we *think* here is surely not what
BdS intends. Thus Prop. 23 has a scholium. BdS notes that this
idea which expresses our Body under a species of eternity (the
word "species" in this phrase has the sense of "form" or "appearance") is a mode of thinking which pertains to a Mind's
being, and which is eternally. We can sense it as well as we can
those things which we have in memory. We do so by means of

demonstrations, which are "a Mind's eyes." This somewhat cryptic remark becomes understandable by a use of it which BdS makes in Chapter 13 of the TTP on p. 170 (178 in Elwes). Demonstrations are a Mind's eyes in the respect that by means of them we see invisible things; for example, *that* God's attributes are aspects of the same thing. Thus by what has gone on in the ETHIC we can *see* that our Minds have a way of experiencing individual things a-temporally.

Insofar as we are aware of the Body in relation to other things we experience them temporally. When, however, we have an idea of the Body under a species of eternity, that is, without relation to other things, we can experience a thing a-temporally or eternally. This is a potency of our Minds which has heretofore been largely ignored, at least by philosophers. When it is at work we are, so to speak, *fully* aware, without distraction by other things either physically or mentally.

We have here a characteristic of knowing intuitively or understanding which was not mentioned in Chapter 7. It is, however, related to one that was: that in knowing intuitively we know singular things. We do not know *of* them by means of universals or any images, which, when we do that, are taken as the objects of knowledge. Thus Prop. 24 is: The more we understand singular things, the more we understand *Being* (BdS has "God"). Knowing things eternally is knowing singulars or Individuals; better: it is knowing an Individual without relation to any thing else.

From Prop. 24 on the going in P. V is simpler than it is in Props. 22 and 23. It is, I think, difficult in the latter because they take us across the bridge from what we ordinarily think of as knowledge (it is of universals and wholly mental) to an awareness of a kind of knowing we come to see with non-dualism: knowing particulars which is also physical.

In Prop. 25 we are told that the highest conatus of a Mind, and its greatest strength lies in knowing things this way. This is, so to speak, true or real knowing, knowing that is like being awake instead of dreaming. The more we do it the more we desire to do it (Prop. 26). With it (Prop. 27) comes the highest

Acquiescence we can have (Def. 25 of Affections, P. III: Acquiescence in oneself is Joy, born from this, that a human being contemplates itself and its potency for acting). The Desire for this way of knowing originates not from vague experience or the use of signs (reading, talking) but from reason; that is, it stems from the clarity and distinctness, or adequate ideas which we achieve by reasoning (Prop. 28 and its demonstration).

Prop. 29 further clarifies the introduction of the notion of eternity or being eternally. Whatever we understand under a species of eternity, we do so without an awareness of our Body as existing temporally but as being eternally. It is, so to speak, with us in this way of knowing, not a part of us. Our being extending and our being thinking are one, not only in conception but in fact. BdS explains in the scholium that we conceive things in two modes: as being in a certain time and place, and in *Being*. These two modes were noted in P. I when BdS spoke of *Natura naturans* and *Natura naturata* (see above). We can perceive things temporally, and related to each other, and eternally or singularly, each in its own activity. Then we see them, not relatively, but absolutely being necessarily what they are.

Insofar as our Mind knows itself and its Body under a species of eternity it knows *Being*, and knows itself to be in *Being*, and to be thought of in terms of *Being* (Prop. 30). It is aware of be-ing. This way of knowing depends on the Mind's awareness that it can be this way; that is, fully consciously, awake and not, as it were, dreaming (Prop. 31). This involves an awareness of non-dualism, or a knowledge of God's attributes (that is, that mind and body are not substances—Dem., Prop. 31). "As each is more powerful in this genus of knowledge, he is better conscious of himself, & of God, that is, he is more perfect and beatific, which will be still more clearly patent from the following" (scholium; again, read "more conscious of himself, & of *Being*;" otherwise you will tend to imagine instead of understand this).

For whatever we understand in this mode of knowing we delight in, and think of God's idea as though it were the cause of that delight (Prop. 32). That is (see Prop. 27), knowing in this way results in Joy (discussed above), accompanied by an idea of oneself, "& consequently also concomitant with God's idea, as if the cause" (Dem., Prop. 32). Here BdS again makes the crucial transition to pointing out that this way of knowing becomes an Affection. In a corollary to the proposition he names it "God's understanding Love." Using the word "God" now as an adjective, this is the highest understanding Love (see above). Notice that we also used the word "God" as an adjective in our statement of the proposition: "God's idea."

Since the word is used like a noun in Prop. 31, that is, *"Being,"* the careful reader will cry out in protest. Come now! Let's at least be consistent. (Pierre Bayle said the same sort of thing in his article on BdS in the Dictionary: Prop. 5, P. I flies in the face of logic; see above.) But you can verify for yourself what BdS is getting at here. We take delight in coming to know some particular thing by being fully conscious of it and only it, especially as we realize that we by our effort are as the cause of this delight and as we experience atonement, at-one-ment, with that thing. For the latter experience is God's idea, the highest idea: the awareness in our oneness or unity with some thing. In the EU BdS called it the knowledge of the union which the Mind has with total Nature. And, as I say, we can all have this experience. Indeed in the scholium to Prop. 34 BdS says that we all do have it: "If we attend to the common opinion of human beings, we shall see that they are, certainly, conscious of their Mind's eternity, but they confound it with duration, and attribute it to imagination, or memory, which they believe remains after death" (see p. 123 above).

This experience is, in other words, what has led us to think confusedly of immortality (and see how many ways there are of describing it: God's idea, knowledge of the union of the Mind with total Nature, God's understanding Love, and others we shall come across). It is the experience of being full of life. In it one loves the so-called "thing in it." Indeed the deeply loving experience is this experience. In imagination, that is, when we read of it, we are inclined to make a mystery of it, and wonder in awe about the union with God. It is only the fully conscious experience of some one thing, accompanied by an awareness of oneself and the feeling of oneness. (A Latin word for "think" is *sentio,* which also means "sense" or "feel." Feeling oneness is also thinking it.) But remember that BdS confessed in the EU that the number of things he had known in this way was small. The experience is down to earth and in the here and now. We all can and do have it, but it is not common.

There is danger here, too, in the use of the word "experience." It can make us think that BdS is talking about ecstasy. There is that there, but mainly he is talking about *a way of living,* the way of human Freedom. In it there may be ecstatic experiences, but more importantly there is a way of knowing that stems from but is beyond the rational. Look back now to p. 135 to the reference to the last six propositions of P. IV and its final scholium. They are all about the free way of life. A free human being meditates on life not on death. The fortitudinous human being "hates no one, is angry with, envious of, indignant with no one, despises no one, and is minimally proud." Where in this is there ecstasy or anything mysterious? (Notice, too, "minimally proud"; not "not proud." It is a matter of degrees.)

This admonition is further answer to the call for consistency. BdS was on to something that is difficult to describe because it involves this other way of knowing as well as (the notion of) unity. Thus our conventional terms have to be stretched beyond their limits and used in a variety of novel ways. This involves breaking down our conventional grammar. Nouns must be turned into adjectives. BdS pointed this out with the word "God" in the TTP. We ourselves are translating adjectives in the Latin to adverbs in the English (Prop. 33: "God's understanding Love is eternally," from *Dei Amor intellectualis . . . est aeternus*). That Latin phrase itself which I have drawn from the Dutch first edition, not from the Latin, has commonly come into English as "the intellectual love of God," which loses its whole point in the cloud of dualism. The word "Affection" is so used that it takes all of P. III to clarify it. Finally a way of *knowing* turns out to be an Affection, that is, the cognitive becomes the affective. And thus we are concerned in P. V with a

[151]

way of living and not simply a kind of experience. See how BdS continues after having identified this way of knowing with loving.

Corollary to Prop. 32: "From this third genus of knowledge necessarily originates God's understanding Love." Prop. 33: God's understanding Love is eternally. Prop. 34: A Mind is subject to passions only while the Body endures. That is to say, we are subject to passions only in so far as we are not realizing the potency of our Minds in understanding. Scholium: People are conscious of their Mind's eternity, but they confound it with duration—and think of immortality.

In Prop. 19 BdS has said that he who loves God cannot expect that God love him. In Prop. 17 he has said that God is exempt from passions. In Prop. 35 he says that God loves himself with infinite understanding Love. Prop. 36 explains this: He does in the respect that and in so far as God can be explicated in terms of individual human beings who are being eternally. God's Love of himself is our understanding Love of particular things (earlier, I said that we would come across other names for God's idea, "God's Love" is one; and note that understanding Love is an active Affection not a passion). We are, remember, modes of *Being*, or God. BdS amplifies on this in the scholium to Prop. 36: From these things we understand in what our "well-being, or beatitude or Freedom consists, namely in constant, & eternal Love toward God, or in the Love of God toward human beings." That is to say, he continues, we understand "how much more able and potent the knowledge of singular things, which I have named *intuitive*, or *of the third genus* [see 2 Schol., Prop. 40, p. 2], is than the universal knowledge, which I have said to be of the second genus." All the talk of God, then, is to help us in understanding this other way of knowing, to explicate some of its properties, and thus to get further understanding.

Nothing in the nature of things can annul this understanding Love (Prop. 37). The axiom of P. IV says that for every thing in nature another more powerful is given which can destroy it. Thus BdS notes in the scholium to Prop. 37 that this axiom applies to singular things in relation to a certain time and place. But this understanding Love is eternally, that is, it is a way of being to which the axiom does not apply. Axioms have their place in the kind of knowledge called "reason" or "of the second genus," not in the kind called "intuitive"; which is another of its characteristics.

Prop. 38: The more we understand things by the second and third genera of knowledge the less passive we are in relation to Affections which are ills and the less we fear death (again, these things are matters of degree). Prop. 39: Those with Bodies apt for plural things, have Minds the maximum part of which is eternally. We have come full circle and the ETHIC is closing on the notion of unity in the form of the union of Mind and Body.

In the Scholium to Prop. 39 BdS summarizes the whole thing in a remarkably simple way, using a term that appears mainly only in P. V: "consciousness." We live in constant change. As we change for the worse we are said to be infelicitous, for the better felicitous. He who dies as an infant is infelicitous. "On the contrary it is attributed to felicity, that we run through the whole space of life with a healthy Mind in a healthy Body." When we are infants we have Bodies apt for few things and maximally dependent on external causes; and a Mind, which considered solely in itself, "is almost *not* conscious of itself, & of God, & of things." As we grow, our Bodies become apt for more things and our Mind becomes "very conscious of itself, & of God, & of things." When we come exceedingly conscious of ourselves, and of things, and of unity (for that is what consciousness of God is), "all that, which is related to its memory, or imagination, [is] scarcely of any moment in respect to understanding."

A central teaching of the ETHIC is that it is human to become increasingly conscious. However, it is central to this teaching that the Body is equally involved with the Mind in this development. The spiritual life, which we strove to understand in the Middle Ages, is the physical life on this earth lived in the human way. In the Middle Ages it seemed to be other-worldly because it was then seen through a cloud or as in a dream.

The perfection of our life lies in being more active than passive (Prop. 40). Even in our passivity, however, reason tells us to "hold as first things Piety, & Religion, & absolutely all the things . . . related to High-spiritedness, & Generosity" (Prop. 41). In the TTP we see that this was the teaching of the Old Testament, though it came in the form of commands. In the New the teaching was not altered. It was simply given a new basis in Love (see Schol., Prop. 68, P. IV). Now with the awareness of understanding or a Mind's eternality we see these things as natural ways of behaving. The love of others as oneself which Christ had taught becomes with this way of knowing God's understanding Love. Then we see that "Beatitude is not virtue's reward, but virtue itself" (Prop. 42).

The last line in the ETHIC reads: *Sed omnia praeclara tam difficilia, quam rara sunt.* This is commonly rendered: "But all things excellent [or some other value-term like "noble"] are as difficult as rare." The more literal translation is more apt. "But all very clear things are as difficult as rare." The ETHIC itself is a very clear example. The more one reads it in Sp's own words, the more this seems the case. Its subject is clarity: the kind of knowing or perceiving that comes with a true idea of unity, that is, with union.

Postscript

Some studies of historical figures are significant mainly for the history of philosophy and for persons who want to know about philosophers. Occasionally, however, a study such as the present one, because of its subject, bears not only in these ways. It may also, and perhaps more importantly, have vital significance for our own times. This is the case with Spinoza. It will both assist with understanding him and accomplish the second purpose in writing this book (see the Preface) if I develop some of the implications of the thinking of BdS for our times. In doing so I shall be continuing with the reflections commenced in the Preface.

1. With some understanding of unity our view of *what is* changes drastically. Instead of seeing our world as made up of discrete things existing independently of each other, we see unity. In the language BdS provided, it is a unity of modes of being. There are not, properly speaking, entities. There is *Being* and modes of being. A tree is an arboreal mode of being. You and I are modes of being, or, more simply human beings. What we have taken to be the real distinctions between things dissolve, and with them the conceptual distinctions between "thing," properties, and actions. Loving, for example, which we commonly take to be an action that some one or thing performs can itself be seen as a mode of being.—This is easy to say, but with time potent in effect. Implications are as follows.

2. There is identity. There is also identifying with. We can identify things or say *what* they are. We can also identify with another mode of being, when what it is is of no moment.

3. There is a kind of knowing that is loving. It is not of universals. In it we know Individuals. There are, then, levels of awareness: imagination and understanding. Imagination is in-

direct awareness and always involves images or representations of things. It includes seeing, hearing, and ratiocinative thinking. Understanding is direct awareness. We can move from images of things to direct awareness, from universals to particulars. In thinking that knowledge is of universals we mistake means of knowing for the objects of knowledge. The objects of knowing or awareness are always particular modes of being; but at first we see them through the cloud of representations of them.

4. The so-called inanimate is no longer inanimate, except for certain purposes. All modes of being are animate. Like us they are mental as well as physical; though, of course, each in its manner or mode: human, equine, lapidary.

5. And so they are all capable of Affections. A sailboat, a navicular being can be joyful—more clearly, can be joyfully.

6. There is a way of humanly being that is active instead of passive, or rather more active than passive.

7. It involves understanding God. In easy parlance this is to see that every mode of being is divine. Thus, to be humanly we are diligent toward every thing, respect, love it. God ceases to be an object and becomes an experience.

God is not dead. The *image* of God is vanishing from some Minds. This is neither lamentable nor a reason for despair. On the contrary, it is preparatory for understanding. The same is true for the dismantling of metaphysics. To have an image of God is to see *Being* through a cloud. With understanding religion and philosophy are found to be not really distinct.

8. Moral responsibility looks different. It has its being in the -domain of the imaginative or immature. I want to say in the domain of children, but that obscures the childishness in adults. The moral commandments are seen as truths when they are understood. As truths they tell us what it is to be humanly. It is to live without killing one's fellow beings, without lying, without covetousness. In positive terms it is to be an Individual who loves its fellow beings. The prejudice about killing animals is sentimental. Awakened we realize that being includes eating.

9. There is not good and ill. There is only what we call good

and ill—while we make comparisons in fulfilling our interests and desires. Considered in itself, without comparison with others, each mode of being simply is.

We hate or disparage ourselves only when we compare ourselves with others. A proper love of self can only become improper pride when we compare ourselves to others. Moral commandments, to repeat, have the form of commandments at a level of awareness when they are not understood.

10. Over a hundred years ago Hegel defined "the Alienated Soul" in *The Phenomenology of Mind.* Later Nietzsche spoke of "the strange contrast between an inner life to which nothing outward corresponds and an outward existence unrelated to what is within."

The philosophical basis for the problem of alienation is the dualistic thinking in which mind and body are not only thought of but taken to the separate entities. With this thinking there is not only the problem of how the mind and the body can interact; there is also the question of how *minds* can interact. The tremendous subjectivity with which this dualism infuses us is one of the most powerful sources of the fact and sense of alienation—not only in the individual but between peoples.

11. This relates to another aspect of our present position in philosophy: the ecological problem. One of its sources is our attitude toward nature. The rise of modern science and technology and the related occurrence of the industrial revolusion (all curiously dependent on dualistic thinking) have been accompanied by an attitude toward nature which is destructive of Nature. (Nature includes human beings *and* all their products, a fact which the distinction between the natural and the manmade has tended to obscure—an obscurity that causes contempt for the man-made.)

This attitude has deeper roots than those in the developments just mentioned. It has roots in the Middle Ages in the rise of Christian thought, when the body was disparaged and the natural world was seen to be merely the stage for the drama of salvation. It is the attitude in which there is combined a contempt for nature with a view that it is to be controlled or

[157]

used. In other words, in the dualistic outlook there is not only the radical separation of mind and body. There is the separation of the human being and nature.

With non-dualism our attitude toward Nature changes. It becomes God's understanding Love. All natural things, including the man-made, come to be respected, and, as I have said, we develop a sense of diligence toward them. The import of this for the ecological problem is clear.

12. It is in non-dualistic thinking that the Minds of the East and the West will come together. The current dialogue between East and West is largely on the level of imagination.

13. Non-dualism is the foundation for recent developments in art and science. In other dualistic terms we could say that it provides the metaphysics for these developments. It is better to say that with non-duality these developments are illuminated.

I have already alluded to the new physics (pp. 96–7). In painting there is the development of non-representational art from cubism on (see Section 3 above). In psychology we have first Freud who cracked the supposedly real distinction between mind and body with the notion of unconscious mental phenomena. Dualistically speaking, an "unconscious idea" is a contradiction in terms (think of our trouble with Sp's use of "idea"). A somewhat parallel development is the increasing, if still fumbling, attention to psychosomatic medicine (fumbling partly because we do not have a language for it, "mind" and "body" have great force). There is, next, the third-force psychology of Abraham Maslow and others. (Maslow might have borrowed from BdS for the title of his book: *Toward a Psychology of Being*.) And finally there is the movement into transpersonal psychology, the study of "transpersonal experiences, that is, ones occupied with other things than oneself . . . [ones in which] to a large extent the subject-object dichotomy is itself transcended." (See Section 2, and the appendix of Huston Smith's *Forgotten Truth*.)

14. Philosophy after reflecting on BdS seems to be a far more individual undertaking than it has been considered to be (see Sections 2, 3, 8, and 11 above). We have thought that individual

philosophers provide us with our meanings or world views. We have also thought that they do this in universal terms that are applicable to all. Now it may be seen that these meanings and systems have been in the imagination. With BdS philosophizing becomes something that each Individual has to do for him or herself. Each Individual has to strive for the realization of non-dualism, for insight into unity.

15. By the time of Descartes thinking had come to be regarded as entirely incorporeal. The original subtitle of the *Meditations* had been "On God's Existence and the Soul's Incorporeality," not "immortality." Still in our day Wittgenstein had to caution that we tend to think of thinking as a gaseous medium and Hannah Arendt writes that it is *"nowhere."*

It is in fact one of the many activities human beings perform. It is no more invisible or incorporeal than feeling and hearing are. More generally, thinking is the activity of becoming conscious and living consciously.

As William James remarked, "thinking" is an equivocal word. "Penny for your thoughts," we say. "Oh, I was just thinking what fun we had yesterday." "Ah, I was thinking of that date tomorrow." "Thinking" is used for a variety of activities: remembering, planning, problem-solving, dealing with the general as opposed to the particular, and, as we know from BdS, dealing with the particular. I suppose that we could call the activity of becoming conscious "philosophical thinking." Arendt said that it is like "the sensation of being alive." With BdS it seems that it is being alive.

In the Preface I reflected that philosophy, except as critical evaluation (pragmatism), conceptual analysis (logical positivism), engagement (existentialism), ordinary-language analysis (English philosophy), seemed finished. In none of these contemporary views of philosophy is there any word of wisdom. Hannah Arendt said: "The thread of tradition is broken and we shall not be able to renew it." We seem also, I thought, to have broken with the tradition of the wise. With BdS a new step on the old way seems possible: the step to non-dualism, or to a new insight into wisdom. Not to greater wisdom or to a redefinition of wisdom, but to more wisdom individually.

Looking at the matter historically, and in these terms, we can see the development of Western philosophic thought since the time of Hume as a destructive criticism of philosophy, in so far as it was taken as an attempt to provide us with an overall *rational* view of the world, or a universal knowledge as Husserl called it, which would constitute wisdom. The critical examination of this attempt developed until it was finally proclaimed in the twentieth century that it had been simply a quest for certainty, or that it is meaningless or inevitably results in meaningless statements. In Hannah Arendt's terms, it was seen that philosophy cannot provide us with the meaning of life. Let us, therefore, leave it and turn to practical matters.

This development, however, may be viewed constructively as well as negatively. What we have been doing in the past two hundred years is becoming aware of the nature and limits of rational thinking or the rational way of being consciously. Speaking, then, in terms of historical development and movements in philosophy, we have gradually moved on from Platonism, Aristotelianism, Cartesianism, or Materialism or Idealism toward mysticism or non-dualism. With BdS we can see that it is not that philosophy died in the twentieth century. Rather it is that it reached the point where a radical new step could be taken. In Sp's terms this is the step from the preoccupation with the rational mode of awareness to an interest in the intuitive. The pragmatists, the positivists, and the existentialists took important steps; but there is, contrary to their belief, still another philosophic step to be taken, one for which their own work prepared.

The matter need not be viewed only in terms of history and movements or positions in philosophy. Let us go along with Hannah Arendt and think of philosophy as the activity of providing us with meanings rather than truths, the latter being considered as the results of science. Then we can see with BdS that we have come to realize that the way of imagination (see Sections 3, 7, and 15 above) is not the way to attain meaning;

"philosophical meaning" we might call it. The way comes with knowing intuitively and understanding. We can then see that philosophizing does not bring us into contact with universals or essences, however these be regarded, as we had thought. It brings us into contact with particular modes of being.

The revolution in our view of philosophy, however, goes deeper than this indicates. For with non-dualism or insight into unity "thinking" is not simply an affair in "the land of the intellect." It is an affair of the whole person. The physicists have a version of non-dualism with Bohr's idea of complementarity. They have abandoned the principle of identity or the notion that they can or even have to specify *what* light, say, is. But philosophical thinking requires more than this. It requires involvement of the total Individual and not simply the brains or intellect; not simply abandonment of the *principle* of identity, but of *identity*.

It requires, in a word, spiritual exercises. Philosophy will no longer be an affair simply of the schools or academies. It will be an affair of something like the monastery or temple. An affair of becoming wise. Not wise in the sense of having universal knowledge, but in the sense of understanding and being an actively loving person. We shall see individual "meaning," not meaning.

16. Under the influence of the dualistic or common way of thinking we are likely to believe that BdS has given us a new and the true way of looking at things as modes of being (see Section 1). However, to think that BdS found a new universal knowledge or metaphysic is to fail to take into account the other way of knowing than the rational: the intuitive (see Section 3 and then reflect that in Section 1 instead of saying "There are not, properly speaking, entities," we should say "There are not, more properly speaking, entities." Unqualified, the statement makes us think that with it we have the final truth.). It is to become a Spinozist instead of whatever *you* are. It is to remain locked in imagination—the ETHIC itself is a work of imagination.

There are times, for example, when it is appropriate and

[161]

useful to regard modes of being as having identities, and others when it is natural to identify with them. In cashing a check we rely on having an identity; in loving we abandon it.

The human Freedom of which BdS spoke includes being able to see things in an infinite variety of ways. It includes Freedom from any "ism," any special general way of thinking of things. I can react to or be involved with any mode of being qua that particular mode of being. I can be with our dog Shasta as a dog, as a four-footed animal, as a hunter, as a guard, or simply as Shasta—that mode of being which we chose to call "Shasta." Here is a reason why mysticism has been said to be ineffable. When we are involved directly with a mode of being, there are no words we can use except proper names. That direct experiencing is lost as soon as we begin to describe it in terms like "dog," "animal," and even "mode of being." With them we then perceive Shasta, say, as through a cloud.

To put it otherwise, when we have a true idea of unity, that is, when we are unified (and it is important to note that it is a matter of degrees), we are detached from any particular mode of thinking, and such detachment is, of course, itself a mode of being. We are neither Aristotelian, a Spinozist, a Buddhist, a Christian, nor even one who sees a dog as a dog. We attain to no-mind. Truth, meaning, substance, identity, all the categories lose their hold on us and we can be with each mode of being simply as *it is*.

Except for its ending that last sentence might have a familiar ring. Hannah Arendt wrote: "I have clearly joined the ranks of those who have for some time been attempting to dismantle metaphysics, and philosophy with all its categories" (see Preface above). She went on, however, to say, "What you are left with, then, is still the past, but a fragmented past, which has lost its certainty of evaluation." Nevertheless, she warns at the last, there are things there that are " 'rich and strange,' " " 'coral,' " and " 'pearls' " that are not to be destroyed (she has been quoting Shakespeare). And she concludes in Auden's words: "Some books are undeservedly forgotten; none are undeservedly remembered."

The attempts of the dismantlers *have* loosened the hold of "philosophy with all its categories." The dismantlers' work, however, has not only left us with the pearls of the past stored in books. It has prepared the way for seeing the other way of thinking, knowing, and living than the rational. When I said that "all the categories lose their hold on us," I cited philosophical categories (truth, etc.). But I also had in mind, as the illustration of Shasta showed, *all* the concepts, *all* the images or representations of things. It is not only that we should not think dualistically that BdS gave us a new metaphysics. It is also that we can be freed of the images of "dog," "human being," "inanimate," and "animate." We are thus left with the pearls of the past *and* the possibility of a new way of thinking and knowing. One of the pearls is "know thyself." Another is "Love thy fellow beings." It is a way of thinking and knowing that is not of the universal but of the particular. "If now the way, which I have shown conducts to this, seem extremely arduous, it can nevertheless be come upon." The more so today, may be added to Sp's observation at the end of the ETHIC. For more of us have broken with the tradition of representational thinking to become aware of the other.

Bibliography and Abbreviations

Translation of BdS in English *

Abbre-
viation

The Ethics of Benedict de Spinoza, D. Van Nostrand,
New York, C. P. Putnam's Sons, 1876, 1888 (trans.
anon., presumed to be Daniel Drake Smith).
The Chief Works of Benedict de Spinoza, trans. & introd.
by R. H. M. Elwes, 2 Vols., Copyright by Dover
Publications, Inc., New York, 1951 (first ed. 1883–
4). Contains:

    A Theological-Political Treatise   TTP
    A Political Treatise (trans. by A. H. Gossett)   TP
    On the Improvement of the Understanding   EU
    The Ethics
    Correspondence (incomplete)
Spinoza Selections, ed. & introd. by John Wild, Charles
Scribner's Sons, New York, 1930. Contains:
    Ethic, trans. by W. H. White and revised by A. H.
      Sterling (1899);
    On the Improvement of the Understanding (Elwes'
      trans.);
    The Short Treatise (Wolf's trans. incomplete);
    Correspondence (Wolf's trans. incomplete)
Ethics, trans. by A. Boyle, introd. by George San-
tayana, incl. *Treatise on the Correction of the Under-
standing,* London, J. M. Dent & Sons Ltd., 1910,
#481 Everyman's Library.

Translations of BdS in French

Oeuvres de Spinoza, traduction et notes par Charles
Appuhn, 4 Vols., Garnier-Flamarrion, Paris, 1964.

——————

* While this volume was in press a fifth translation of the ETHIC
came to my attention: *Spinoza and his Environment,* A Critical Essay
with a Translation of the Ethics, Henry Smith, Cincinnati, Robert
Clarke & Co., 1886.

Translations of BdS in German

Several volumes in *Der Philosophischen Bibliothek,* Verlag von Felix Meiner in Hamburg

Editions in Latin of BdS

Opera Posthuma, B.d.S., cIɔIɔcLXXVII
This was printed in Amsterdam in 1677 by Jan Rieuwerts, who earlier had printed *Descartes' Principles* and *The Theological-Political Treatise* (both in Latin) & a trans. of each in Dutch. The OP contains:

Ethica Ordine Geometrico Demonstrata	ETHIC
Tractatus Politicus	TP
De Intellectus Emendatione	EU
Epistolae Doctorum Quorundum Verorum	Letters
ad B.d.S et Auctoris Responsiones	
Compendium Grammatices Linguae Hebraeae	

Opera, ed. by C. H. Bruder, Leipzig, 1843, 2 Vols.
Contains: *PrincipiaPhilosophiae, Cogitata Metaphysica, Ethica, EU, TP, Epistolae.*

Spinoza Opera, Im Auftrag Der Heidelberger Akadamie Der Wissenschafter, Herausgegeben von Carl Gebhardt, Heidelberg, 1925, 4 Vols.   Geb
This text presents the OP in Latin with variations in brackets in Dutch where there are differences between the OP and the NS. Geb conjectures that the Latin manuscript from which the ETHIC in the OP was printed was a different one from that on which the Dutch trans. in the NS was based, the latter being older but containing corrections in SP's hand (there are no extant mss. of the ETHIC). Thus Geb's ETHIC is now regarded as the definitive text of the ETHIC. It is the one I followed in my trans. However, I also referred to the OP and the NS, making further corrections. Thus my Latin text of the ETHIC differs from Geb's.

The four volumes also contain all of Sp's other writings, plus those attributed to him such as *The Short Treatise,* and the little treatises on the rainbow and on chances; as well as thorough notes on the texts, their histories, and comparisons. The version of *Descartes' Principles* in Vol. I was the basis for the English trans. of the work in the 1960's by Frank A. Hayes, and by H. E. Wedeck. The third English trans. by A. I. Britan in 1905 was based on the Latin ed. of Sp's works by Vloten-Land of 1895, Amsterdam.

Geb's edition of the TTP contains all the extant Annotations to that work made by BdS after its publication. Hoping that he could correct misunderstandings of the work and clarify some of its points, BdS began making notes on it shortly after its first printing in 1670. He intended to publish these (see Letters 68 and 69), but this never happened. The Annotations came down to us by various means and Geb first collated and published them all.

The version of *Descartes' Principles* contains additions made to that work by BdS when its Dutch trans. by Pieter Balling appeared in 1664 (the first ed. in Latin was 1663). This makes it in effect a second edition of *Descartes' Principles* (as, also in effect, the Dutch trans. was).

Editions of BdS in Dutch

De Nagelata Schriften, van B.d.S. M. DC. LXXVII (a Dutch trans. by Hendrik Glasemaker of the OP except for the Hebrew Grammar). NS

A new translation prepared by a committee in Holland for the 300th Anniversary of Sp's death in 1977.

English translations relating to BdS by A. Wolf

The Correspondence of Spinoza, trans., ed., introd., and annot. by
A. Wolf, George Allen & Unwin, Ltd., London, 1928; reis-
sued by Russell & Russell, New York, 1966.

Spinoza's Short Treatise on God, Man, & his Well-Being, trans., ed.,
introd., and comment. by A. Wolf, plus a biography of BdS
by Wolf, George Allen & Unwin Ltd., London, 1910; reis-
sued by Russell & Russell, New York, 1963 (contains a history
of the mss. of the Short Treatise and notes. Wolf was a de-
voted scholar of BdS and his works are mines of information
about BdS and his contemporaries. Wolf's library and papers
are at U.C.L.A., making the latter's library on BdS one of the
best in the world.).—The attribution of the Short Treatise to
BdS is doubtful. At best it came from another's hand who
talked with BdS, made notes, and perhaps had seen an early
draft of the ETHIC. Possibly the Short Treatise was trans. by
Wolf, and included by Geb, because there was great en-
thusiasm for it after it was discovered in the 1860's. A
hundred years later more sober appraisal of it is possible.

The Oldest Biography of Spinoza, A. Wolf, George Allen & Unwin
Ltd., London, 1927. Contains the French text of *La Vie de Feu
Monsieur Spinoza* (Life of the Recent Mr. Spinoza) by J. M.
Lucas, trans. by A. Wolf, plus some of the materials from
Freudenthal's *Lebensgeschichte.*

Other Works

Before Philosophy, by Henri Frankfort and Others, Penguin
Books, A198, 1949.

The Philosophical Works of Descartes, trans. by E. S. Haldane and
G. R. T. Ross, 1st ed. Cambridge University Press, 1911; repr.
with corrections, 1931; paper 1970, 2 Vols.

Oeuvres de Descartes, pub. by C. Adam & P. Tannery, Paris, *Lib-
rarie Philosophique.* 10 Vols. (Descartes' complete writings).

The Dictionary Historical and Critical of Mr. Peter Bayle, second ed.,
Vol. the fifth, London, MDCCXXXVIII.

Ein Denkerleben, Spinoza, a fictional biography by Berthold Au-
erbach, trans. by F. Nicholson, Henry Holt & Co., 1882. Au-
erbach also translated the OP into German.

Die Lebensgeschichte Spinoza's, J. Freudenthal, Leipzig, Von Veit
& Comp., 1899 (contains materials, letters, etc. written about
BdS during and shortly after his life, as well as a list of the
books in his library at his death (pp. 160–64). Freudenthal
also wrote a biography of BdS, *Das Lebens Spinozas,* published
in a second edition by Gebhardt in 1927, *Curis Societatis
Spinozanae.*

The Three Pillars of Zen, by Philip Kapleau, John Weatherhill,
Tokyo, 1st ed. 1965 (now in Harper Torchbooks).

Spinoza, by Sir Fred. Pollock, London, C. Kegan Paul & Co.,
1880, 2nd ed. 1889 (Reprint Library, Dubuque, Iowa, contains Colerus' biography of BdS).

*Spinoza mercator et autodidactus. Oorkonden en andere authentieke
documenten betreffende des wijsgeers jeugd en diens betrekkingen,
verzameld door . . .* (charters and other authentic documents
concerning the youth of the philosopher and his relations,
collected by . . .) A. M. Vaz Dias et W. G. van der Tak, La
Haye, 1932. (Contains the information that BdS was a merchant for several years before his excommunication; and not,
as legend had it, studying for the rabbinate. It raises the
question of the extent to which he was self-educated.)

Philosophical Investigations, Ludwig Wittgenstein, trans. by
G. E. M. Anscombe, Basil Blackwell, Oxford, 1953. In this
book, continuing from *The Blue and the Brown Books,*
Wittgenstein works at dissolving mind-body dualism as it occurs in our thinking about such things as the meaning of a
word. For this he employs a "therapeutic" technique consisting mainly of presenting examples and illustrations of the
bewitchment of our understanding by our language.

Instructions for Practical Living, by Wang Yang-ming, trans. with
notes by Wing-tsit Chan, Columbia University Press, New
York, 1963. Wang (1472–1529) is regarded by Chinese scholars as a neo-Confucian. I have found him mainly a Ch'an
Buddhist and the *Instructions* a fine accompaniment to *zazen.*

See "Wang Yang-ming and Meditation," P. Wienpahl, Journal of Chinese Philosophy, Vol. 1, No. 2, March, 1974. I compared Wang to BdS in "Spinoza and Wang Yang-ming," *Religious Studies,* Vol. 5, No. 1, October, 1969.

The Matter of Zen, Paul Wienpahl, New York University Press, 1964.* Some articles of possible interest are: "Ch'an Buddhism, Western Thought, and the Concept of Substance," *Inquiry,* Vol. 14, Nos. 1 and 2, Summer, 1971; "Spinoza and Mental Health," *Inquiry,* Vol. 15, Nos. 1 and 2, Summer, 1972; "On Translating Spinoza," *Speculum Spinozanum 1677–1977,* ed. by Siegfried Hessing, Routledge & Kegan Paul, London, 1977; and "Spinoza and Mysticism," *Spinoza's Philosophy of Man,* ed. Jon Wetlesen, Universitetsforlaget, 1978, Oslo, Norway.

Webster's New International Dictionary of the English Language, Unabridged, Second Edition, C. & C. Merriman, Co., 1946.

The Oxford English Dictionary, Oxford University Press.—(Abbrev. "O.D.")

A Latin Dictionary, C. Lewis and C. Short, Oxford, Impression of 1969.

Abbreviations

Def.—Definition	P.—Part
Dem.—Demonstration	Prop.—Proposition
Schol.—Scholium	

---

* On p. 43 there is a reference to a Letter 13 bis. A holograph of this letter by BdS appeared in the Spring of 1975. The letter is to L. Meijer and concerns the publication of *Descartes' Principles.* It is dated 26 July, 1663, and has been published in Hessing's *Speculum Spinozanum.*

Appendix

This appendix is provided for three reasons. Containing only the definitions, axioms, postulates, and propositions of the ETHIC, it gives the reader an experience of the work different from that obtained by reading it in its entirety. Secondly, with the Latin version of the propositions on pages facing the English, it is a compendium of aids for reading with greater accuracy the extant English translations of Sp's writings. Finally, if the reader will take the pains to compare the Latin and English versions of the propositions, he or she will have an experience of the ETHIC which cannot come from reading the English alone.

This latter is not so arduous a task as it may appear to those who have had no Latin. From the Preface you know that a principle in the translation is that of using wherever possible English words that have Latin roots. Thus, generally, the Latin version of a proposition can be easily made out and the words corresponding to the English words found. A few further hints for this will be found below. The reader may then check the Latin, if that be desired, with the help of a Latin dictionary. More importantly, you will come to see how the direction of Sp's thinking forces the rendition of nouns and adjectives in the Latin into verbal forms in the English, that is, into participles and adverbs, if we are to catch the spirit of this thinking. Of course, this phenomenon is much more apparent and powerful when the entire work is read in this manner. But reading the propositions only is impressive.

Let me say a word about the first reason for presenting these parts of the ETHIC. They are, as it were, the skeleton of Sp's thinking, which he fleshed out with prefaces, appendices, demonstrations, and scholia. With the flesh removed one finds the bare bones reveal two themes: that of unity and that of the distinction between imagination as a way of knowing and understanding as a way of knowing. As we have now seen, these themes complement each other. They are, as it were, the two great insights in the ETHIC. Given them, human experience may be observed with new eyes or with open eyes. This observation occurs in most of the scholia in Parts III, IV, and V. The scholia in Parts I and II are occupied mainly with clarifying or explicating the two insights. By means of the latter, as it were, one comes to see and understand the spiritual or "religious" dimension of human being in everyday lives: in the active as distinct from the passive Affections, and in understanding as distinct from imagination. Meanwhile it is also clear that the last three parts of the ETHIC were necessary for full explication of understanding, since it is affective as well as cognitive.

We have seen that the germ of Sp's insight into unity can be put in a grammatical way. If there is not more than one substance, then properly speaking the verb "to be" should always be used actively and never as a copula. This in turn means that modifiers should be adverbs instead of adjectives. In Latin, generally speaking, adjectives and nouns end in "a," "m," and "s." Adverbs end in "e" and "o." However, sometimes these are endings for nouns and adjectives. To avoid confusion the "e" and the "o" in the ETHIC are accented, è, when they are part of an adverb. This information, plus the context, should enable the reader to distinguish adverbs from adjectives in the Latin text. You will thus be able to tell easily where an adverb occurs in the English for an adjective in the Latin.

Consider next prepositions. Where prepositions occur in parentheses in the English there is no corresponding preposition in the Latin. This marks the presence of the ablative case in the Latin, a case we do not have in English. The preposition used in parentheses is suggestive only. The ablative case may be translated by using various English prepositions: by, in, with, from, for, and even others. Indeed in the ablative we have in effect a preposition which combines the use of one or more prepositions in English. This is a matter of crucial importance in Parts III to V in the ETHIC. Thus, BdS speaks of our being affected (by) some Affection. This could also read: being affected (with) some Affection, or being affected (in) some Affection. In fact a reader should think of a combination of all these. Translators commonly ignore the occurrence of the ablative and supply one of their own prepositions. The care with which the ETHIC was written, Sp's own comments on grammar, and the effect of his thinking on grammar require other treatment.

Some occurrences of prepositions are followed in a parenthesis by varations of the preposition in Latin. Thus, "by" may be followed by (*a*), (*ab*), or (*ex*) (*a* is used before consonants, *ab* before vowels in Latin). *a* can mean "from" when used with active verbs. It can mean "by" (indicating agency) when used with passive verbs. For example, he goes from(*ab*) here to there; she was loved by(*a*) Paul. This fact subtly changes the use of the English "by." In some cases this change is philosophically important; for example, Prop. VI, P. I: One substance cannot be produced by(*a*) another substance. In the German translations this comes out that one substance cannot be produced *from* another; in English translations both "by" and "from" have been used. It is crucial that a reader should be aware of both possibilities.

a or *ab* can also mean "in relation to" (as in the Explication of Def. 3, P. II). When you bear this in mind, phrases like "this was determined by(*a*) God," Sp's so-called "determination" takes on a different aspect.

All uses of "by" in Sp's parenthetical references to previous propositions translate the Latin preposition *per* which is otherwise rendered "by means of." In certain instances it is properly translated "through."

Where "from" occurs alone (that is, not followed by *a* or *ab*), it translates the preposition *ex*. Occasionally "according to" seems preferable, as when BdS has *ex dictamine rationis* (according to the dictate of reason). In such cases "according to" is followed by (*ex*).

The use of the ampersand (&) in the OP is retained. It is a version of "and," but there are cases where "&" is different from "and" (it is stronger). The ampersand was widely used in seventeenth-century printing, but its use as different from "and" in the ETHIC is rigorous and is therefore retained. (The device was very likely due to Meijer, not to BdS.)

As noted in the Preface, the Latin participle of the verb "to be," *essentia,* is translated "being" rather than "essence." The infinitive, *esse* (to be), is translated "be-ing," when used nominatively, to distinguish it from the translation of *essentia.* Another participle of *esse, ens,* is translated *"being"* to distinguish it from "be-ing" and "being." The reader will find these distinctions philosophically important. To match the translation of *essentia, existentia* is translated "existing" instead of the more customary "existence."

Latin nouns often admit of an active and a passive version. Thus *cogitatio* can be rendered "thinking" (an act of) or "thought." In such cases I have employed the active form.

The Latin word *potis* (root *pot*) forms a family of words which BdS uses with great effect—an effect that can be got into English only by being aware of this. Thus, *potis* is in *potentia* (potency), *potestas* (power), *possum* (can, be able to, have the power to), *compos* (share in), and *potior* (become partaker of), to list only several. All of these meanings can come into play when any one of these words is used in the ETHIC. This is lost sight of when *possum* is translated "I can." It is also lost sight of when we speak of being a partaker of something. However, to take one example, in the context of BdS "he can swim" has the ring of "he becomes a partaker of swimming." "Potency," then, means both to have power and to be able to.

Any work is enriched by the study of the etymology of crcial words in it, for this helps to restore these words to the metaphors from which they arose and which have long since been forgotten. This is particularly true of the ETHIC. Throughout his writings BdS exercised great care with the language he used (to the extent that he apologizes for clumsy constructions which are necessary to convey his meaning). He also wrote a grammar of the Hebrew language. No one who writes a grammar can fail to be aware of the ways in which he says things. So too the reader of BdS should pay particular attention to the way BdS says a thing and to his use of terms.

There is an example in the text of the word *amicitia* which only apparently loses its root in "love" (*amo*) when it comes into English as "friendship." Because of this I was not unhappy when I found that Sp's *libertas* (freedom) could not go into English as "liberty" because there is no corresponding adjective (*liber* in Latin) in English. The word had to become "freedom" because of "free," which in turn comes from a root meaning "love." Still, the root of *libertas* is *lib* which gave BdS *libido* (urge) and *Libido* by which he refers to "Desire, & Love in mingling bodies" (Def. 48, P. III). *Lib* also gives Latin *libet* which means "it pleases."

The genitive or possessive case can be preposed to or follow the word with which it is grammatically connected. Thus we can speak of Paul's house or the house of Paul. The same is true of Latin. Our translation follows Sp's preposing of the case as far as this is possible without undue clumsiness. The results are often surprisingly important, as in "God's idea," "God's Love," etc. When care is taken in reading BdS the Latin should always finally be consulted for the occurrence of preposing which does not come easily into English.

NB. Following is the title-page for the ETHIC as it occurs in the OP and in Geb. Observe that it has the ETHIC "demonstrated in Geometrical order." In the table of contents in the OP, which Geb does not reproduce, we read: *Hoc Opere continentur* I. *Ethica, More Geometrico demonstrata* [etc.]. "(In) this work are contained I. Ethic, demonstrated (in) the Geometrical Manner." The difference between "order" and "manner" is significant; or rather their interchangeability is. When BdS speaks of "the order of Nature" he does not mean "order" as we ordinarily think of it. He means rather the course or manner of Nature. In Appendix, P. I he tells us that, since human beings were persuaded that "all things that happen, happen on account of them," they "were bound to form these notions (by) which they explicate the natures of things, to wit Good, Ill, Order, Confusion, Heat, Cold, Pulchritude, & Deformity" (p. 81; 79 in Elwes). "And because those who do not understand the nature of things, but only imagine things, affirm nothing concerning things, & take imagination for understanding, on that account, ignorant of the nature of things and of themselves, they firmly believe that order is in things . . . as if order were something (in) nature except with respect to our imagination" (p. 82; 79 in Elwes). He concludes the discussion (p. 83; 80 in Elwes): "And thus we see that all the notions (by) which the vulgar are accustomed to explicate nature are only modes of imagining, and that they do not indicate any thing's nature, but only the constitution of imagination; & because they have names, as if they were *beings* existing outside imagination, I call them *beings* not *of reason* but of imagination." Notice that BdS says *"all* the notions" (emphasis added). This includes the notions called "universal" which are discussed in Schol. 1, Prop. 40, P. II, that is notions like Human Being, Dog, Horse, etc. When we understand or intuitively know a particular horse, we are aware of Prince (or whatever we call that singular Individual). We are only aware of him as a horse in imagination. Thus Appendix, P. I closes on a consequence of the notion of unity as it is explicated in P. I.

The title-page of the NS in translation reads: "ETHIC, divided into five parts; in which is treated I. of God. II. Of the human SOUL [ZIEL, the word with which *mens* is translated throughout the NS]. III. Of the Nature and ORIGIN of AFFECTIONS. IV. Of Human SERVITUDE. V. of Human FREEDOM. All arranged and demonstrated in a Geometrical order."

[177]

ETHIC
Demonstrated in Geometrical Order,
AND
Divided into five Parts,
in which is treated,

ETHICA
Ordine Geometrico demonstrata,
ET
In quinque Partes distincta,
in quibus agitur

ETHICS
First Part
CONCERNING GOD

Definitions.

I. By means of *cause of itself* I understand that, whose being involves existing, or that, whose nature cannot be conceived, unless exist*ing*.

II. That thing is said *finite in its genus,* which can be terminated (by) another of the same nature. E.g., a body is said *finite,* because we can always conceive another greater. So thinking is terminated (by) other thinking. Yet body is not terminated (by) thinking, nor thinking (by) body.

III. By means of *substance* I understand that, which is in itself, & is conceived by means of itself: that is that, whose conceiving does not need conceiving another thing, by(*a*) which it is bound to be formed.

IV. By means of *attribute* I understand that, which an understanding perceives concerning a substance, as if constituting its being.

V. By means of *mode* I understand affections of a substance, or that, which is in another, by means of which also it is conceived.

VI. By means of *God* I understand *Being* absolutely infinitely, that is, substance being established (in) infinite attributes, each of which expresses being eternally, & infinitely.

Explication.

I say *absolutely infinitely, <u>not</u> in its genus;* for concerning whatever is infinitely only in its genus we can deny infinite attributes [(that is, we can conceive infinite attributes which do not belong to the same nature)]; (concerning—tr.) that however which is absolutely infinitely, whatever expresses being, & involves no negation pertains to its being.

NB. "Exist*ing*" in l. 3 to distinguish *"existentiam"* from *"existens."*— The "is" in Defs. 3 and 5 is an active verb. Modes have their being in another.

ETHICES
Pars Prima
DE DEO

Definitiones.

I. Per *causa sui* intelligo id, cujus essentia involvit existentiam, sive id, cujus natura non potest concipi, nisi existens.

II. Ea res dicitur *in suo genere finita,* quae aliâ ejusdem naturae terminari potest. Ex. gr. corpus dicitur *finitum,* quia aliud semper majus concipimus. Sic cogitation aliâ cogitatione terminatur. At corpus non terminatur cogitatione, nec cogitatio corpore.

III. Per *substantiam* intelligo id, quod in se est, & per se concipitur: hoc est id, cujus conceptus non indiget conceptus alterius rei, à quo formaris debeat.

IV. Per *attributum* intelligo id, quod intellectus de substantiâ percipit, tanquam ejusdem essentiam constituens.

V. Per *modum* intelligo substantiae affectiones, sive id, quod in alio est, per quod etiam concipitur.

VI. Per *Deum* intelligo Ens absolutè infinitum, hoc est, substantiam constantem infinitis attributis, quorum unumquodque aeternam, & infinitam essentiam exprimit.

Explicatio.

Dico *absolutè infinitum,* non autem *in sui genere;* quicquid enim in suo genere tantùm infinitum est, infinita de eo attributa negare possumus [dat is, men kan onëindige toeëigeningen bevatten, die tot des zelfs natuur niet behore]; quod autem absolutè infinitum est, ad ejus essentiam pertinet, quicquid essentiam exprimit, & negationem nullam involvit.

NB. There are no italics in the OP. In Def. 6 *"Ens"* is not capitalized in the OP or Geb. The addition in brackets is from the NS (see p. 183 for this).

VII. That thing will be said *free,* which exists solely from its nature's necessity, & is determined to acting solely by(*a*) itself: *necessary* however, or rather *constrained,* which is determined by (*a*) another to existing, & operating (in) a certain, and determined mode.

VIII. By means of *eternity* I understand existing itself, in so far as it is conceived to follow necessarily solely from an eternal thing's definition.

Explication.

For such existing, like a thing's being, is conceived as an eternal verity, and on this account cannot be explicated by means of *duration,* or *time,* even if duration be conceived without beginning, & end.

Axioms.

I. All things, which are, are either in themselves, or in another.

II. That, which cannot be conceived by means of another, is bound to be conceived by means of itself.

III. From a given determined cause an effect necessarily follows, & on the contrary, if no determined cause be given, it is impossible that an effect follow.

IV. Knowledge of effect depends on knowledge of cause, & involves it.

V. Things which have nothing common with each other, also cannot be understood by means of each other, or conceiving of one does not involve conceiving of the other.

VI. A true idea is bound to agree with its ideate.

VII. Whatever can be conceived as not exist*ing,* of that being does not involve existing.

VII. Ea res *libera* dicetur, quae ex solâ suae naturae necessitate existit, & à se solâ ad agendum determinatur: *necessaria* autem, vel potius *coacta,* quae ab alio determinatur ad existendum, & operandum certo, ac determinato modo.

VIII. Per *aeternitatem* intelligo ipsam existentiam, quatenus ex solâ rei aeternae definitione necessariò sequi concipitur.

Explicatio.

Talis enim existentia, ut aeterna veritas, sicut rei essentia, concipitur, proptereáque per *durationem,* aut *tempus* explicari non potest, tametsi duratio principio, & sine carere concipiatur.

Axioms.

I. Omnia, quae sunt, vel in se, vel in alio sunt.

II. Id, quod per aliud non potest concipi, per se concipi debet.

III. Ex datâ causâ determinatâ necessariò sequitur effectus, & contrà, si nulla detur determinata causa, impossibile est, ut effectus sequitur.

IV. Effectûs cognitio à cognitione causae dependet, & eandem involvit.

V. Quae nihil commune cum se invicem habent, etiam per se invicem intelligi non possunt, sive conceptus unius alterius conceptum non involvit.

VI. Idea vera debet cum suo ideato convenire.

VII. Quicquid, ut nonexistens, potest concipi, ejus essentia non involvit existentiam.

NB. The end of Def. VII in the OP and Geb reads: *certâ, ac determinatâ ratione.* I change *"ratio"* to *"modus"* on the basis of the NS.

Propositions.

Prop. I. A substance is prior (by) nature to its affections.

Prop. II. Two substances having diverse attributes, have nothing common between them.

Prop. III. If things have nothing common between them, one of them cannot be cause of the other.

Prop. IV. Two, or plural distinct things are distinguished between one another, either according to(*ex*) diversity of attributes of the substance, or according to diversity of their affections.

Prop. V. In the nature of things there cannot be given two or plural substances of the same nature or attribute.

Prop. VI. One substance cannot be produced by(*ab*) another.

Prop. VII. To exist pertains to the nature of a substance.

Prop. VIII. Every substance necessarily is infinitely.

Prop. IX. To the extent that each thing has more of reality, or be-ing, plural attributes appertain to it.

Prop. X. Each attribute of one substance is bound to be conceived by means of itself.

Prop. XI. God, or substance being established (in) infinite attributes, of which each expresses being eternally, & infinitely, exists necessarily.

Prop. XII. No attribute of a substance can be truly conceived, from which it would follow that a substance can be divided.

Prop. XIII. A substance absolutely infinite is indivisibly.

Prop. XIV. Besides God no substance can be given, nor be conceived.

> *Corol. 1°.* It follows clearly hence I°. that God is uniquely, that is (*by Defin.* 6) that in the nature of things only one substance is given, and that it is absolutely infinitely, as we have already intimated in *Schol. of Prop.* 10.
>
> *Corol. II°.* It follows II°. that the extended thing, & the thinking thing are either God's attributes, or (*by Axiom* 1) affections of attributes of God.

Prop. XV. Whatever is, is in God, & nothing can be, nor be conceived without God.

Propositiones.

Prop. I. Substantia prior est naturâ suis affectionibus.

Prop. II. Duae substantiae, diversa attributa habentes, nihil inter se commune habent.

Prop. III. Quae res nihil commune inter se habent, earum una alterius causa esse non potest.

Prop. IV. Duae, aut plures distinctae, vel inter se distinguuntur ex diversitate attributorum substantiarum, vel ex diversitate earundem affectionum.

Prop. V. In rerum naturâ non possunt dari duae, aut plures substantiae ejusdem naturae, sive attributi.

Prop. VI. Una substantia non potest produci ab alia substantiâ.

Prop. VII. Ad naturam substantiae pertinet existere.

Prop. VIII. Omnis substantia est necessariò infinita.

Prop. IX. Quò plus realitas, aut esse unaquaeque res habet, eò plura attributa ipsi competunt.

Prop. X. Unumquodque unius substantiae attributum per se concipi debet.

Prop. XI. Deus, sive substantia constans infinitis attributis, quorum unumquodque aeternam, & infinitam essentiam exprimit, necessariò existit.

Prop. XII. Nullum substantiae attributum potest verè concipit, ex quo sequatur, substantiam posse dividi.

Prop. XIII. Substantia absolutè infinita est indivisibilis.

Prop. XIV. Praeter Deum nullum dari, neque concipi potest substantia.

> *Corol. I.* Hinc clarissimè sequitur I°. Deum esse unicum, hoc est (*per Defin.* 6) in rerum natura non nisi unam substantiam dari, eamque absolutè infinitam esse, ut in *Scholio Prop.* 10. jam innuimus.

> *Corol. II.* Sequitur II°. rem extensam, & rem cogitantem, vel Dei attributa esse, vel (*per Axiom.*1.) affectiones attributorum Dei.

Prop. XV. Quicquid est, in Deo est, & nihil sine Deo esse, neque concipi potest.

Prop. XVI. From the necessity of the divine nature countless things in countless modes (that is, all things which can fall under an infinite understanding) are bound to follow.

    Corol. I. It follows hence that God is the efficient cause of all things, which can fall under an infinite understanding.

    Corol. II. It follows II°. that God is cause by means of himself, *not* by means of accident.

    Corol. III. It follows III°. that God is absolutely first cause.

Prop. XVII. God acts solely from laws of his nature, & [is] constrained by no one.

Prop. XVIII. God is the immanent cause of all things, *not* transient.

Prop. XIX. God, or all God's attributes are eternally.

Prop. XX. God's existing and his being are one & the same.

Prop. XXI. All things, which follow from the absolute nature of some attribute of God, have been bound to exist always, & infinitely, or are by means of the same attribute eternally, & infinitely.

Prop. XXII. Whatever follows from some attribute of God, in so far as it is affected (by) a mode of such a kind that it exists both necessarily, & infinitely by means of that attribute, is also bound to exist both necessarily, & infinitely.

Prop. XXIII. Every mode, which exists both necessarily, & infinitely, is bound to follow necessarily, either from the absolute nature of some attribute of God, or from some attribute affected (by) a mode, which exists both necessarily, & infinitely.

NB. In Prop. 17 the "is" in brackets is added from the NS., in which the proposition also reads: "God acts solely in virtue of [*uit kracht van*] the laws of his nature."—See p. 100 above for the use of the propositions on this page.—In the opening lines of Preface, P. IV quoted above on p. 128 BdS says, "for a human being subject to Affections is not dependent on itself, but on fortune."—BdS uses the notion of cause by accident in P. III in discussing the sources of Affections. See, for example, Dem., Prop. 36.

Prop. XVI. Ex necessitate divinae naturae, infinita infinitis modis (hoc est, omnia, quae sub intellectum infinitum cadere possunt) sequi debent.

Corol. I. Hinc sequitur, Deum omnium rerum, quae sub intellectum infinitum cadere possunt, esse causam efficientum.

Corol. II. Sequitur II°. Deum causam esse per se, non verò per accidens.

Corol. III. Sequitur III°. Deum esse absolutè causam primam.

Prop. XVII. Deus ex solis suae naturae legibus, & à nemine coactus agit.

Prop. XVIII. Deus est omnium rerum causa immanens, non verò transiens.

Prop. XIX. Deus, sive omnia Dei attributa sunt aeterna.

Prop. XX. Dei existentia, ejus'que essentia unum & idem sunt.

Prop. XXI. Omnia, quae ex absoluta natura alicujus attributi Dei sequuntur, semper & infinita existere debuerunt, sive per idem attributum aeterna, & infinita sunt.

Prop. XXII. Quicquid ex aliquo Dei attributo, quatenus affectum est tali modo, qui & necessariò, & infinitus per idem existit, sequitur, debet quoque & necessariò, & infinitum existere.

Prop. XXIII. Omnis modus, qui & necessariò, & infinitus existit, necessariò sequi debuit, vel ex absolutâ naturâ alicujus attributi Dei, vel ex aliquo affecto modo, qui & necessariò, & infinitus existit.

NB. Corollaries included for text. In Cor. I, Pr. 14 OP and Geb have commas after *non* and *substantiam*. Following Bruder I omit them. NS read: in nature there is no more, than a unique substance. In Pr. 21 the adjective *infinita* is used adverbially to modify *existere*.

NB. In Prop. 22 an adjective and an adverb (*infinitus, necessariò*) are both used as modifiers of a verb (*existit*). In Geb and the OP *"modificio"* and *"modificatio"* are used instead of *"afficio"* and *"modus."* The same is true in the third line of Prop. 23. I make the change on the basis of the NS.

Boyle and Elwes used "modification" instead of "affection" throughout their translations of the ETHIC.

Prop. XXIV. The being of things produced by(*a*) God does not involve existing.

Prop. XXV. God is not only efficient cause of things' existing, but also of (things'—tr.) being.

Prop. XXVI. A thing, which is determined to be operating something, has been necessarily so determined by(*a*) God; & one which is not determined by (*a*) God cannot determine itself to operating.

Prop. XXVII. A thing, which is determined by(*a*) God to operating something, cannot rendered itself undetermined.

Prop. XXVIII. Every singular thing, or any thing whatever, which is finitely, & has a determined existing, cannot exist, and not be determined to operating, unless it is determined to existing, & operating by(*ab*) another cause, which also is finitely, & has a determined existing: & again this cause also cannot exist nor be determined to operating, unless it is determined to existing, & operating by(*ab*) another, which also is finitely, & has a determined existing, & so ad infinitum.

Prop. XXIX. In the nature of things no contingent thing is given, but all things are determined from the necessity of the divine nature to existing, & operating (in) a certain mode.

Prop. XXX. Understanding, finite (in) act or infinite (in) act, is bound to comprehend God's attributes, and God's affections, & nothing other.

Prop. XXXI. Understanding (in) act, whether it be finitely or infinitely, as also will, desire, love, &c., are bound to be related to Natura naturata, *not* to [Natura] naturans.

Prop. XXXII. Will cannot be called *free cause,* but only *necessary.*

NB. In Props. 22 and 23 Geb and the OP have "modify" and "modification" instead of "affect" and "mode." I make the change on the basis of the NS. *Natura naturans* and *Natura naturata* are the only phrases I do not translate, trying to give them English citizenship. In the NS Prop. 29 reads: In nature there is no "contingency" with *"Contingentia"* listed in the margin. Glazemaker usually renders *in rerum natura* with *in de natuur* and *datur* (is given) with "is."

Prop. XXIV. Rerum à Deo productarum essentia non involvit existentiam.

Prop. XXV. Deus non tantùm est causa afficiens rerum existentiae, sed etiam essentia.

Prop. XXVI. Res, quae ad aliquid operandum determinata est, à Deo necessariò sic fuit determinata; &, quae à Deo non est determinata, non potest se ipsam ad operandum determinari.

Prop. XXVII. Res, quae à Deo ad aliquid operandum determinata est, se ipsam indeterminatam redder non potest.

Prop. XXVIII. Quodcunque singulare, sive quaevis res, quae finita est, & determinatam habet existentiam, non, potest existere, nec ad operandum determinari, nisi existendum, & operandum determinetur ab aliâ causâ, quae etiam finita est, & determinatam habet existentiam: & rursùs haec causa non potest etaim existere, neque ad operandum determinari, nisi ab aliâ, quae etiam finita est, & determinatam habet existentiam, determinetur ad existendum, & operandum, & sic in infinitum.

Prop. XXIX. In rerum naturâ nullum datur contingens, sed omnia ex necessitate divinae naturae determinata sunt ad certo modo existendum, & operandum.

Prop. XXX. Intellectus actu finitus, aut actu infinitus Dei attributa, Deique affectiones comprehendere debet, & nihil aliud.

Prop. XXXI. Intellectus actu, sive is finitus sit, sive infinitus, ut & voluntas, cupiditas, amor, &c. ad Naturam naturatam, non verò ad naturantem, referri debent.

Prop. XXXII. Voluntas non potest vocari *causa libera,* sed tantùm *necessaria.*

Corol. I. It follows hence I°. that God does not operate from freedom of will.

Prop. XXXIII. Things could have been produced by(*a*) God (*in*) no other mode, and (in) no other order than they are produced.

Prop. XXXIV. God's potency is his being itself.

Prop. XXXV. Whatever we conceive to be in God's power necessarily is.

Prop. XXXVI. Nothing exists from whose nature some effect does not follow.

ETHIC'S
Second Part,
Concerning the
Nature, & Origin
of
MIND

Definitions.

I. By means of *body* I understand a mode, which expresses God's being, in so far as it is considered as an extending thing, (in) a certain, & determined mode; see Corol., Prop. 25, P. I.

II. I say that it pertains to the being of some thing which given, the thing is necessarily posited, & which removed, the thing is necessarily annulled; or that, without which the thing, & vice versa which without the thing can neither be, nor be conceived.

NB. Corol., Prop. 25 is: "Particular things are nothing but affections of God's attributes, or modes (by) which God's attributes are expressed (in) a certain, & determined mode."—*"Extensa"* is translated "extending" because of Sp's philosophy. In Corol. Prop. 14, P. I "extended thing" referred to Descartes' terms.—The corollary to Prop. 32 is included because it was referred to on p. 101.

Corol. I. Hinc sequitur I°. Deum non operari ex libertate voluntatis.

Prop. XXXIII. Res nullo alio modo, neque alio ordine à Deo produci potuerunt, quàm producti sunt.

Prop. XXXIV. Dei potentia est ipsa ipsius essentia.

Prop. XXXV. Quicquid concipimus in Dei potestate esse, id necessariò est.

Prop. XXXVI. Nihil existit, ex cujus naturâ aliquis effectus non sequatur.

ETHICES

Pars Secunda,

DE

Natura, & Origine

MENTIS

Definitiones.

I. Per *corpus* intelligo modum, que Dei essentiam, quatenus, ut res extensa, consideratur, certo, & determinato modo expimit; *vid. Coroll. Prop. 25, p.* I.

II. Ad essentiam alicujus re id pertinere dico, quo dato res necessariò ponitur, & quo sublato res necessariò tollitur; vel id, sine quo res, & vice versa quod sine re nec esse, nec concipi potest.

III. By means of *idea* I understand a Mind's conceiving, which the Mind forms, on account of (the fact that—tr.) it is a thinking thing.

Explication.

I say *conceiving* rather than *perception,* because the noun for perception seems to indicate that a Mind is passive in relation to an object. Yet *conceiving* seems express an action of the Mind.

IV. By means of *adequate idea* I understand an idea which, in so far as it is considered in itself without relation to the object, has all the properties or intrinsic denominations of a true idea.

Explication.

I say *intrinsic* to exclude that which is extrinsic, namely agreement of an idea with its ideate.

V. Duration is indefinite continuation of existing.

Explication.

I say *indefinite,* because it can by no means be determined by means of an existing thing's nature itself, and also not by(a) an efficient cause, which to wit necessarily posits, *not* annuls a thing's existing.

VI. By means of *reality* and *perfection* I understand the same.

VII. By means of *singular thing* I understand things, which are finitely, & have a determined existing. But if plural Individuals [or singulars] so concur in one action that all are simultaneously cause of one effect, I consider them all to that extent one singular thing.

NB. The explication of Def. 3 produces the translation of *"conceptus"* by "conceiving." "Conceptus" is a verbal form, *"perceptio"* a nominal form. In Ax. 3 "Affections" translates "affectûs." See p. 99 above. Def. 5 could read: "Duration is existing's indefinite continuation."

III. Per *ideam* intelligo Mentis conceptum, quem Mens format, propterea quòd res est cogitans.

Explicatio.

Dico potius *conceptum,* quàm *perceptionem,* quia perceptionis nomen indicare videtur, Mentem ab objecto pati. At *conceptus* actionem Mentis exprimere videtur.

IV. Per *ideam adaequatam* intelligo ideam, quae, quatenus in se sine relatione ad objectum consideratur, omnes verae ideae proprietates, sive denominationes intrinsecas habet.

Explicatio.

Dico *intrinsicas,* ut illam secludam, quae extrinseca est, nempe convenientam ideae cum suo ideato.

V. Duratio est indefinita existendi continuatio.

Explicatio.

Dico *indefinitam,* quia per ipsam rei existentis naturam determinari nequaquam potest, neque etaim à causâ efficiente, quae scilicet rei existentiam necessariò ponit, non autem tolit.

VI. Per *realitatem,* & *perfectionem* idem intelligo.

VII. Res singulares intelligo, res, quae finitae sunt, & determinatum habent extentiam. Quòd si plura Individua [of bezonderen/Singularia] in unâ actione ità concurrant, ut omnia simul unius effectûs sint causa, eadem omnia eatenus, ut unam rem singularem, considera.

NB. There are no italics in Geb and the OP except for "vid. Coroll. Prop. 25. p. I." in Def. 1. The corollary is: Res particulares nihil sunt, nisi Dei attributorum affectiones, sive modi, quibus Dei attributa certo, & determinato modo exprimuntur.

Axioms.

I. The being of a human being does not involve existing necessarily, that is, from nature's order it can happen that this or that human being exist as well as that it not exist.

II. A human being thinks [; or otherwise, we know that we think].

III. Modes of thinking like love, desire, or (by) whatever name of Affections of spirit they are designated, are not given, unless there is given in the same Individual an idea of a thing loved, wanted, &c. Yet an idea can be given, although no other mode of thinking be given.

IV. We sense that a certain [our, in the NS] body is affected (in) many modes.

V. We sense, or perceive no singular things [or nothing of nature natured] except bodies, & thinking's modes.

See Postulates after the 13th Proposition.

Propositions.

Prop. I. Thinking is an attribute of God, or God is a thinking thing.

Prop. II. Extension is an attribute of God, or God is an extending thing.

Prop. III. In God there is necessarily given the idea of his being, as well as of all things which necessarily follow from his own being.

Prop. IV. The idea of God from which countless things (in) countless modes follow, can only be uniquely.

Prop. V. The formal be-ing of ideas acknowledges God for cause in so far only as he is considered as a thinking thing, & not in so far as he is explicated (by) another attribute. That is, ideas of God's attributes as well as ideas of singular things do not acknowledge their ideates, or things perceived for efficient causes, but God himself in so far as he is a thinking thing.

[194]

Axioms.

I. Hominis essentia non involvit necessariam existentiam, hoc est, ex naturae ordine, tam fieri potest, ut hic, & ille homo existat, quàm ut not existat.

II. Homo cogitat [; of anders, wy weten dat wy denken].

III. Modi cogitandi, ut amor, cupiditas, vel quicunque nomine affectûs animi insigniuntur, non dantur nisi in eodem Individuo detur idea rei amatae, desideratae, &c. At idea dari potest, quamvis nullus alius detur cogitandi modus.

IV. Nos corpus quoddam [onz] multis modis affici sentimus.

V. Nullas res singulares [of niets van de genatuurde natuur/ natura naturata] praeter corpora, & cogitandi modos, sentimus, nec percipimus.

Postulata vide post 13. *Propositionem.*

Propositiones.

Prop. I. Cogitatio attributum Dei est, sive Deus est res cogitans.

Prop. II. Extensio attributum Dei est, sive Deus est res extensa.

Prop. III. In Deo datur necessariò idea, tam ejus essentiae, quàm omnium quae ex ipsius essentiâ necessariò sequuntur.

Prop. IV. Idea Dei, ex quâ infinita infinitis modis sequuntur, unica tantùm esse potest.

Prop. V. Esse formale idearum Deum, quatenus tantùm, ut res cogitans, consideratur, pro causâ agnoscit, & non, quatenus alio attributo explicatur. Hoc est, tam Dei attributorum, quàm rerum singularium ideae non ipsa ideata, sive res perceptas pro causâ efficiente agnoscunt, sed ipsum Deum, quatenus est res cogitans.

NB. There are no italics in Geb and the OP. Additions in brackets are from the NS which had the important Latin words in the margins.

Prop. VI. Any attribute's modes have God for cause, in so far as he is considered under that attribute whose modes they are, and not in so far as he is considered under any other attribute.

Prop. VII. Order, & connection of ideas is the same as order, & connection of things.

Prop. VIII. Ideas of non-existing things, or modes are bound to be comprehended in God's infinite idea in the same way as the formal beings of singular things, or modes are contained in God's attributes.

> *Corollary.* It follows hence that, as long as singular things do not exist, unless in so far as they are comprehended in God's attributes, their objective be-ing, or ideas also do not exist, unless in so far as God's infinite idea exists; & where singular things are said to exist, not only in so far as they are comprehended in God's attributes, but in so far as they are also said to endure, their ideas also involve existing, by means of which they are said to endure.

NB. On p. 194 we see that the postulates for P. II, on *Mind,* are in the section of the scholium of Prop. 13 that is on *bodies.* This non-dualism is also evident in Prop. 7. There is no causal connection between Mind and Body because they are attributes not substances. I have included the corollary to Prop. 8 because it more clearly says that Thinking cannot exist without Extending and vice versa than does the proposition (see pp. 78 and 80 above). However, the demonstration of Prop. 8 says that it is patent from Prop. 7. In the scholium to Prop. 8 BdS says that the matter cannot be illustrated with an example because it is unique. He was fully aware of the fact that non-dualism is bound to seem odd to dualists. For example, we have been able to see that stones as well as human beings are expressed under the attribute of Thinking. BdS did this by using the word "idea" in the sense of "form" as well as to refer to a psychological occurrence.

The term "objective be-ing" is from the 17th C. and is equivalent to "idea." It contrasts with "formal be-ing," which refers to a thing or a mode outside a Mind. Thus, a horse's formal be-ing or reality is the horse. Its objective be-ing or reality is an idea of the horse in someone's Mind.

Prop. VI. Cujuscunque attributi modi Deum, quatenus tan-tùm sub illo attributo, cujus modi sunt, & non, quatenus sub ullo alio consideratur, pro causâ habent.

Prop. VII. Ordo, & connexio idearum idem est, ac ordo, & connexio rerum.

Prop. VIII. Ideae rerum singularum, sive modorum non exis-tentium ita debent comprehendi in Dei infinitâ ideâ, ac rerum singularium, sive modorum essentiae formales in Dei attributis contientur.

> *Corollarium.* Hinc sequitur, quòd, quamdiu res singulares non existunt, nisi quatenus in Dei attributis comprehen-duntur, earum esse objectivum, sive ideae, non existunt, nisi quatenus infinita Dei idea existit; & ubi res singulares dicuntur existere, non tantùm quatenus in Dei attributis comprehenduntur, 'sed quatenus etiam durare dicuntur, earum ideae etiam existentiam, per quam durare dicuntur, involvent.

NB. In Prop. 4, if we followed the NS we would read: "Dei idea" instead of "Idea Dei;" that is, "God's idea" instead of "The idea of God." Props. 5 and 6 with the phrases *"alio attributo"* (another attri-bute) and *"cujuscunque attributi modi"* (any attribute's modes) suggest more than two attributes. *"Alius"* generally means "other" of several (*"alter"* is the other of two). However, there are exceptions. In the NS *"cujuscunque"* is rendered by *"yder"* (any, each). Still, there is *"sub ullo alio"* (under any other) in Prop. 6. But all this is to be thrown by grammar and our preconceptions. Philosophically speaking, there are and can only be two attributes, as BdS himself said. See p. 83 and its quotation from Letter 64.

Prop. IX. An idea of a singular thing, actually existing, has God for cause, not in so far as he is infinitely, but in so far as he is considered (as—tr.) affected (by) another idea of a singular thing actually existing, of which God is also the cause, & so ad infinitum.

Prop. X. The be-ing of substance does not pertain to the being of a human being, or substance does not constitute the form of a human being.

Prop. XI. The first thing, which constitutes a human Mind's actual be-ing, is nothing other than an idea of some singular thing actually existing.

Prop. XII. Whatever befalls in the object of the idea constituting a human Mind is bound to be perceived by(*ab*) the human Mind, or an idea of this thing will necessarily be given in the Mind: that is, if the object of the idea constituting a human Mind be a body, nothing could befall in the body which is not perceived by(*a*) the Mind [, or unless an idea of it is in the mind].

Prop. XIII. The object of the idea constituting a human Mind is the Body, or a certain mode of Extension actually existing, & nothing other.

Definition. When several bodies of the same, or diverse magnitude are so coerced by(*a*) the rest, that they press on each other, or if they are moved (with) the same, or diverse degrees of celerity, so that they communicate their motions to each other (in) some certain ratio [mode—in NS], we shall say that these bodies are united with each other, & that they all together compose one body, or Individual, which is distinguished from(*a*) the rest by means of this union of bodies.

NB. The definition of "Individual" is Sp's paradoxical definition of the atom. In it identity is dispensed with. In Prop. 12 "body" is not capitalized because it is not yet identified as a human Body. Finally, the placement of articles before "idea" is tricky. If the word has the sense of "form" "the" should be used. Otherwise "an."

Prop. IX. Idea rei singularis, actu existentis, Deum pro causâ habet, non quatenus infinitus est, sed quatenus aliâ rei singularis actu existentis ideâ affectus consideratur, cujus etiam Deus est causa, quatenus aliâ tertiâ affectus est, & sic ad infinitum.

Prop. X. Ad essentiam hominis non pertinet esse substantiae, sive substantiam formam hominis non constituit.

Prop. XI. Primum, quod actuale Mentis humanae esse constituit, nihil aliud est, quàm idea rei alicujus singularis actu existentis.

Prop. XII. Quicquid in objecto ideae, humanam Mentem constituentis, contingit, id ab humanâ Mente debet percipi, sive ejus rei dabitur in Mente necessariò idea: hoc est, si objectum ideae, humanam Mentem constituentis, sit corpus, nihil in eo corpore poterit contingere, quod à Mente non percipiatur [, of zonder dat dar af een denkbeelt in de ziel is].

Prop. XIII. Objectum ideae, humanam Mentem constituentis, est Corpus, sive certus Extensionis modus actu existens, & nihil aliud.

Definitio. Cùm corpora aliquot ejusdem, aut diversae magnitudinis à reliquis ità coërcentur, ut invicem incumbant, vel si eodem, aut diversis celeritatis gradibus moventur, ut motûs suos invicem certâ quadâm ratione communicent, illa corpora invicem unita dicemus, & omnia simul unum corpus, sive Individuum componere, quod à reliquis per hanc corporum unionem distinguitur.

Postulates.

I. A human Body is composed of a great many Individuals (of diverse nature), of which each is mightily composite.

II. Of the Individuals, from which a human Body is composed, certain are fluid, certain soft, & certain, finally, hard.

III. Individuals, composing a human Body, & consequently a human Body itself is affected by(a) external bodies (in) a great many modes.

IV. A human Body needs, that it be conserved, a great many other bodies, by(a) which it is continually quasi regenerated.

V. When a fluid part of a human Body is so determined by (a) an external body that it often impinges on another soft part, it mutates the plane of this, & imprints on it as it were certain vestiges of the impelling external body.

VI. A human Body can move external bodies (in) a great many modes, and dispose them (in) a great many modes.

Propositions.

Prop. XIV. A human Mind is apt for perceiving a great many things, & the more apt to the extent that its Body can be disposed (in) plural modes.

Prop. XV. The idea, which constitutes the formal be-ing of a human Mind, is not simple, but composed from a great many ideas.

Prop. XVI. An idea of any mode whatever, (by) which a human Body is affected by (a) external bodies, is bound to involve the nature of the human Body, & simultaneously the nature of the external bodies.

Postulata.

I. Corpus humanum componitur ex plurimis (diversae naturae) Individuis, quorum unumquodque valdè compositum est.

II. Individuorum, ex quibus Corpus humanum componitur, quaedam fluida, quaedam mollia, & quaedam denique dura sunt.

III. Individua, Corpus humanum componentia, & consequentur ipsum humanum Corpus à corporibus externis plurimis modis afficitur.

IV. Corpus humanum indiget, ut conservetur, plurimis aliis corporibus, à quibus coninuò quasi regeneratur.

V. Cùm Corporis humani pars fluida à corpore externo determinatur, ut in aliam mollem saepe impingat, ejus planum mutat, & veluti quaedam corporis externi impellentis vestigia eidem imprimit.

VI. Corpus humanum potest corpora externa plurimis modis movere, plurimisque modis disponere.

Propositiones.

Prop. XIV. Mens humana apta est ad plurima percipiendum, & eò aptior, quò ejus Corpus pluribus modis disponi potest.

Prop. XV. Idea, quae esse formale Mentis constituit, non est simplex, sed ex plurimis ideis composita.

Prop. XVI. Idea cujuscunque modi, quo Corpus humanum à corporibus externis afficitur, involvere debet naturam Corporis humani, & simul natural corporis externi.

NB. In Postulate I *"Individuis"* is not capitalized in either Geb or the OP. The definition and the postulates are in the long scholium to Prop. 13, which is about bodies.

NB. In Prop. 16 *"corporibus"* is mistakenly capitalized in Geb and the OP.

NB. BdS uses the postulates in accounting for mental operations. For example, #5 is used in connection with imagination and memory. Prop. 17 on the following page forms the basis for his wide sense of "imagination."

Prop. XVII. If a human Body is affected (in) a mode, which involves the nature of some external body, a human Mind will contemplate that external body as actually exist*ing*, or as being present to it, until the Body is affected (in) another mode, which excludes this body's existing or presence.

Prop. XVIII. If a human Body has been affected simultaneously by(*a*) two, or plural bodies, when the Mind afterward imagines some one of them, it will immediately also recollect the others.

Prop. XIX. A human Mind does not cognize the human Body itself, and does not know it exists, unless by means of ideas of affections, (by) which the Body is affected.

Prop. XX. There is also given in God an idea or knowledge of a human Mind, which follows in God (in) the same mode, & is related to God (in) the same mode as an idea or knowledge of a human Body.

Prop. XXI. This idea of a Mind is united to the Mind (in) the same mode as the Mind itself is united to the Body.

Prop. XXII. A human Mind perceives not only the Body's affections, but also these affections' ideas.

Prop. XXIII. A Mind does not cognize itself, unless in so far as it perceives the Body's affections' ideas.

Prop. XXIV. A human Mind does not involve adequate knowledge of the parts composing the human Body.

Prop. XXV. An idea of any affection whatever of a human Body does not involve an external body's adequate knowledge.

Prop. XXVI. A human Mind perceives no external body, as actually exist*ing*, unless by means of affections of its Body.

Prop. XXVII. An idea of any affection whatever of a human Body does not involve adequate knowledge of the human Body itself.

Prop. XVII. Si humanum Corpus affectum est modo, qui naturam corporis alicujus externi involvit, Mens humana idem corpus externum, ut actu existens, vel ut sibi praesens, contemplabitur, donec Corpus afficiatur alio modo, qui ejusdem proporis existentiam, vel praesentiam secludat.

Prop. XVIII. Si Corpus humanum à duobus, vel pluribus corporibus simul affectum semel, ubi Mens postea eorum aliquod imaginabitur, statim & aliorum recordabitur.

Prop. XIX. Mens humana ipsum humanum Corpus non cognoscit, nec ipsum existere scit, nisi per ideas affectionum, quibus Corpis afficitur.

Prop. XX. Mentis humanae datur etiam in Deo idea, sive cognitio, quae in Deo eodem modo sequitur, & ad Deum eodem modo refertur, ac idea sive cognitio Corporis humani.

Prop. XXI. Haec Mentis idea eodem modo unita est Menti, ac ipsa Mens unita est Corpori.

Prop. XXII. Mens humana non tantùm Corporis affectiones, sed etiam harum affectionum ideas percipit.

Prop. XXIII. Mens se ipsam non cognoscit, nisi quatenus Corporis affectionum ideas percipit.

Prop. XXIV. Mens humana partium, Corpus humanum componientum, adaequatam cognitionem involvit.

Prop. XXV. Idea cujuscunque affectionis Corporis humani adaequatam corporis externi cognitionem non involvit.

Prop. XXVI. Mens humana nullum corpus externum, ut actu existens, percipit, nisi per ideas affectionum sui Corporis.

Prop. XXVII. Idea cujuscunque affectionis Corporis humani adaequatum ipsius humani Corporis cognitionem non involvit.

NB. In the fourth line of Prop. 17 all the Latin editions that I have seen mistakenly have *"affectu"* where we have *"alio modo."* The NS correctly has *"op een andere wijze* (in another mode)" with *"modus"* in the margin for *"wijze."*

Prop. XXVIII. Ideas of affections of a human Body, in so far as they are related only to a human Mind, are not clear, & distinct, but confused.

Prop. XXIX. An idea of the idea of any affection whatever of a human Body does not involve a human Mind's adequate knowledge.

Prop. XXX. We can have only quite inadequate knowledge concerning the duration of our Body.

Prop. XXXI. We can have no, unless quite inadequate, knowledge concerning the duration of singular things which are outside us.

Prop. XXXII. All ideas, in so far as they are related to God, are true.

Prop. XXXIII. There is nothing positive in ideas on account of which they are said *false*.

Prop. XXXIV. Every idea which is absolute, or adequate, or perfect in us, is true.

Prop. XXXV. Falsity consists in the privation of knowledge, which inadequate, or mutilated & confused ideas involve.

Prop. XXXVI. Inadequate, & confused ideas are consequent (with) the same necessity as are adequate, or clear, and distinct ideas.

NB. Observe the use of "ideas" in Prop. 22—It is a consequence of the notion of unity that ideas in so far as they are related to God, that is, in reality, are true. See Ax. 6, P. I. Hence another account of falsity is required. A "false" idea is a mutilated or confused one. Hence the metaphor of dreaming with open eyes and gradually awakening.— With the comma after *"nullam"* in Prop. 30 it reads: We can have no, unless quite inadequate, knowledge concerning the duration of our Body.—Properly speaking, Prop. 34 reads: Every idea which is absolutely, or adequately, or perfectly in us, is truly. Here, as well as in the version above, "truly" equals "really." The same may be observed of Prop. 32. Once the impact of Sp's insight on grammar is clear, these grammatical considerations lose importance. Prior to it they are of great importance.

Prop. XXVIII. Ideae affectionum Corporis humani, quatenus ad humanam Mentem tantùm referuntur, non sunt clarae, & distinctae, sed confusae.

Prop. XXIX. Idea ideae cujuscunque affectionis Corporis humani adaequatam humanae Mentis cognitionem non involvit.

Prop. XXX. Nos de duratione nostri Corporis nullam nisi admodùm inadaequatam cognitionem habere possumus.

Prop. XXXI. Nos de duratione rerum singularium, quae extra nos sunt, nullam, nisi admodùm inadaequatam cognitionem habere possumus.

Prop. XXXII. Omnes ideae, quatenus ad Deum referuntur, verae sunt.

Prop. XXXIII. Nihil in ideis positivum est propter quod *falsae* dicuntur.

Prop. XXXIV. Omnis idea, quae in nobis est absoluta, sive adaequata, & perfecta, vera est.

Prop. XXXV. Falsitas consistit in cognitionis privatione, quam ideae inadaequatae, sive mutilatae, & confusae involvunt.

Prop. XXXVI. Ideae inadaequatae, & confusae eadem necessitate consequuntur, ac adaequatae, sive clarae, ac distinctae ideae.

NB. In Geb and the OP there is a comma after *"nullam"* in Prop. 30. I follow Bruder in omitting it. He also omits it in Prop. 31. There are no italics in Prop. 33 in Geb or the OP.

Prop. XXXVII. That, which is common to all things (*concerning these see Lemma 2 above*), and which is equally in the part, and in the total constitutes no singular thing's being.

Prop. XXXVIII. Those things, which are common to all things, and which are equally in the part, and in the total, cannot be conceived, unless adequately.

Prop. XXXIX. That, which is common, & proper to a human Body, & to certain external bodies, by(*a*) which a human Body is accustomed to be affected, and which is equally in any part whatever of these, and in the total, of this an adequate idea will also be in the Mind.

Prop. XL. Whatever ideas in a Mind follow from ideas, which are adequate in it, are also adequate.

NB. In Schol. 1 of Prop. 40 BdS gives a thoroughly nominalistic account of what he calls "transcendental terms" and "universal notions." The first are: *Being, Thing,* etc. Examples of the second are: *Human being, Horse, Dog,* etc. In Schol. 2 he distinguishes knowledge from vague experience, from signs, and calls these *knowledge of the first genus, opinion,* or *imagination.* A third sort of knowledge which he calls *knowledge of the second genus* and *reason,* arises from this, "that we have universal notions, and adequate ideas of the properties of things." The latter are common notions. Thus, universal notions and common notions are the foundations of our reasoning. In this definition there is a mistake in the OP, which has never been corrected and is of crucial importance. The Latin text reads: *ex eo, quod notiones communes, rerumque proprietatum ideas adaequatas habemus* (from this, that we have common notions, and adequate ideas of the properties of things). This is, of course, redundant. The text should read: *ex eo, quod notiones universales, rerumque proprietatum ideas adaequatas habemus.* Furthermore, it does read correctly in the NS with "*notiones univerales*" indicated in the margin. Geb noted this, but apparently did not see its significance. For he did not alter his Latin text from that of the OP, a thing he frequently did when the text of the NS and the sense indicated it.

In both Geb and the OP Schol. 2 is one long paragraph. In the NS it is broken into four paragraphs, so that each of the four modes of knowing occupies a paragraph. Thus, when BdS introduces intuitive knowing with "*Besides these two* genera of knowledge [i.e., opinion and reason] there is given a third," it comes in a separate paragraph (em-

[Cont. on p. 208]

Prop. XXXVII. Id, quod omnibus commune (*De his vide supra Lemma* 2.), quodque aequè in parte, ac in toto est, nullius rei singularis essentiam constituit.

Prop. XXXVIII. Illa, quae omnibus communia, quaeque aequè in parte, ac in toto sunt, non possunt concipi, nisi adaequatè.

Prop. XXXIX. Id, quod Corpore humano, & quibusdam corporibus externis, à quibus Corpus humanum affici solet, commune est, & proprium, quodque in cujuscunque horum parte aequè, ac in toto est, ejus etiam idea erit in Mente adaequata.

Prop. XL. Quaecunque ideae in Mente sequuntur ex ideis, qua in ipsâ sunt adaequatae, sunt etiam adaequatae.

NB. Lemma 2 is in the section on bodies after Prop. 13. It reads: *Omnia Corpora quibusdam conveniunt.* All bodies agree in certain things. In Letter 10 BdS discusses axioms and definitions. Nowhere that I know does he say anything about lemmas. I have the impression that he regarded them as he did axioms and common notions, which are the subject of Props. 37 through 39. All the axioms in the ETHIC are examples of common notions. Thus, motion and rest are *not* common notions, but *that* all bodies move or are at rest is a common notion. However, so also is: a true idea is bound to agree with its ideate (Ax. 6, P. I). Prop. 37 is of great importance in understanding common notions. Something which is common to all things constitutes the being of no singular thing, which is to say that it is not what we call a property.—In Prop. 38 Bruder omits the comma after "*concipi.*" In translation this becomes: those things, which are common to all things, and which are equally in the part, and in the total, can only be conceived adequately.

Intuitive knowing is introduced in Schol. 2, Prop. 40 thus: *Praeter haec duo cognitionis genera datur, ut in sequentibus ostendam, aliud tertium, quod* SCIENTIAM INTUITIVAM *vocabimus. Atque hoc cognoscendi genus precedit ab adaequata idea essentiae formalis quorundam Dei attributorum ad adaequatam cognitionem essentiae rerum.* (Besides these two genera of knowledge there is given, as I shall show in the following, another a third, which we shall call *knowing intuitively.* And this genus of cognizing proceeds from(*ab*) an adequate idea of the formal being of certain of God's attributes to adequate knowledge of the being of things.)

[207]

Prop. XLI. Knowledge of the first genus is the unique cause of falsity, of the second however, & of the third is necessarily true.

Prop. XLII. Knowledge of the second, & third, & not of the first genus teaches us to distinguish true from(*a*) false.

Prop. XLIII. He, who has a true idea, simultaneously knows he has a true idea, and cannot doubt concerning the thing's verity.

Prop. XLIV. It is not of the nature of Reason to contemplate things as contingent, but as necessary.

Prop. XLV. Each idea or any body, or singular thing whatever, actually existing, necessarily involves God's eternally, & infinitely being.

Prop. XLVI. Knowledge of the eternally, & infinitely being of God, which each idea involves, is adequate, & perfect.

Prop. XLVII. A human Mind has adequate knowledge of the eternally, & infinitely being of God.

Prop. XLVIII. There is in a Mind no absolute, or free will, but a Mind is determined to willing this, or that by(*a*) a cause, which is also determined by(*ab*) another, & this again by(*ab*) another, & so ad infinitum.

Prop. XLIX. In a Mind no volition, or affirmation, & negation is given except that which an idea, in so far as it is an idea, involves.

Corol.: Will, & understanding are one, & the same.

[Cont. from p. 206]

phasis added). It is clear that BdS actually thought of two sorts of knowing: imagination and understanding. Knowing intuitively is described thus: it "proceeds from (*ab*) an adequate idea of the formal being of certain of God's attributes to adequate knowledge of the being of things."

Prop. XLI. Cognitio primi generis unica est falsitatis causa, secundi autem, & tertii est necessariò vera.

Prop. XLII. Secundi, & tertii, & non primi generis cognitio docet nos verum à falso distinguere.

Prop. XLIII. Qui veram habet ideam, simul scit se veram habere, nec de rei veritate potest dubitare.

Prop. XLIV. De naturâ Rationis non est res, ut contingentes, sed, ut necessarias, contemplari.

Prop. XLV. Unaquaeque cujuscunque corporis, vel rei singularis, actu existentis idea Dei aeternam, & infinitam essentiam necessariò involvit.

Prop. XLVI. Cognitio aeternae, & infinitae essentiae Dei, quam unaquaeque idea involvit, est adaequata, & perfecta.

Prop. XLVII. Mens humana adaequatam habet cognitionem aeternae, & infinitae essentiae Dei.

Prop. XLVIII. In Mente nulla est absoluta, sive libera voluntas; sed Mens ad hoc, vel allud volendum determinatur, à causà, quae etiam ab aliâ determinata est, & haec iterùm ab aliâ, & sic in infinitum.

Prop. XLIX. In Mente nulla datur volitio, sive affirmatio, & negatio praeter illam, quam idea, quatenus idea est, involvit.

Coral.: Voluntas, & intellectus unum, & idem sunt.

ETHICS
Third Part,
CONCERNING
the Origin, & Nature
of AFFECTIONS

Definitions.

I. I name that *adequate cause,* whose effect can be clearly, & distinctly perceived by means of it. However I call that *inadequate,* or *partial,* whose effect cannot be understood solely by means of it.

II. I say that we are active, when something happens inside us, or outside us, of which we are an adequate cause, that is (*by preced. Defin.*), when something in us, or outside us follows from our nature, which can be clearly, & distinctly understood solely by means of the latter. Yet I say on the contrary that we are passive, when something happens to us, or when something follows from our nature, of which we are only partially the cause.

III. By means of *Affection* I understand a Body's affections, (by) which this Body's potency for acting is augmented, or diminished, helped, or coerced, & simultaneously these affections' ideas.

And thus if we are able to be an adequate cause of some of these affections, then I understand by means of Affection *an action, otherwise a passion.*

Postulates.

I. A human Body can be affected (in) many modes, (by) which the potency for its own acting is augmented, or diminished, & also (in) others which render the potency for its acting neither greater nor less.

II. A Human Body can experience many mutations, & nonetheless retain objects' impressions, or vestiges (*concerning which things see Post.* 5, *p.* 2), & consequently these things' images; *whose Defin.* see Schol. Prop. 17, *p.* 2.

ETHICES
Pars Tertia
DE
Origine, & Naturâ,
AFFECTUM

Definitiones.

I. *Causam adaequatam* appello eam, cujus effectus per ipsam potest clarè, & distinctè per eandem percipi. *Inadaequatam* autem, seu *partialem* illam voco, cujus per ipsam solam intelligi nequit.

II. Nos tum agere dico, cùm aliquid in nobis, aut extra nos fit, cujus adaequata sumus causa, hoc est (*der Defin. praeced.*) cùm ex nostrâ naturâ aliquid in nobis, aut extra nos sequitur, quod per eandem solam potest clarè, & distinctè intelligi. At contra nos pati dico, cùm in nobis aliquid fit, vel ex nostrâ naturâ aliquid sequitur, cujus nos non, nisi partialis, sumus causa.

III. Per *Affectum* intelligo Corporis affectiones, quibus ipsius Corporis agendi potentia augetur, vel minuitur, vel coërcetur, & simul harum affectionum ideas.

Si itaque alicujus harum affectionum adaequata possimus esse causa, tum per Affectum *actionem intelligo, aliàs passionem.*

Postulata.

I. Corpus humanum potest multis affici modis, quibus ipsius agendi potentia augetur, vel minuitur, & etiam aliis, qui ejusdem agendi potentiam nec majorem, nec minorem reddunt.

II. Corpus humanum multas pati potest mutationes, & nihilominus retinere objectorum impressiones, seu vestigia (*de quibus vide Post. 5, p. 2*), & consequenter easdem rerum imagines; *quarum Defin. vide Schol. Prop. 17, p. 2.*

NB. The words being defined are not in italics in Geb or the OP.

Propositions.

Prop. I. Our Mind is active in certain things, but in fact passive in others, namely in so far as it has adequate ideas, it is to that extent necessarily active in certain things; & in so far as it has inadequate ideas, it is to that extent necessarily passive in others.

Prop. II. A Body cannot determine the Mind to thinking, nor the Mind the Body to motion, or quiet, nor to some (if there is any) other thing.

Prop. III. A Mind's actions originate solely from adequate ideas; passions however depend solely on inadequate ideas.

Prop. IV. Nothing can be destroyed, unless by(*a*) an external cause.

Prop. V. To the extent that things are of contrary nature, that is, to the extent that they cannot be in the same subject, to that extent one is able to destroy the other.

Prop. VI. Each thing, as far as it is in it, endeavors to persevere in its be-ing.

Prop. VII. The conatus, (by) which each thing endeavors to persevere in its be-ing, is nothing except the thing itself's actual being.

NB. In Props. 46 and 47, P. II (p. 208) the NS reads; "God's being eternally, & infinitely" instead of "the eternally, & infinitely being of God."

For the capitalizing of "Affection" see p. 99 above.

The definitions referred to in Postulate II from Schol., Prop. 17, P. II are: "we shall call a human Body's affections, of which the ideas represent external bodies as if present to us, *things' images,* even if they do not reproduce the figures of things. And when a Mind contemplates bodies in this fashion, we shall say, *it imagines.*"

In Prop. I, P. III we have: "Our Mind is active." It can read: "Our Mind acts." We also have it that a Mind "has" (*habet*) adequate ideas. In Latin *"habere"* is often used like *"eese"* (to be). We can, therefore think here: the Mind *is* adequate ideas. And this is correct. For BdS a Mind is its ideas, it is not some thing that has ideas. See Props. I–13, P. II.

Propositiones.

Prop. I. Mens nostra quaedam agit, quaedam verò patitur, nempe quatenus adaequatas habet ideas, eatenus quaedam necessariò agit, & quatenus ideas habet inadaequatas, eatenus necessariò quaedam patitur.

Prop. II. Nec Corpus Mentem ad cogitandum, nec Mens Corpus ad motum, neque ad quietem, nec ad aliquid (si quid est) aliud determinare potest.

Prop. III. Mentis actiones ex solis ideis adaequatis oriuntur; passiones autem à solis inadaequatis pendent.

Prop. IV. Nulla res, nisi à causâ externâ externa, potest destrui.

Prop. V. Res eatenus contrariae sunt naturae, hoc est, eatenus in eodem subjecto esse nequeunt, quatenus una alteram potest destruere.

Prop. VI. Unaquaeque res, quantum in se est, in suo esse perseverare conatur.

Prop. VII. Conatus, quo unaquaeque res in suo esse persevevare conatur, nihil est praeter ipsius rei actualem essentiam.

Prop. VIII. The conatus, (by) which each thing endeavors to persevere in its be-ing, involves no finite, but indefinite time.

Prop. IX. A Mind, in so far as it has clear, & distinct ideas, as well as in so far as it has confused ideas, endeavors to persevere in its be-ing for a certain indefinite duration, & is conscious of this its conatus.

Prop. X. An idea, which excludes our Body's existing, cannot be given in our Mind, but is contrary to it.

Prop. XI. Whatever augments our Body's potency for acting, or diminishes, helps or coerces it, an idea of this thing augments, or diminishes, helps or coerces our Mind's potency for thinking.

Prop. XII. A Mind, as much as it can, endeavors to imagine the things which augment, or help the Body's potency for act-ing.

Prop. XIII. When a Mind imagines things, which diminish, or coerce the Body's potency for acting, it endeavors, as much as it can, to recollect things, which exclude their existing.

Prop. XIV. If a Mind has been simultaneously affected (by) two Affections, when it is affected afterwards (by) one or the other of them, it will be affected (by) the other.

Prop. XV. Any thing whatever can by means of accident be cause of Joy, Sadness, or Desire.

Prop. XVI. Solely from this, that we imagine some thing similar to an object, which customarily affects the Mind (with) Joy, or Sadness, although that, in which the thing is similar to the object, is not an efficient cause of these Affections, we shall nevertheless love or hate it.

NB. Beginning with Prop. 12 in P. III Elwes translates *"imaginor"* and its cognates by "conceive" and its cognates. This is due to SP's broad use of "imagine," *which must be kept in mind at all times.*—In the Schol. to Prop. 18 BdS defines "time" in terms of tense; i.e., a thing is called past because we have been affected by it, etc.—Note that the names of Affections are capitalized, signifying extraordinary use.

Prop. VIII. Conatus, quo unaquaeque res in suo esse perseverare conatur, nullum tempus finitum, sed indefinitum involvit.

Prop. IX. Mens tam quatenus claras, & distinctas, quàm quatenus confusas habet ideas, conatur in suo esse perseverare indefinitâ quâdam duratione, & hujus sui conatus est conscia.

Prop. X. Idea, quae Corporis nostri existentiam secludit, in nostrâ Mente dari nequit, sed eidem est contraria.

Prop. XI. Quicquid Corporis nostri agendi potentiam auget, vel minuit, juvat, vel coërcit, ejusdem rei idea Mentis nostrae cogitandi potentiam auget, vel minuit, juvat, vel coërcit.

Prop. XII. Mens, quantùm potest, ea imaginari conatur, quae Corporis agendi potentiam augent, vel juvant.

Prop. XIII. Cùm Mens ea imaginatur, quae Corporis agendi potentiam minuunt, vel coërcent, conatur, quantùm potest, rerum recordari, quae horum existentiam secludunt.

Prop. XIV. Si Mens duobus affectibus simul affecta fuit, ubi postea eorum alterutro afficietur, afficietur etiam altero.

Prop. XV. Res quaecunque potest esse per accidens causa Laetitiae, Tristitiae, vel Cupiditas.

Prop. XVI. Ex eo solo, quòd rem aliquam aliquid habere imaginamur simile objecto, quod Mentem Laetitiâ, vel Trisitiâ afficere solet, quamvis id, in quo res objecto est similis, non sit horum affectuum efficiens causa, eam tamen amabimus, vel odio habebimus.

Prop. XVII. If we imagine that a thing, which customarily affects us (with) an Affection of Sadness, has something similar to another, which customarily affects us (with) an equally great Affection of Joy, we shall hate, & love it simultaneously.

Prop. XVIII. A human being is affected (with) the same Affection of Joy, & Sadness from an image of a past, or future thing as from an image of a present thing.

Prop. XIX. He, who imagines that, that which he loves, is destroyed will be saddened; if however that it is conserved, he will rejoice.

Prop. XX. He who imagines that, that which he hates, is destroyed will rejoice.

Prop. XXI. He who imagines that, which he loves, affected (by) Joy, or Sadness, is also affected (by) Joy, or Sadness; and both these Affections will be greater, or less in the one loving according as they are greater, or less in the thing loved.

Prop. XXII. If we imagine that someone affects (with) Joy a thing, which we love, we shall be affected (with) Love toward him. If on the contrary we imagine that he affects it (with) Sadness, we shall contrariwise be affected (with) Hate against him.

Prop. XXIII. He who imagines that which he hates affected (with) Sadness will rejoice; if on the contrary he imagines it to be affected (with) Joy, he will be saddened; & both these Affections will be greater, or less according as its contrary is greater, or less in that which he hates.

Prop. XXIV. If we imagine that someone affects (with) Joy a thing, which we hate, we shall also be affected (with) Hate towards him. If on the contrary we imagine that he affects this thing (with) Sadness, we shall be affected (with) Love toward him.

Prop. XXV. We endeavor to affirm concerning us, and concerning a thing loved all that we imagine affects us, or a thing loved (with) Joy; & on the contrary to deny all that which we imagine affects us, or a thing loved (with) Sadness.

Prop. XVII. Si rem, quae nos Tristitias affectu afficere solet, aliquid habere imaginamur simile alteri, quae nos aequè magno Laetitiae affectu solet afficere, eandem odio habebimus, & simul amabimus.

Prop. XVIII. Homo ex imagine rei praeteritas, aut futurae eodem Laetitiae, & Tristitiae affectu afficitur, ac ex imagine rei praesentis.

Prop. XIX. Qui id, quod amat, destrui imaginatur, contristabitur; si autem conservari, laetabitur.

Prop. XX. Qui id, quod odio habet, destrui imaginatur, laetabitur.

Prop. XXI. Qui id, quod amat, Laetitiâ, vel Tristiâ affectum imaginatur, Laetitiâ, vel Tristitiâ afficietur; & uterque hic affectus major, aut minor erit in amante, prout uterque major, aut minor est in re amata.

Prop. XXII. Si aliquem imaginamur Laetitiâ afficere rem, quam amamus, Amore erga eum afficiemur. Si contrà eundem imaginamur Tristitiâ eandem afficere, econtra Odio etiam contra ipsum afficiemur.

Prop. XXIII. Qui id, quod odio habet, Tristitiâ affectum imaginatur, laetabitur; si contrà idem Laetitiâ affectum esse imaginetur, contristabitur; & uterque hic affectus major, aut minor erit, prout ejus contrarius major, aut minor est in eo, quod odio habet.

Prop. XXIV. Si aliquem imaginamur Laetitia afficere rem, quam odio habemus, Odio etiam erga eum. Si contrà eundem imaginamur Tristitia eandem rem afficere, Amore erga ipsum afficiemur.

Prop. XXV. Id omne de nobis, deque re amatâ affirmare conamur, quod nos, vel rem amatam Laetitiâ afficere, imaginamur; & contrà id omne negari, quod nos, vel rem amatam Tristitiâ afficere, imaginamur.

Prop. XXVI. We endeavor to affirm concerning a thing, which we hate, all that which we imagine affects it (with) Sadness; & on the contrary to deny that which we imagine affects it (with) Joy.

Prop. XXVII. From this, that we can imagine a thing similar to us, & which we have pursued (with) no Affection to be affected (with) some Affection, we are (by) that itself affected (with) a similar Affection.

Prop. XXVIII. We endeavor to promote all that which we imagine conduces to Joy, so that it may happen; *but* we endeavor to remove, or destroy that which we imagine is repugnant to it, or conduces to Sadness.

Prop. XXIX. We shall also endeavor to act all that which we imagine human beings look on with Joy, & on the contrary we shall be averse to act that to which we imagine they are averse.

Prop. XXX. If one has acted something which he imagines affects the rest (with) Joy, he will be affected (with) Joy, concomitant with an idea of himself as if the cause; or he will contemplate himself (with) Joy. If on the contrary he has acted something which he imagines affects the rest (with) Sadness, he will on the contrary contemplate himself with Sadness.

Prop. XXXI. If we imagine that someone loves, or desires, or hates something, which we ourselves love, desire, or hate, we shall (by) that itself love, &c. the thing more constantly. If however we imagine that he is averse to that which we love, or on the contrary, [that he loves that which we hate,] then we shall experience Fluctuation of Spirit.

Prop. XXXII. If we imagine that someone is Joyful (with) some thing, of which solely one can be partaker, we shall endeavor to effect it, that he does not partake of that thing.

NB. Prepositions in parentheses indicate the ablative case in Latin. Compare, e.g., Props. 21 and 22. I have used "by" and "with," but even "in" is possible.—BdS has a footnote to Prop. 29: I understand here, and in the following human beings whom we have pursued with no Affection.—This reminds us that even so-called inanimate things can be affected with certain simple Affections. Reread, e.g., Props. 21–2.

Prop. XXVI. Id omne de re, quam odio habemus, affirmare conamur, quod ipsam Tristitiâ afficere imaginamur, & id contrà negare, quod ipsam Laetitiâ afficere imaginamur.

Prop. XXVII. Ex eo, quòd rem nobis similem, & quam nullo affectu prosecuti sumus, aliquo affectu affici imaginamur, eo ipso simili affectu afficimur.

Prop. XXVIII. Id omne, quod Laetitiam conducere imaginamur, conamur promovere, ut fiat; quod verò eidem repugnare, sive Tristitiam conducere imaginamur, amovere, vel destruere conamur.

Prop. XXIX. Nos id omne etiam agere conabimur, quod homines cum Laetitiâ aspicere imaginamur, & contrà agere aversabimur, quod homines aversari imaginamur.

Prop. XXX. Si quis aliquid egit, quod reliquos Laetitiâ afficere imaginatur, is Laetitiâ, concomitante ideâ sui, tanquam causâ, afficietur; sive ipsum cum Laetitiâ contemplabitur. Si contrà aliquid egit, quod reliquous Tristitiâ afficere imaginatur, se ipsum cum Tristitiâ contra contemplabitur.

Prop. XXXI. Si aliquem amare, vel cupere, vel odio habere aliquid, quod ipsi amamus, cupimus, vel odio habemus, eo ipso rem constantiùs amabimus, &c. Si autem id, quod amamus, eum aversari imaginamur, vel contrà, [dat hy't geen bemint, 't welk wy haten,] tum Animi Fluctuationem patiemur.

Prop. XXXII. Si aliquem re aliquâ, quâ unus solus potiri potest, gaudere imaginamur, conabimur efficere, ne ille illâ re potiatur.

Prop. XXXIII. When we love a thing similar to us, we endeavor, as much as we can, to effect it, that it loves us in return.

Prop. XXXIV. The greater the Affection (with) which we imagine a thing loved to be affected toward us, the more we shall glory in ourselves.

Prop. XXXV. If one imagines that another joins himself to a thing loved (with) the same or a tighter Friendship than that (by) which he himself partook alone, he will be affected (with) Hate toward the very thing loved, & will envy that other.

Prop. XXXVI. He, who recollects a thing (by) which he was once delighted, desires to partake of it with the same circumstances as (those—tr.) when he was first delighted (by) it.

Prop. XXXVII. Desire, which originates through Sadness, or Joy, and through Hate, or Love, is greater as the Affection is greater.

Prop. XXXVIII. If one begins to hate a thing loved, so that Love is plainly abolished, he will pursue it from a comparable cause, (with) greater Hate than if he had never loved it, & the greater as the antecedent Love was greater.

Prop. XXXIX. He, who hates someone, will endeavor to inflict ill on him, unless he fears that from this a greater ill will originate for himself; & on the contrary he, who loves another, will endeavor (by) the same law to benefit him.

Prop. XL. He, who imagines that he is hated by(*ab*) another, and does not believe that he has given him any cause for Hate, will hate him in return.

Prop. XLI. If one imagines himself to be loved by(*ab*) someone, and believes that he has not given any cause for it, he will love him in return.

NB. In Prop. 35 "Friendship" is the name of an Affection by reason of its capital letter. BdS nowhere discusses friendship as an Affection. In Descartes' *The Passions of the Soul* it is a passion. Later in the ETHIC *"Amicitia"* is not capitalized. This may be an unfinished aspect of the ETHIC.

Prop. XXXIII. Cùm rem nobis similem amamus, conamur, quantum possumus, efficere, ut nos contrà amet.

Prop. XXXIV. Quò majori affectu rem amatam erga nos affectam esse imaginamur, èo magis gloriabimur.

Prop. XXXV. Si quis imaginatur rem amatam eodem, vel arctiore vinculo Amicitiae, quo ipse eâdem solus potiebatur, alium sibi jungere, Odio erga ipsam rem amatam afficietur, & illi alteri invidebit.

Prop. XXXVI. Quo rei, quâ semel delectatus est, recordatur, cupit eâdem cum iisdem potiri circumstantiis, ac cùm primò ipsâ delectatus est.

Prop. XXXVII. Cupiditas, quae prae Tristitiâ, vel Laetitiâ, praeque Odio, vel Amore oritur, eò major, quò affectus major est.

Prop. XXXVIII. Si quis rem amatam odio habere inceperit, ità ut Amor planè aboleatur, eandem majore Odio, ex pari causâ, prosequetur, quàm si ipsam nunquam amavisset, & eò majori, quò Amor antea major fuerat.

Prop. XXXIX. Qui aliquem odio habet, ei malum inferre conabitur, nisi ex eo majus sibi malum oriri timeat; & contrà, qui aliquem amat, ei eâdem lege benefacere conabitur.

Prop. XL. Qui se odio habere ab aliquo imaginatur, nec se ullam odii causam illi dedisse credit, eundem odio contrà habebit.

Prop. XLI. Si quis ab aliquo se amari imaginatur, nec se ullam ad id causa dedisee credit, eundem contrà amabit.

NB. In Prop. 38 the second *"Odio"* is not capitalized in Geb and the OP. It should be since it is the name of an Affection. In Prop. 39 *"odio"* is capitalized in Geb and the OP. It should not be because it is part of the verb *"odio habere"* (to hate).

Prop. XLII. He who, moved (by) Love, or Hope of Glory, has conferred a benefit on someone, will be saddened if he sees that the benefit is received (in) ungrateful spirit.

Prop. XLIII. Hate is augmented (by) reciprocal Hate, & can on the contrary be effaced (by) Love.

Prop. XLIV. Hate, which is plainly overcome, passes into Love; & the Love on this account is greater than if Hate had not preceded it.

Prop. XLV. If one imagines that someone similar to himself is affected (with) Hate for a thing similar to himself, which he loves, he will hate him.

Prop. XLVI. If one has been affected (with) Joy, or Sadness (by) someone of a certain class, or nation diverse from(*a*) his, concomitant with an idea of him under the universal name of his class, or nation, as if the cause: he will love, or hate not only that but all (persons—tr.) of that class, or nation.

Prop. XLVII. Joy, which originates from this, that to wit we imagine a thing, which we hate destroyed, or affected (with) another ill, does not originate without any Sadness of spirit.

Prop. XLVIII. Love, & Hate, e.g., toward Peter, is destroyed, if the Sadness which the latter, & the Joy which the former involves, is joined to an idea of another cause; & to that extent one or the other is diminished, in so far as we imagine that Peter was not solely the cause of one or the other.

Prop. XLIX. Love, & Hate toward a thing, which we imagine to be free, are each bound to be greater from a comparable cause, than toward a necessary (thing—tr.).

Prop. L. Every thing whatever can by means of accident be a cause of Hope, or Dread.

Prop. LI. Diverse human beings can be diverse-modally affected by(*ab*) one and the same object, & one and the same human being can be diverse-modally affected by(*ab*) and the same object at diverse times.

NB. BdS distinguishes between Dread and Fear in the ETHIC (Schol., Prop. 39), i.e., between *Metus* and *Timor*. He does not in his other writings.

Prop. XLII. Qui in aliquem, Amore, aut Spe Gloriae motus, beneficium contulit, contristabitur, si viderit, beneficium ingrato animo accipi.

Prop. XLIII. Odium reciproco augetur, & Amore contrà deleri potest.

Prop. XLIV. Odium, quod Amore planè vincitur, in Amorem transit; & Amor proptera major est, quàm Odium non praecessit.

Prop. XLV. Si quis aliquem sibi similem Odio in rem sibi similem, quam amat, affectum esse imaginatur, eum odio habebit.

Prop. XLVI. Si quis ab aliquo cujusdam classis, sive nationis à suâ diversae, Laetitiâ, vel Tristitiâ affectus fuerit, concomitante ejus ideâ, sub nomine universali classis, vel nationis, tanquam causâ: is non tantùm illum, sed omnes ejusdem classis, vel nationis amabut, vel odio habebit.

Prop. XLVII. Laetitia, quae ex eo oritur, quòd scilicet rem, quam odimus, destrui, aut odio malo affici imaginamur, non oritur absque ullâ animi Tristitiâ.

Prop. XLVIII. Amor, & Odium, ex. gr. erga Petrum destruitur, si Tristitia, quam hoc, & Laetitia, quam ille involvit, ideae alterius causae jungatur; & eatenus uterque diminuitur, quatenus imaginamur Petrum non solum fuisse alterutrius causam.

Prop. XLIX. Amor, & Odium erga rem, quam liberam esse imaginamur, major ex pari causâ uterque debet esse, quàm erga necessariam.

Prop. L. Res quaecunque potest esse per accidens Spei, aut Metûs causâ.

Prop. LI. Diversi homines ab uno, eodemque objecto diversimodè affici possunt, & unus, idemque homo ab uno, eodemque objecto potest diversis temporibus diversimodè affici.

NB. In Prop. 42 "*Spe*" is not capitalized in Geb or the OP. Given the irregularity of capitalizing in the 17th C., the small number of these errors is remarkable.

Prop. LII. An object, which we have previously seen together with others, or which we imagine has nothing except what is common to plural things, we shall not contemplate for as long as one alvm we imagine has something singular.

Prop. LIII. When a Mind contemplates it itself, and its potency for acting, it rejoices, & the more so as it imagines itself, and its potency for acting more distinctly.

Prop. LIV. A Mind endeavors to imagine those things only, which posit the potency for its own acting.

Prop. LV. When a Mind imagines its impotence, it is (by) that itself saddened.

Prop. LVI. There are given as many species of Joy, Sadness, & Desire, & consequently of each Affection which is composed from these, such as Fluctuations of Spirit, or which is derived from these, namely of Love, Hope, Dread, &c., as there are species of objects by(a) which we are affected.

NB. In Prop. 53 BdS is preparing the way for discussing the active Affections in Props. 58 and 59. In Prop. 57 he uses "Individual," the term defined in the section on bodies after Prop. 13, P. II. In Props. 58 and 59 he provides another of the things that distinguish an action from a passion: passions stem from the three primary passive Affections of Joy, Sadness, and Desire; active Affections are based only on Joy and Desire (the latter are also associated with clear and distinct or adequate ideas, the former with confused or inadequate ideas). It is a striking fact that in three of the four extant English translations of the ETHIC (Elwes', White's, and Boyle's) this distinction is blurred because the translator substituted "Sadness" for "Desire" in either Prop. 58 or 59 or both. (The fourth translation, D. D. Smith's, got this right, but has "soul" instead of "mind" for *"Mens"* in P. V.—"mind" was used in P. II.) As noted in the chapter on Affections, BdS distinguished passive from active Affections in part because of his distinction between imagination and understanding. Understanding or knowing intuitively has almost invariably been missed by readers of BdS. This, in turn, means that the notion of unity has either been ill-understood or itself missed.

The Schol. to Prop. 59 provides the definitions of High-spiritedness and Generosity. There is then a 13-page section called "Definitions of Affections," in which most of the Affections discussed in the scholia of

[Cont. on p. 226]

Prop. LII. Objectum, quod simul cum aliis antea vidimus, vel quod nihil habere imagin amur, nisi quod commune est pluribus non tamdiu contemplabimur, ac illud quod singulare habere imaginamur.

Prop. LIII. Cùm Mens se ipsam, suamque agendi potentiam contemplatur, laetatur, & eò magis, quò se, suamque agendi potentiam distinctiùs imaginatur.

Prop. LIV. Mens ea tantùm imaginari conatur, quae ipsius agendi potentiam ponunt.

Prop. LV. Cùm Mens suam impotentiam imaginatur, eo ipso contristatur.

Prop. LVI. Laetitiae, Tristitiae, & Cupiditatis, & consequenter uniuscujusque affectûs, qui ex his componitur, ut Animi Fluctuationis, vel qui ab his derivatur, nempe Amoris, Odii, Spei, Metûs, &c., tot species dantur, quot sunt species objectorum, à quibus afficimur.

NB. *"Animi Fluctuationis"* in Prop. 56 is not capitalized in Geb or the OP. It is capitalized elsewhere, sometimes only the "F," sometimes both the "F" and the "A." Apparently the author of this device was not clear whether Fluctuations of Spirit were Affections. They are, as Prop. 56 indicates. See Prop. 17 in the schol. of which BdS defines "Fluctuations of Spirit" as referring to the "constitution of the Mind which originates to wit from two contrary Affections."

In Prop. 57 *"Individui"* is not capitalized in GEB or the OP.

Observe on the facing page that in the translation of Prop. 53, for example, we have "its potency for acting" for *"suam agendi potentiam."* If we follow the preposing of the genitive case, the English should read: "its acting's potency." This construction is not peculiar to BdS. It occurs, for example, in Descartes' Latin. However, in this case *and with BdS* "its acting's potency" is particularly apt, for it helps with the notion that a Mind is not a thing. I have not used it in the translation of the proposition because it occurs in other contexts where its employment is excessively clumsy and I had to decide against it in the interests of consistency. Variations of this sort are limitless in translating the ETHIC, a fact that makes the presence of the Latin text for the careful reader a necessity. This is, of course, always true, but it is particularly true of BdS since the direction of his thinking strains conventional grammar—if it does not require a new grammar.

Prop. LVII. Any Affection you please of each Individual is discrepant from(*a*) an Affection of another only in so far as the being of the one differs from the being of the other.

Prop. LVIII. Besides Joy, & Desire, which are passions, other Affections of Joy, & Desire are given which relate to us in so far as we are active.

Prop. LIX. Among all the Affections, which are related to a Mind in so far as it is active, there are none which are not related to Joy, or Desire.

ETHIC'S
Fourth Part,
CONCERNING
Human Servitude, or the
FORCES OF AFFECTIONS

Definitions.

I. By means of *good* I understand, what we know for certain to be useful to us.

II. By means of *ill* however, that which we know for certain to be an impediment to our sharing some good.

III. I call singular things *contingent,* in so far as, while we attend solely to their being, we come upon nothing which necessarily posits their existing, or which necessarily excludes it.

IV. I call the same singular things *possible,* in so far as, while we attend to the causes from which they are bound to be produced, we do not know whether they are determined to be producing them.

[Cont. from p. 224]

P. III are defined. This section is capped by a "Generic Definition of *Affection.*" A study of the latter reveals that the bulk of P. III is a view of human behavior based on the insights into unity and intuitive knowing. It is not a theory of the Affections. Even study of only the propositions in P. III shows this.

Prop. LVII. Quilibet uniuscujuscunque Individui affectus ab affectu alterius tantùm discrepat, quantùm essentia unius ab essentiâ alterius differt.

Prop. LVIII. Praeter Laetitiam, & Cupiditatem, quae passiones sunt, alii Laetitiae, & Cupiditatis affectûs dantur, qui ad nos, quatenus agimus, referuntur.

Prop. LIX. Inter omnes affectûs, qui ad Mentem, quatenus agit, referentur, nihil sunt, quam qui ad Laetitiam, vel Cupiditatem referentur.

ETHICES

Pars Quarta,

DE

Servitute Humana, seu de Affectuum

VIRIBUS

Definitiones.

I. Per *bonum* id intelligam, quod certò scimus nobis esse utile.

II. Per *malum* autem id, quod certò scimus impedire quominùs boni alicujus simus compotes.

III. Res singulares voco *contingentes,* quatenus, dum ad earum solam essentiam attendimus, nihil invenimus, quod earum esitentiam necessariò ponat, vel quod ipsam necessariò secludat.

IV. Easdem res singulares voco *possibiles,* quatenus, dum ad causas, ex quibus produci debent, attendimus, nescimus, an ipsae determinatae ad easdem producendum.

In Schol. 1, Prop. 33, P. I, I made no difference between *possible,* & *contingent,* because there was no need there to distinguish between these accurately.

V. By means of *contrary Affections* in the ff. I understand those, which draw a human being diversely, although they are of the same genus, such as Luxury, & Avarice, which are species of Love; and are not contraries (by) nature, but by means of accident.

VI. What I understand by means of *Affection toward a thing future, present, & past,* I have explicated in Schol. 1, & 2, Prop. 18, P. III.

VII. By means of *end, (in) cause of which we do something,* I understand Appetite.

VIII. By means of *virtue,* & *potency* I understand the same, that is (*by Prop. 7, p. 3*), virtue, in so far as it is related to a human being, is a human being's being itself, or nature, in so far as it has a power for effecting certain things, which can be understood solely by means of its nature's laws.

Axioms.

No singular thing is given in the nature of things, than which another more potent, & stronger is not given. But for any given thing whatever another more potent is given, by(*a*) which that given thing can be destroyed.

N B. BdS notes that he discusses *good* and *ill* in the Preface to P. IV. He also discusses them in the appendix to P. I (see note, p. 177 above). The relativity of these terms and the identification of virtue and potency are consequences of the notion of unity. But otherwise, with understanding we see that morals and morality are matters of concern on the level of imagination, but not on that of understanding.—For the reference in Def. 6 see p. 214 above, note. "Its" in the last line of Def. 8 refers to either "human being" or "being" since a human being is its being. However, when "being" occurs in the phrase "nature or being" the whole phrase has a meaning close to that of "essence," the conventional English translation of *essentia.*

In Schol. 1, Prop. 33, p. I inter *possibile, & contingens* nullam feci differentiam, quia ibi non opus erat haec accuratè distinguere.

V. Per *contrarios affectûs* in seqq. intelligam eos, qui hominem diversum trahunt, quamvis ejusdem sint generis, ut Luxuries, & Avaritia, quae Amoris sunt species; nec naturâ, sed per accidens sunt contrarii.

VI. Quid per *affectum erga rem futuram, praesentem, & praeteritam* intelligam, explicui in Schol. 1, & 2, Prop. 18, p. 3, quod vide.

VII. Per *finem cujus causa aliquid facimus,* Appetitum intelligo.

VIII. Per *virtutem, & potentiam* idem intelligo, hoc est (*per Prop. 7, p.* 3), virtus, quatenus ad hominem refertur, est ipsa hominis essentia, seu natura, quatenus potestatem habet, quaedam efficiendi, quae per solas ipsius naturae leges possunt intelligi.

Axioma.

Nulla res singularis in rerum naturâ datur, quâ potentior, & fortior non detur alia. Sed quâcunque datâ datur alia potentior, a quâ illa data potest destrui.

NB. There are no italics in Geb or the OP. The names of the Affections in Def. 5 are not capitalized in the latter texts, nor is *"Appetitum"* in Def. 7.

Propositions.

Prop. I. Nothing, which a false idea has positively, is annulled (by) the presence of truth, in so far as [it is] truth.

Prop. II. We are passive, in so far as we are a part of Nature, which cannot be conceived by means of itself without others.

Prop. III. The force, (with) which a human being perseveres in existing, is limited, & infinitely surpassed by(*a*) the potency of external causes.

Prop. IV. It cannot happen that a human being not be Nature's part, & that it can experience no mutations, unless these can be understood solely by means of its nature, and it can be their adequate cause.

Prop. V. The force, & increment of any passion whatever, and its perseverance in existing is not defined (by) the potency (with) which we endeavor to persevere in existing, but (by) an external cause's potency compared with ours.

Prop. VI. The force of some passion, or Affection can surpass the rest of a human being's actions, or potency, so that the Affection adheres pertinaciously to the human being.

Prop. VII. An Affection can neither be coerced, nor annulled, except by means of an Affection contrary to, & stronger than the Affection to be coerced.

Prop. VIII. Knowledge of good, & ill is nothing other than an Affection of Joy, or Sadness, in so far as we are conscious of it.

Prop. IX. Affection, whose cause we imagine to be there before us in the present, is stronger than if we were to imagine it not to be there.

NB. The addition in brackets in Prop. 1 is from the NS.—The famous *"Deus sive Natura"* occurs in the OP in Preface, P. IV, but not in the NS, though it occurs there too later in scholia. Remember that BdS did not mean by "Nature" what is ordinarily meant (see p. 47 above).

Propositiones.

Prop. I. Nihil, quod idea falsa positivum habet, tollitur praesentiâ veri, quatenus verum.

Prop. II. Nos eatenus patimur, quatenus Naturae sumus pars, quae per se se absque aliis non potest concipi.

Prop. III. Vis, quâ homo in existendo perseverat, limitata est, & à potentiâ causarum externarum infinitè superatur.

Prop. IV. Fieri non potest, ut homo non sit Naturae pars, & ut nullas possit pati mutationes, nisi, que solam suam naturam possint intelligi, quarunque adaequata sit causa.

Prop. V. Vis, & incrementum cujuscunque passiones, ejusque in existendo perseveranita non definitur potentiâ, quâ nos in existendo perseverare conamur, sed causae externae potentiâ cum nostrâ comparatâ.

Prop. VI. Vis alicujus passionis, seu affectûs reliquas hominis actiones, seu potentiam superare potest, ità ut affectus pertinaciter homini adhaereat.

Prop. VII. Affectus nec coërceri, nec tolli potest, nisi per affectum contrarium, & fortiorem affectus coërcendo.

Prop. VIII. Cognitio boni, & mali nihil aliud est, quàm Laetitiae, vel Tristiiae affectûs, quatenus ejus sumus conscii.

Prop. IX. Affectus, cujus causam in praesenti nobis adesse imaginamur, fortior est, quàm si eandem non adesse imaginaremur.

Prop. X. We are more intensely affected toward a future thing which we imagine will shortly not be future than if we were to imagine its time of existing longer distant from(*a*) the present; & we are also more intensely affected (by) memory of a thing which we imagine to be not long passed than if we were to imagine it long passed.

Prop. XI. Affection toward a thing which we imagine as necessary, other things being equal, is more intense than toward one possible, or contingent, or not necessary.

Prop. XII. Affection toward a thing, which we know does not exist in the present, & which we imagine as possible, other things being equal, is more intense than toward a contingent thing.

Prop. XIII. Affection toward a contingent thing, which we know does not exist in the present, other things being equal, is more remiss than Affection toward a past thing.

Prop. XIV. True knowledge of good, & ill, in so far as it is true, can coerce no Affection, but only in so far as it is considered an Affection.

Prop. XV. Desire, which originates from true knowledge of good, & ill, can be assuaged, or coerced (by) many other Desires, which originate from Affections (with) which we are in conflict.

Prop. XVI. Desire, which originates from knowledge of good, & ill, in so far as this knowledge respects the future, can be more facilely coerced, or assuaged (by) Desire of things which are in the present sweet.

Prop. XVII. Desire, which originates from true knowledge of good, & ill, in so far as this is about contingent things, can be more facilely coerced than Desire for things which are present.

Prop. XVIII. Desire, which originates from Joy, other things being equal, is stronger than Desire, which originates from Sadness.

Prop. XIX. Each according to the laws of his nature necessarily has an appetite for, or is averse to that which he judges to be good, or ill.

Prop. X. Erga rem futuram, quàm cito affuturam imaginamur, intensiùs afficimur, quàm si ejus existendi tempus longiùs à praesenti distare imaginaremur; & memoriâ rei, quam non diu praeterisse imaginamur, intensiùs etiam afficimur, quam si eandem diu praeterisse imaginaremur.

Prop. XI. Affectus erga rem, quam ut necessariam imaginamur, caeteris paribus, intensior est, quàm erga possibilem, vel contingentem, sive non necessariam.

Prop. XII. Affectus erga rem, quam scimus in praesenti non existere, & quam ut possibiliem imaginamur, caeteris paribus, intensior est, quàm erga contingentem.

Prop. XIII. Affectus erga rem contingentem, quam scimus in praesenti non existere, caeteris paribus, remission est, quàm praeteritam.

Prop. XIV. Vera boni, & mali cognitio, quatenus vera, nullum affectum coërcere potest, sed tantùm, quatenus ut affectus consideratur.

Prop. XV. Cupiditas, quae ex verâ boni, & mali cognitione oritur, multis aliis Cupiditatibus, quae ex affectibus, quibus conflictamur, oriuntur, restingui, vel coërceri potest.

Prop. XVI. Cupiditas, quae ex cognitione boni, & mali, quatenus haec cognitio futurum respicit, oritur, faciliùs rerum Cupiditate, quae in praesentiâ suaves sunt, coërceri, vel restingui potest.

Prop. XVII. Cupiditas, quae oritur ex verâ boni, & mali cognitione, quatenus haec circa res contingentes versatur, multò adhuc faciliùs coërceri potest, Cupiditate rerum, quae praesentes sunt.

Prop. XVIII. Cupiditas quae ex Laetitiâ oritur, caeteris paribus, fortior est Cupiditate, quae ex Tristitiâ oritur.

Prop. XIX. Id unusquisque ex legibus suae naturae necessariò appetit, vel aversatur, quod bonum, vel malum esse judicat. .

Prop. XX. The more each endeavors, & is able to seek what is useful to him, that is, to conserve his be-ing, the more he is endowed with virtue; & on the contrary in so far as each neglects what is useful to him, that is, to conserve his be-ing, he is to that extent impotent.

Prop. XXI. No one can desire to be beatifically, to act well, & to live well, who does not simultaneously desire to be, to act, & to live, that is, to actually exist.

Prop. XXII. No virtue can be conceived prior to this (namely the conatus for conserving oneself).

Prop. XXIII. A human being, in so far as it is determined to acting something from this, that it has inadequate ideas, cannot be said absolutely to act from virtue; but only, in so far as it is determined from this, that it understands.

Prop. XXIV. To act absolutely from virtue is nothing other than to act, to live, to conserve one's be-ing (these three signify the same) according to(*ex*) the conduct of reason, and that from the foundation of seeking what is useful to one.

Prop. XXV. No one endeavors to conserve his or her be-ing (in) cause of another thing.

Prop. XXVI. Whatever we endeavor according to reason, is nothing other than to understand; and a Mind, in so far as it uses reason, does not judge another thing useful to it, except that which conduces to understanding.

NB. Elwes is again using "conceive" to translate *"imaginor."*—Schol. Prop. 17 summarizes with the quotation from Ovid (see p. 128 above).—The equation of being, acting and living well in Prop. 21 merits the split infinitive at its end. The NS has "really to exist" (*daat wezentlijk te wezen*—literally: really beingly to be).

NB. I take it that the first half of Prop. 26 defines understanding in so far as it is regarded as an Affection. Other translators, for example, Charles Appuhn, read it differently: every effort in which reason is the principle in us has no other object than knowledge [*connaissance;* elsewhere Appuhn uses *entendre* to translate *intelligere*]. However, I think that understanding is whatever we endeavor according to or from reason. See pp. 112 and 126 above. It is a mistake to regard understanding as only cognitive, a dualistic mistake. It is also affective,

[Cont. on p. 236]

Prop. XX. Quò magis unusquisque sum utile quaerere, hoc est, sum esse conservare conatur, & potest, eò magis virtute praeditus est; & contrà quatenus unusquisque sum utile, hoc est, suum esse conservare negligit, eatenus impotens.

Prop. XXI. Nemo potest cupere beatum esse, bene agere, & bene vivere, qui simul cupiat, esse, agere, & vivere, hoc est, actu existere.

Prop. XXII. Nulla virtus potest prior hâc (nempe conatus sese conservandi) concipi.

Prop. XXIII. Homo, quatenus ad aliquid agendum deter-minatur, ex eo, quòd ideas habet inadaequatas, non potest abso-lutè dici, ex virtute agere; sed tantùm, quatenus determinatur ex eo, quòd intelligit.

Prop. XXIV. Ex virtute absolutè agere nihil aliud in nobis est, quàm ex dictu rationis agere, vivere, suum esse conservare (haec tria idem significant), idque ex fundamento proprium utile quaerendi.

Prop. XXV. Nemo suum esse alterius rei causâ conservare conatur.

Prop. XXVI. Quicquid ex ratione conamur, nihil aliud est, quàm inteligere; nec Mens, quatenus ratione utitur, aliud sibi utile esse judicat, nisi id, quod ad intelligendum conducit.

Prop. XXVII. We know nothing for certain to be good, or ill, except that which really conduces to understanding, or which can impede our understanding.

Prop. XXVIII. A Mind's highest good is God's knowledge, & a Mind's highest virtue is to cognize God.

Prop. XXIX. Any singular thing whatever, whose nature is entirely diverse from(*a*) ours, can neither help, nor coerce our potency for acting, & absolutely no thing can be good, or ill for us, unless it has something common with us.

Prop. XXX. No thing can be ill by means of that which it has common with us; but in so far as it is ill for us, to that extent it is contrary to us.

Prop. XXXI. In so far as some thing agrees with our nature, to that extent it is necessarily good.

Prop. XXXII. In so far as human beings are subject to passions, to that extent they cannot be said to agree in nature.

Prop. XXXIII. Human beings can be discrepant (in) nature, in so far as they are in conflict with Affections which are passions, & to that extent also one and the same human being is variable, & inconstant.

Prop. XXXIV. In so far as human beings are in conflict with Affections which are passions, they can be contrary to each other.

Prop. XXXV. In so far as human beings live according to(*ex*) the conduct of reason, to that extent only do they always necessarily agree (in) nature.

Prop. XXXVI. The highest good of those, who follow virtue continuously, is common to all, and all can be equally joyful (in) it.

Prop. XXXVII. A good, for which each who follows virtue continuously has an appetite for himself, he will desire for the rest of human beings, & the more, as he will have greater God's knowledge.

[Cont. from p. 234]

a quite different way of knowing from what we ordinarily think of as knowing.

Prop. XXVII. Nihil certò scimus bonum, aut malum esse, nisi id, quod ad intelligendum reverâ conducit, vel quod impedire potest, quominùs intelligamus.

Prop. XXVIII. Summum Mentis bonum est Dei cognitio, & summa Mentis virtus Deum cognoscere.

Prop. XXIX. Res quaecunque singularis, cujus natura à nostrâ prorsus est diversa, nostram agendi potentiam nec juvare, nec coërcere potest, & absolutè res nulla potest nobis bona, aut mala, nisi commune aliquid nobiscum habeat.

Prop. XXX. Res nulla per id, quod cum nostrâ naturâ commune habet, potest esse mala; sed quatenus nobis mala est, eatenus est nobis contraria.

Prop. XXXI. Quatenus res aliqua cum nostrâ naturâ convenit, eatenus necessariò bona est.

Prop. XXXII. Quatenus homines passionibus sunt obnoxii, non possunt eatenus dici, quòd naturâ conveniant.

Prop. XXXIII. Homines natura discrepare possunt, quatenus affectibus, qui passiones sunt, conflictantur, & eatenus etiam unus, idemque homo varius est, & inconstans.

Prop. XXXIV. Quatenus homines affectibus, qui passiones sunt, conflictantur, possunt invicem esse contarii.

Prop. XXXV. Quatenus homines ex dictu rationis vivunt, eatenus tantùm naturâ semper necessariò conveniunt.

Prop. XXXVI. Summum bonum eorum, qui virtutem sectantur, omnibus commune est, eoque omnes aequè gaudere possunt.

Prop. XXXVII. Bonum, quod unusquisque, qui sectatur virtutem, sibi appetit, reliquis hominibus etiam cupiet, & eò magis, quò majorem Dei habuerit cognitionem.

Prop. XXXVIII. That, which so disposes a human Body that it can be affected (in) plural modes, or which renders it apt for affecting external bodies (in) plural modes, is useful to a human being, & the more useful as the Body is rendered the more apt by(*ab*) it for it to be affected, and to affect other bodies (in) plural modes, & on the contrary that is noxious which renders the Body less apt for this.

Prop. XXXIX. Things which effect it, that the ratio of motion, & quiet, which a human Body's parts have to each other, is conserved are good; & on the contrary those ill which effect it, that a human Body's parts should have another ratio of motion, & quiet to each other.

Prop. XL. Things which conduce to human beings' common Society, or which effect it, that human beings live in concord, are useful; those on the contrary ill, which induce discord into a Civic Body.

Prop. XLI. Joy is not directly ill, but good; Sadness however is directly ill.

Prop. XLII. Hilarity cannot have an excess, but is always good; & on the contrary Melancholy is always ill.

Prop. XLIII. Titillation can have an excess, & be ill; Dolor however, can be good, to the extent that Titillation, or Joy is ill.

Prop. XLIV. Love, & Desire can have an excess.

Prop. XLV. Hate can never be good.

NB. It must never be forgotten that knowledge of God is not knowledge of some thing. It is the experience of unity or union, which is God's or the highest kind of knowing (Prop. 37). Thus in the scholia of Prop. 37 BdS discusses Society and a Civic Body (see TP, Chp. 3).—In Prop. 41 we might read: "A Joy is not an ill." However, Joy is a way of behaving.—Titillation or Hilarity is an Affection of Joy related simultaneously to Mind & Body; Dolor or Melancholy is a similar Affection of Sadness. However, in Titillation & Dolor only a part of a human being is affected; in Hilarity & Melancholy all the parts are comparably affected (see Schol. Pr. 11, P. III). Here again the notion of unity or the whole is playing a part. See Prop. 60.

Prop. XXXVIII. Id, quod Corpus humanum ità disponit, ut pluribus modis possit affici, vel quod idem aptum reddit ad corpora externa pluribus modis afficiendum, homini est utile; & eò utilius, quò Corpus ab aptius redditur, ut pluribus modis afficiatur, aliaque corpora afficiat, & contrà id noxium est, quod Corpus ad haec minùs aptum reddit.

Prop. XXXIX. Quae efficiunt, ut motûs, & quietis ratio, quam Corpris humani partes ad invicem habent, conservetur, bona sunt; & ea contrà mala, quae efficiunt, ut Corporis humani partes aliam ad invicem motûs, & quietis habeant rationem.

Prop. XL. Quae ad hominem communem Societam conducunt, sive quae efficiunt, ut homines concorditer vivant, utilia sunt; & ill contrà mala, quae discordiam in Civitatem inducunt.

Prop. XLI. Laetitia directè mala non est, sed bona; Tristitia autem contrà directè est mala.

Prop. XLII. Hilaritas excessum habere nequit, sed semper bona est, & contrà Melancholia semper est mala.

Prop. XLIII. Titillatio excessum habere potest, & mala esse; Dolor autem eatenus potest esse bonus, quatenus Titillatio, seu Laetitia est mala.

Prop. XLIV. Amor, & Cupiditas excessum habere possunt.

Prop. XLV. Odium nunquam potest esse bonum.

NB. In the third line of Prop. 38 *corpora* is mistakenly capitalized in Geb and the OP.—Some of the names of the Affections sound odd in English, but BdS defines all the Affections carefully so that we know what the names refer to. We must also keep in mind that "Affection" is extremely broadly used by BdS.

Prop. XLVI. He, who lives according to(*ex*) the conduct of reason, endeavors, as much as he can, to compensate another in his Hate, Anger, Contempt, &c. (with) Love, or Generosity in return.

Prop. XLVII. Affections of Hope, & Dread cannot be good by means of themselves.

Prop. XLVIII. Affections of Esteem, & Despite are always ill.

Prop. XLIX. Esteem facilely renders the human being, who is esteemed, proud.

Prop. L. Commiseration in a human being, who lives according to(*ex*) the conduct of reason, is by means of itself ill, & useless.

Prop. LI. Favor is not repugnant to reason; but can agree with it & originates from it.

Prop. LII. Acquiescence in oneself can originate from reason, & solely Acquiescence which originates from reason is the highest which can be given.

Prop. LIII. Humility is not a virtue, or does not originate from reason.

Prop. LIV. Penitence is not a virtue, or does not originate from reason; but he, who repents what he has done is doubly miserably, or impotent.

Prop. LV. Maximum Pride, or Abjection is maximum ignorance of self.

Prop. LVI. Maximum Pride, or Abjection indicates maximum impotence of spirit.

Prop. LVII. The proud man loves the presence of parasites, or adulators, however he hates that of the generous.

NB. For *Love* see p. 124 and for *Generosity* p. 125. *Esteem* is to think more than justly of another through Love. *Despite* is to think less than justly of another through Hate. *Favor* is Love toward someone who benefits another. *Commiseration* is Sadness, concomitant with an idea of an ill, which has eventuated for someone we imagine to be similar to us. *Humility* is Sadness due to contemplating one's impotence. *Pride* is to think more than justly of oneself through Self-love. *Abjection* is to

[Cont. on p. 242]

Prop. XLVI. Qui ex dictu rationis vivit, quantùm potest, conatur alterius in ipsum Odium, Iram, Contemptum, &c., Amore contrà, sive Generositate compensare.

Prop. XLVII. Spei, & Metûs affectûs non possunt esse per se boni.

Prop. XLVIII. Affectûs Existimationis, & Despectûs semper mali sunt.

Prop. XLIX. Existimatio facilè hominem, qui existimatur, superbum reddit.

Prop. L. Commiseratio in homine, qui ex dictu rationis vivit, per se mala, & inutilis est.

Prop. LI. Favor rationi non repugnat; sed cum eâdem convenire, & ab eâdem oriri potest.

Prop. LII. Acquiescentia in se ipso ex ratione oriri potest, & ea sola Acquiescentia, quae ex ratione oritur, summa est, quae potest dari.

Prop. LIII. Humilitas virtus non est, sive ex ratione non oritur.

Prop. LIV. Poenitentia virtus non est, sive ex ratione non oritur; sed is, quem facti poenitet, bis miser, seu impotens est.

Prop. LV. Maxima Superbia, vel Abjectio est maxima sui ignorantia.

Prop. LVI. Maxima Superbia, vel Abjectio maximum animi impotentia inddicat.

Prop. LVII. Superbus parasitorum, seu adulatorum praesentiam amat, generosorum autem odit.

NB. The second occurrence of *Acquiescentia* in Prop. 52 is not capitalized in Geb or the OP.

Prop. LVIII. Glory is not repugnant to reason, but can originate from(*a*) it.

Prop. LIX. To all actions, to which we are determined from an Affection which is a passion, we can be determined without it by(*a*) reason.

Prop. LX. Desire, which originates from Joy, or Sadness, which is related to one or some, *not* to all the Body's parts, does not have a reference to the utility of the total human being.

Prop. LXI. A Desire, which originates from reason, cannot have an excess.

Prop. LXII. In so far as a Mind conceives a thing according to(*ex*) reason's dictate, it is equally affected, whether the idea be of a thing future, or past, or present.

[Cont. from p. 240]

think less than justly of oneself through Sadness. Acquiescence in oneself (*Acquiescentia in se ipso*) is Joy, born from this, that a human being contemplates itself, & its potency for acting. BdS has two definitions of *Penitence:* Sadness with an idea of oneself as if the cause (Schol. Pr. 51, P. III), and: Sadness with an idea of something done which we believe we did from the Mind's free decree (Def. 27, P. III). The last five Affections center about the idea of what BdS calls an "internal cause" (see Prop. 30, P. III & Schol.) the others about the idea of an external cause. The last five are closely interrelated and are related to an Affection Geb obliterates in his text: *Acquiescentia in se ipsa* (Acquiescence itself in self) because he thinks "*ipsa*" is a misprint for "*ipso*" (Schol. Prop. 51, P. III). It is not. *Acquiescence itself in self* is: Joy concomitant with an idea of oneself as if the cause. It and Penitence are "vehement" Affections "because human beings believe themselves to be free." Sp's analysis of these Affections is marvellous but incomplete. Self-love can become Acquiescence itself in self or Pride. With understanding the former can become Acquiescence in oneself (*in se ipso*). Pride is thus one of the worst of the passions partly because it stems from the same source as one of the highest sorts of Acquiescence (Prop. 52). We are thus easily deceived by it.—BdS notes that Humility and Penitence, while not virtues, are useful to society (see p. 134 above).

NB. Glory is Joy, concomitant with some action of ours, which we imagine that others praise.

Prop. LVIII. Gloria rationi non repugnat, sed ab eâ oriri potest.

Prop. LIX. Ad omnes actiones, ad quas ex affectu, qui passio est, determinatur, possumus, absque eo à ratione determinari.

Prop. LX. Cupiditas, quas oritur ex Laetitiâ, vel Tristitiâ, quae ad unam, vel ad aliquot, non autem ad omnes Corporis partes referetur, rationem utilitatis totius hominis non habet.

Prop. LXI. Cupiditas, quae ex ratione oritur, excessum habere nequit.

Prop. LXII. Quatenus Mens ex rationis dictamine res concipit, aequè afficitur, sive idea sit rei futurae, vel praeteritae, sive praesentis.

Prop. LXIII. He, who is conducted (by) Dread, & acts a good so that he may avoid an ill, is not conducted (by) reason.

Prop. LXIV. Knowledge of an ill is inadequate knowledge.

Prop. LXV. According to(*ex*) reason's conduct we shall follow the greater of two goods, & the lesser of two ills.

Prop. LXVI. According to(*ex*) reason's conduct we shall have an appetite for a greater future good compared with a lesser present one, & a lesser present ill compared with a future greater one.

Prop. LXVII. A free human being thinks concerning no thing less than concerning death, & its sapience is a meditation not of death, but of life.

Prop. LXVIII. If human beings were born free, they would form no conceiving of good, & ill, as long as they were free.

Prop. LXIX. A human being's virtue is discerned as equally great in declining as in surmounting perils.

Prop. LXX. A free human being, who lives among the ignorant, studies to decline their benefits, as much as it can.

Prop. LXXI. Solely human beings are very grateful toward each other.

Prop. LXXII. A free human being never acts (by) fraud, but always with fidelity.

Prop. LXXIII. A human being who is conducted (by) reason, is freer in a civic body, where it lives according to(*ex*) common decree, than it is in solitude where it complies solely with itself.

Prop. LXIII. Qui Metus ducitur, & bonum, ut malum vitet, agit, is ratione non ducitur.

Prop. LXIV. Cognitio mali cognitio adaequata.

Prop. LXV. De duobus bonis majus, & de duobus malis minus ex ratione ductu sequemur.

Prop. LXVI. Bonum majus futuram prae minor praesenti, & malum praesens minus prae majori futuro ex rationis ductu appetemus.

Prop. LXVII. Homo liber de nullâ re minùs, quàm de morte cogitat, & ejus sapientia non mortis, sed vitae meditatio est.

Prop. LXVIII. Si homines liberi nascerentur, nullum boni, & mali formarent conceptum, quamdiu liberi essent.

Prop. LXIX. Hominis liberi virtus aequè magna cernitur in declinandis, quàm in superandis periculis.

Prop. LXX. Homo liber, qui inter ignaros vivit, eorum, quantum potest, beneficia declinare studet.

Prop. LXXI. Soli homines liberi erga se invicem gratissimi sunt.

Prop. LXXII. Homo liber nunquam dolo malo, sed semper cum fide agit.

Prop. LXXIII. Homo qui ratione ducitur, magis in civitate, ubi ex communi decreto vivit, quàm in solitudine, ubi sibi soli obtemperat, liber est.

NB. Geb lacks *"se"* in Prop. 71.

ETHIC'S
Fifth Part,
CONCERNING
the Potency of Understanding, or
concerning Human Freedom

AXIOMS.

I. If two contrary actions are excited in the same subject, a mutation will necessarily be bound to happen, either in both, or solely in one, until they cease to be contrary.

II. An effect's potency is defined (by) the potency of its cause, in so far as its being is explicated, or defined by means of its cause's being.

This Axiom is patent from Prop. 7, Part 3.

Propositions.

Prop. I. According as thinkings, & things' ideas are ordered, & concatenated in a Mind, so exactly are the Body's affections, or the thing's images ordered, & concatenated in the Body.

Prop. II. If we move an emotion, or an Affection away from(*ab*) a thinking of an external cause, & join it to other thinkings, then Love, or Hate toward the external cause, & also Fluctuations of Spirit, which originate from these Affections, will be destroyed.

Prop. III. An Affection which is a passion, ceases to be a passion at the same time that we form its clear, & distinct idea.

Prop. IV. There is no affection of the Body of which we cannot form some clear, & distinct conceiving.

Prop. V. An Affection toward a thing, which we imagine simply, & not as necessary, or possible, or contingent is, other things being equal, the maximum of all.

NB. Sp's notion of axioms is reflected in the line after Ax. 2—Elwes again translates *"Imaginor"* with "conceive." Prop. 1 is helpful with Sp's notion of imagination.

ETHICS
Pars Quinta,
DE
Potentia Intellectûs, seu de Liber-
tate Humanâ

AXIOMATA.

I. Si in eodem subjecto duae contrariae actiones excitentur, debebit necessariò vel in utràque, vel in unâ solâ mutatio fieri, donec desinant contrariae esse.

II. Effectûs potentia definitur potentiâ ipsius causae, quatenus ejus essentia per ipsius causae essentiam explicatur, vel definitur.

Patet hoc Axioma ex Prop. 7, Part. 3.

Propositiones.

Prop. I. Prout cogitationes rereumque ideae ordinantur, & concatenantur in Mente, ità Corporis affectiones, seu rerum imagines ad amussim ordinantur, & concatenantur in Corpore.

Prop. II. Si animi commotionem, seu affectum a causae exter- nae cogitatione amoveamus, & aliis jungamus cogitationibus, tum Amor, seu Odium erga causam externam, ut & Animi Fluctuationes, quae ex his affectibus oriuntur, destruentur.

Prop. III. Affectus, qui passio est, desinit esse passio, simulat- que ejus claram, & distinctam formamus ideam.

Prop. IV. Nulla est Corporis affectio, cujus aliquam clarum, & distinctam non possumus formare conceptum.

Prop. V. Affectus erga rem, quam simpliciter, & non ut neces- sarium, neque possibilem, neque ut contingentem imaginamur, caeteris paribus, omnium maximus.

NB. *"Corporis"* in Prop. 1 is not capitalized in Geb or the OP; nor is *"Animi Fluctuationes"* in Prop. II.

Prop. VI. In so far as a Mind understands all things as necessary, to that extent it has greater potency in Affections, or is less passive in relation to them.

Prop. VII. Affections, which originate, or are excited from reason, if there is reference to time, are more potent than those which are related to singular things, which we contemplate as absent.

Prop. VIII. To the extent that some Affection is excited by (a) plural concurrent causes, it is greater.

Prop. IX. An Affection, which is related to plural, & diverse causes, which the Mind contemplates together with the Affection itself, is less noxious, & we are less passive by means of it, & we are less affected toward each cause, than another equally great Affection, which is related solely to one, or to fewer causes.

Prop. X. As long as we are not in conflict (with) Affections, which are contrary to our nature, we have the power for ordering, & concatenating the Body's affections according to an order for understanding.

Prop. XI. To the extent that some image is related to plural things, the more frequent it is, or the more often it is vigorous, & the more it occupies the Mind.

Prop. XII. Things' images are more facilely joined to images, which are related to things, which we understand clearly, & distinctly, than to others.

Prop. XIII. To the extent that some image is joined to plural others, the more often it is vigorous.

Prop. XIV. A mind can effect it, that all the Body's affections, or things' images are related to God's idea.

Prop. VI. Quatenus Mens res omnes, ut necessarias intelligit, eatenus majorem in affectûs potentiam habet, seu minùs ab iisdem patitur.

Prop. VII. Affectûs, qui ex ratione oriuntur, vel excitantur, si ratio temporis habeatur, potentiores sunt iis, qui ad res singulares referuntur, quas ut absentes contemplamur.

Prop. VIII. Quò affectus aliquis à pluribus causis concurrentibus excitatur, èo major est.

Prop. IX. Affectus, qui ad plures, & diversas causas refertur, quas Mens cum ipso affectus simul contemplatur, minùs noxius est, & minùs per ipsu, patimur, & arga unamquamque causam minus afficimur, quàm alius aequè magnus affectus, qui ad unam solam, vel pauciores causas refertur.

Prop. X. Quamdiu affectibus, qui nostrae naturae sunt contrarii, non conflictamur, tamdiu ptestatem habemus ordinandi, & concetanandi Corporis affectiones secundùm ordinem ad intellectum.

Prop. XI. Quò imago aliqua ad plres res refertur, eò frequentior est, seu saepiùs viget, & Mentem magis occupat.

Prop. XII. Rerum imagines facilius imaginibus, quae ad res referuntur, quas clarè, & distinctè intelligimus, junguntur, quàm aliis.

Prop. XIII. Quò imago aliqua pluribus aliis juncta est, eò saepiùs viget.

Prop. XIV. Mens efficere potest, ut omnes Corporis affectiones, seu rerum imagines ad Dei ideam referantur.

NB. All other Latin Texts have *"simul"* before *"concurrentibus"* in Prop. 8 (reading in English: plural concurrent causes simultaneously). This is redundant and the NS does not have the corresponding Dutch word. In the ETHIC a proposition is usually repeated in the last line of its demonstration. The last line of the demonstration of Prop. 8 has *"fortior"* (stronger) instead of *"major."* The same is true in the NS. The use of *"animi commotionem"* (see Prop. 2) is also extremely rare in the ETHIC (it means "emotion"). That it should occur in a proposition, together with what we have just observed in Prop. 8, suggests the unpolished character of Part V.

Prop. XV. He, who understands himself, and his Affections clearly, & distinctly, loves God, & the more so, as he understands himself, and his Affections.

Prop. XVI. This Love toward God is bound to occupy a Mind maximally.

Prop. XVII. God is exempt from passions, and is not affected (with) any Affection of Joy, or Sadness.

Prop. XVIII. No one is able to hate God.

Prop. XIX. He, who loves God, is unable to endeavor that God love him in return.

Prop. XX. This Love toward God can neither be defiled (with) an Affection of Envy, nor (with) an Affection of Jealousy; but it is fomented the more, as we imagine plural human beings joined with God (in) the same bond of Love.

Prop. XXI. A Mind is able to imagine nothing, nor to recollect past things, except while the Body endures.

Prop. XXII. In God nevertheless there is necessarily given an idea, which expresses this, & that human Body's being under eternity's species.

Prop. XXIII. A human Mind cannot be absolutely destroyed with the Body, but something remains, which is eternally.

Prop. XXIV. The more we understand singular things, the more we understand God.

NB. Notice that in Prop. 8., for example, *"pluribus"* is translated "plural" instead of "many" as in other translations. But more than one is enough. It is the difference between plurality and unity that counts, not many and one. Notice, too, that in Prop. 16 BdS uses "maximally" not "completely." Things are always matters of degree for him.—In Prop. 10 "understanding" translates *"intellectum,"* the noun. "The" or "an" before it is, therefore, grammatically correct; but philosophically in BdS incorrect, for there is not a faculty, the understanding. This is another of the many examples of how Sp's thinking changes our grammar, and hence our thinking. See Letter 83: "For up to now it has been permitted me to dispose nothing concerning these things in order." The change in his thinking from the ordinary made his task almost impossible.

Prop. XV. Qui se, suosque affectûs clarè, & distinctè intelligit, Deum amat, & eò nagis, quò se, suosque affectûs magis intelligit.

Prop. XVI. Hic erga Deum Amor Mentem maximè occupare debet.

Prop. XVII. Deus expers est passionum, nec ullo Laetitiae, aut Tristitiae affectu afficitur.

Prop. XVIII. Nemo potest Deum odio habere.

Prop. XIX. Qui Deum amat, conari non potest, ut Deus ipsum contrà amet.

Prop. XX. Hic erga Deum Amor, neque Invidiae, neque Zelotypiae affectu imaginari potest; sed eò magis fovetur, quò plures homines eodem Amoris vinculo cum Deo junctos imaginamur.

Prop. XXI. Mens nihil imaginari potest, neque rerum praeteritarum recordari, nisi durante Corpore.

Prop. XXII. In Deo tamen datur necessariò idea, quae hujus, & illius Corporis humani essentiam sub aeternitatis specie exprimit.

Prop. XXIII. Mens humana non potest cum Corpore absolutè destrui; sed ejus aliquid remanet, quod aeternum est.

Prop. XXIV. Quò magis res singulares intelligimus, eò Deum intelligimus.

NB. In Prop. 24 Geb adds a clause from the NS: [*of wy ook meer verstant van God heben*] (or we also have more understanding of God). Translated Prop. 24 in the NS reads: "The more we understand singular things, the more also we understand God, or have more understanding of God." Geb has thus distorted the proposition with his addition at the end of the Latin. I omit the addition in favor of indicating the difference between the OP and the NS in a note.

Prop. XXV. A Mind's highest conatus, and highest virtue is to understand things (by) the third genus of knowledge.

Prop. XXVI. The more apt a Mind is for understanding things (by) the third genus of knowledge, the more it desires to understand things (by) this very genus of knowledge.

Prop. XXVII. From this third genus of knowledge originates the highest Acquiescence of Mind, that can be given.

Prop. XXVIII. The conatus, or Desire for cognizing things (by) the third genus of knowledge cannot originate from the first, yet certainly from the second genus of knowledge.

Prop. XXIX. Whatever a Mind understands under a species of eternity, it understands not from this, that it conceives the Body's present actual existing, but from this, that it conceives the Body's being under a species of eternity.

Prop. XXX. Our Mind, in so far as it cognizes itself, & the Body under eternity's species, to that extent necessarily has God's knowledge, and knows itself to be in God, & to be conceived by means of *God.*

Prop. XXXI. The third genus of knowledge depends on the Mind, as if on a formal cause, in so far as the Mind itself is eternally.

NB. Elwes has "conceive" instead of "imagine" in Prop. 21.—In Prop. 23 "remains" means "left over."—In Prop. 20 we have "joined with God (in) the same bond of Love." The ablative case in the Latin allows "(by) the same bond of Love," but notice that this does not unite us all, "God" included, in the bond. "Toward God" at the beginning of the proposition throws us because of our preconceptions and prejudices. Think of "Toward *Being.*"—In Prop. 26 we have "(by) the third genus." It could be "(in) the third genus."—In Prop. 30 I have "God" in italics because we are conceived by "God" or *"Being."* Of course, "conceived" here might mean to refer to the act that produces off-spring, though it probably does not because "to be & to be conceived" is a common phrase in the ETHIC.—With Prop. 21 BdS leaves the remedies for Affections, or what reason or understanding can do among the Affections (note: not "over" them), and turns to a Mind's being eternally, intuitive knowing, or the third genus of knowledge, that is, human Freedom.

Prop. XXV. Summus Mentis conatus, summaque virtus est res intelligere tertio cognitionis genere.

Prop. XXVI. Quò Mens aptior ad res tertio cognitionis genere intelligendum, eò magis cupit, res eodem hôc cognitionis genere intelligere.

Prop. XXVII. Ex hôc tertio cognitionis genere summa, quae dari potest, Mentis Acquiescentia oritur.

Prop. XXVIII. Conatus, seu Cupiditas cognoscendi res tertio cognitionis genere, oriri non potest ex primo, at quidam ex secundo cognitionis genere.

Prop. XXIX. Quicquid Mens sub specie aeternitatis intelligit, id ex eo non intelligit, quòd Corporis praesentem actualem existentiam concipit, sed ex eo, quòd Corporis essentiam concipit sub specie aeternitatis.

Prop. XXX. Mens nostra, quatenus se, & Corpus sub aeternitatis specie cognoscit, eatenus Dei cognitionem necessariò habet, scitque se in Deo esse, & per *Deum* concipi.

Prop. XXXI. Tertium cognitionis genus pendet à Mente, tanquam à formali causâ, quatenus Mens ipsa aeterna est.

NB. In Prop. 27 *"Acquescentia"* is not capitalized in Geb or the OP.

Prop. XXXII. Whatever we understand (by) the third genus of knowledge, we delight in it, & concomitant certainly with God's idea, as if the cause.

Prop. XXXIII. God's understanding Love, which originates from the third genus of knowledge, is eternally.

Prop. XXXIV. A Mind is only subject to Affections, which are related to passions, while the Body endures.

Prop. XXXV. God loves himself with infinitely understanding Love.

Prop. XXXVI. A Mind's understanding Love toward God is God's Love itself, (by) which God loves himself, not in so far as he is infinitely, but in so far as he can be explicated by means of *the being of a human Mind, considered under a species of eternity,* that is, a Mind's understanding Love toward God is part of the infinite Love (with) which God loves himself.

NB. Notice again the prepositions in parentheses. Prop. 35, for example, may read: God loves himself (in) infinitely understanding Love. Note next in the latter that "infinitely understanding Love" is a variation of "God's understanding Love." When "God" is used as an adjective it means "highest" or some other superlative.

BdS introduces the phrase "God's understanding Love" in the Corollary to Prop. 32, explaining that "from the third genus of knowledge necessarily originates God's understanding Love. For from this genus of knowledge originates Joy, concomitant with God's idea, as if the cause, that is, God's Love, not in so far as we imagine him as present, but in so far as we understand that God is eternally, and this is what I call *God's understanding Love.*" In the TTP the phrase appears in the form: "God's understanding knowledge." This kind of Love and this kind of knowing are one and the same. Note the contrasting of imagination with understanding, and *in so far as we understand* that *Being* is eternally. A clearer statement of union than this corollary is hard to come by. With it we realize that the distinction between imagination and understanding, or the making of that distinction, is itself a form of the expression of union.

The portion of Prop. 36 is in italics (it is not in Geb or the OP) because it is being mentioned rather than used. That is, "the being of a human Mind, considered under a species of eternity" is a way of

[Cont. on p. 256]

Prop. XXXII. Quicquid intelligimus tertio cognitionis genere, eo delectamur, & quidem Dei ideâ, tanquam causâ.

Prop. XXXIII. Dei Amor intellectualis, qui ex tertio cognitionis genere oritur, est aeternus.

Prop. XXIV. Mens non nisi durante Corpore obnoxia est affectibus, qui ad passiones referuntur.

Prop. XXXV. Deus se ipsum Amore intellextuali infinito amat.

Prop. XXXVI. Mentis Amor intellectualis erga Deum est ipse Dei Amor, quo Deus se ipsum amat, non quatenus infinitus est, sed quatenus per *essentiam humanae Mentis, sub specie aeternitatis,* explicari potest, hoc est, Mentis erga Deum Amor intellectualis pars est infiniti Amoris, quo Deus se ipsum amat.

NB. In Prop. 32 other Latin texts, including Geb and the OP, have *"ideâ Dei"* instead of *"Dei ideâ"* (idea of God, not God's idea). I follow the reading in the NS, but the change is philosophically sound. Of course, as noted before, once we follow Sp's insight into unity these grammatical differences do not matter. At first, however, and for some time, they are helpful. In Prop. 32 other Latin texts have *"Amor Dei intellectualis."* The authorities for my change are again the NS and philosophy. "God's understanding Love" is more accurate than "the understanding Love of God." (In Elwes this is "the intellectual Love of God.")

In Prop. 34 *"Corpore"* is not capitalized in Geb or the OP. In Prop. 36 the same is true of *"Amoris"* in the last line. In Prop. 37 Appuhn, the French translator, and I capitalize *"Naturâ."* It is not in Geb or the OP. However, BdS sometimes used *"in naturâ"* as an abbreviation for *"in rerum naturâ"* (in the nature of things), and the latter also fits in the proposition. The phrase means roughly: as things are. Nature, that is, Nature is God or *Being* for BdS. For dualists it is the natural world, often excluding our Minds and generally regarded as inanimate, or largely so.

Prop. XXXVII. Nothing in Nature is given, which is contrary to this understanding Love, or which can annul it.

Prop. XXXVIII. To the extent that a Mind understands plural things (by) the second, & third genera of knowledge, it is less passive in relation to Affections, which are ill, & it fears death less.

Prop. XXXIX. He, who has a Body apt for a great many things, has a Mind, whose maximum part is eternally.

Prop. XL. The more of perfection each thing has, the more it is active, & the less it is passive, & on the contrary, the more it is active, the more perfect it is.

Prop. XLI. Although we did not know our Mind to be eternally, we would nevertheless hold as first things Piety, & Religion, & absolutely all the things, which we have shown in the Fourth Part to be related to High-spiritedness & Generosity.

Prop. XLII. Beatitude is not virtue's reward, but virtue itself; and we are not joyful (in) it because we coerce libidos; but on the contrary because we are joyful (in) it, we can on that account coerce libidos.

But all things very clear are as difficult as rare.—ETHIC'S last line.

[Cont. from p. 254]

thinking of God which helps us to see that it may be said that God loves himself. He does in so far as he is a human Mind. In so far as he is infinitely, however, the expression makes no sense. In the schol. of Prop. 17, P. I BdS warns that terms like "will" and "understanding" do not apply to God in at all the same way that they apply to human beings. Thinking that they do is ordinary anthropomorphism.

NB. We become less passive and fear death less. A maximum part of a Mind can be eternally. For BdS things are matters of degree not absolutes.

Remember that in Latin *"habere"* (to have) and *"esse"* (to be) are sometimes interchangeable. Thus, a form of Prop. 39 is: He who is

[Cont. on p. 258]

Prop. XXXVII. Nihil in Naturâ datur, quod huic Amori intellectuali sit contrarium, sive quod ipsum possit tollere.

Prop. XXXVIII. Quò plures res secundo, & tertio cognitionis genere Mens intelligit, eò minùs ipsa ab affectibus, qui mali sunt, patitur, & mortem minus timet.

Prop. XXXIX. Qui Corpus ad plurima aptum habet, is Mentem habet, cujus maxima pars est aeterna.

Prop. XL. Quò unaquaeque res plus perfectionis habet, eò magis agit, & minùs patitur, & contrà quò magis agit, eò perfectior est.

Prop. XLI. Quamvis nesciremus, Mentem nostram aeternam esse, Pietatem tamen, & Religionem, & absolute omnia, quae Animisitem, & Generositatem referri ostendimus in Quartâ Parte, prima haberemus.

Prop. XLII. Beatitudo non est virtutis praemium, sed ipsa virtus; nec eâdem gaudemus, quia libidines coërcemus; sed contrà quia eâdem gaudemus, idèo libidines coërcere possumus.

Sed omnia praeclara tam difficilia, quàm rara sunt.

[Cont. from p. 256]

extending aptly for many things, is thinking which is maximally eternally.

Note that Prop. 40 refers to each thing, not simply to human beings. There is unity at work. Further, according to Def. 6, P. II Prop. 40 has it that the more active we are, the more real we are. A translation of *"ens"* (*being*) is "thing." A translation of *"res"* is "thing." *"Res"* is the root of "real."

"Whatever we desire, & act, of which we are cause, in so far as we have an idea of God, or in so far as we cognize God, I relate to Religion." "The Desire for benefitting, which is engendered (by) this, that we live according to the conduct of reason, I call *Piety."* These are from Schol. 1, Prop. 37, P. IV. For High-spiritedness and Generosity see p. 125 above.

BdS uses "libido" generally in the sense of a blind urge (see p. 54 above). He also uses the word as the name of an Affection: "Libido is also Desire, & Love in mingling bodies" (Def. 43, P. III).

With imagination ETHIC'S last line reads: but all things noble [or, excellent] are as difficult as rare. With understanding it reads as above. Etymologically speaking, for "preclare" the O.D. lists: 1) very clear, 2) distinguished, illustrious. The relation of (2) to clear and distinct is evident. Philosophically speaking, an aim of the ETHIC is clarity, i.e., knowing intuitively.

Index

"a," "an" discussed 105, 198 note; example 124

abbreviations 165–7, 170

Abjection Def. 240 note

ablative 172, 218 note, 252 note

acceptance of being 88; see Acquiescence

Acquiescence in oneself Def. 149; and Pride 127, 240 note

Acquiescence itself in self 240 note

Acquiescence of Mind 252 (Prop. 27)

action Def. 123; none in Desc. 123, 125; from passion 127, 138; Sp on 210–2 (Defs. 2, 3 and Props. 1–3)

active, being 210 (Def. 2), 147–9

adjectives, as adverbs 71, 86, 151, 171, 172, 187 note; see also "be, to," *Being, essentia,* attribute, "Mind"

adverbs, for adjectives; see adjectives

aeternitatis, sub specie, used 46; meaning of "species" in 147, 149, 252–3

affection, see 180 in def. of "mode"; see also "Affection" [Sp gives an early def. of the term in CM P. I, Ch. 3]; "modification"

"Affection" explained 99; complex referent 124, 151, 192 note, 224 note, 238 note

Affections, Def. 122, 210; capitalizing names of 52, 122, 214 note; discussed 121–7; knowledge of 138; in animals 123; all things "have" 122–3, three primary passive 124; two primary active 125; defined by no number 124; passive discussed 124, 138–41, Props. 1–57 P. III (pp. 210–26); active 125–7, 224 note, 226–7 (Props. 58, 59); what good and ill in 134, 232–44 (Props. 18–66); no theory of 226

note; which affect whole or part of us 238 note; see also cause, internal and external

affectus, see "Affection," affection, *afficio*

afficio 99, 187 note

agent, where an action 20, 31, 58, 68; see also notion

aids for reading BdS in tr. xii; and *essentia* 65, 77; adjectives as adverbs 71; capitalization of "mind" and "body" 51, 75–6; "God" as adjective 7, 46, 88, 151–2; "Affection" for "emotion" 99; articles 105; use of "imag." 108; see also adjectives; being 174; see also Elwes, the whole Appendix and Index

Alexander the Great, empire and death 3

alienation, problem of 33, 90, 157; see also dualistic thinking

altruism, dissolves 133

Ambition Def. 138; passion into action 138

Amicitia, tr. 126, 175

ampersand 173

analysis, ordinary-language 16, 159

analytic, see synthetic

angels, Sp on 38, 43

Anger, impediment to true knowledge 135; understanding it 138

animals, and Affections 123; not killing a prejudice 156 [in Sp Schol. 1, Prop. 37, P. IV]

animate, all thing are 1, 78ff., 156, 163, 218 note

Annot. 34; and annotations 45; in TTP 129, 144; see also commandments, moral, morality, understanding

Anselm, St. 23

[259]

demonstrations, nature of xii, 27, 56; a Mind's eyes 148; more than, needed 62, 77–8, 87, 88, 89, 92, 94, 103; postscript passim but espec. 160–1

Derision, an impediment to true knowledge 135

Descartes, R., and implications of Copernicus 13; and true knowledge 13; and Hobbes' failures 15; his idea of God peculiar 22–5; his idea of self a fiction 25, 93, 103 (see also fiction, imagination); quoted on God and Soul 16; quoted on his proof 27; and union of mind and body 77; and attributes 83–4; and motion 87; his *Discourse* 34, 106; his philosophy examined by BdS 40–1; compared with BdS 117; on passions 123, 126, 220 note; BdS on will in 137; "new philosophy" of Ch. 2

Descartes' Principles quoted on understanding 16, 71; described 40–1, 43; English tr. of 41, 167; and plural Gods 62; and "being" and "existing" 64; and distinctions 81; mentioned 107; and letters 121; and Meijer 53

Desires, Def. 124; an Affection 124; primary, for passions, and for actions 125; mistreated 125, 224 note; can be excessive 134

determinism, a main aspect of Sp's so-called 66, 139, 190–1 (Def. 2); 173 (on *a* and *ab*); see also cause by accident, individuality, "necessary," properties; will, free

Deus sive Natura, see God or Nature

Dewey, J., Sp and influence of Darwin ix–x

Dias, A. M. Vaz, and BdS as merchant 36, 169

distinctions, real, modal, rational, attributive 82; no real 85, 142, 155; between the modes of knowing not real 139–40; making between imagination and understanding an

expression of unity 254 note; see also dualism, non-dualism

Dolor, Def. 238 note; affects only part of us 238 note

doubt, Desc.'s reasons for 18, 25, 26, 29–30; and experience of being 23; and existence of God 28; absence of = knowing God 28, 238 note; see also certitude, see imagination

dreaming, in Desc. 18, 29; while awake ("blinded by images") 27, 30; metaphor of and knowing 28, 116, 119, 138 (experience but not distinctly see), 148, 149, 172, 204 note; see also awake, mythopoesis, passim

dualism, of form and matter and spirit and flesh 16, 73; and form and individuals 73; Def. 31–2; discussed 137, 147; problems of 33, 157; explanation of by BdS 114; Sp on 121; cloud of 151; and word usage 122; problems of do not appear in BdS 57; and Wittgenstein 169; and "nature" 255 note; and unconscious ideas 158; see also non-dualism

dualistic thinking, affects our understanding 81, 127, 139–40; and alienation 157; and systems of philosophy or metaphysics 161–2

duration, Def. 192–3 (Def. 5), 182–3 (Explication of Def. 8), a Mind's without relation to the body 145; and immortality 152; see also eternity

dying, see death

East-West communication, and BdS 158

Ecclesiastes, quoted 129

ecology, problem of 157

ecstasy, experience of and being eternally 147; qualified 151

ego, Def. 90, and substance compared 93; see also identity

egolessness, Def. 90–91; expressed in ETHIC 93–4, 98–101, 184–90

idea of a self-contradiction 24; two ideas of in Desc. 27; as *a* being 6, 23, 25ff., 49, 64, 93–5, 102; idea of deepened by BdS 57; as Being in BdS 57, 64, 70, 85, 152, 252 note, passim (and see, of course, "God" Def. of); as exemplar of true life 93, 102; as exemplar of human nature 54–5, 93–4, 127, 131, 134; and self-understanding or knowledge 94–5; existence of in Desc. 22–3; and doubt 28; an improper question 64; *exists necessarily* as example 56 (and see 184–5, Prop. 11), = Prop. 5 of P. I 61–2, 64; genderless 51; is eternally 100, 186–7 (Prop. 19); as material, Sp on 39, 43; an extending thing 194–5 (Prop. 2); has no properties 63; what can be properly said of 98, 101; *idea of* and Moses 6; as a person unclear 26; in Desc. 22, 32; peculiar in Desc. 22, 24, 130; in Middle Ages 8–9; dissolves when true 130, 140–1; imagined vs. understood 47, 57, 95, 130, 133–4, 140, 156; in the "new philosophy" 24, 34; is uniquely: in Desc. 31, 41, 62–3, = God exists necessarily 64, 66, 68, 71, 97–8, 101, 141, 145, 184–5 (Prop. 14 and Corols.); knowledge of = absence of doubt 28, 238 note; to know = to be fully consciously 88, 130, 238 note; knowledge of is not knowledge of some thing 238 note; understanding = understanding singular things 149–50; has no free will 190–1 (Corol.); is not dead 156; see also attribute, *Being*, egolessness, Nature, preposing, properites, substance

God's idea 150, 152, 254–5 (Prop. 32); names in Sp 6, 51; understanding Love 38, 151ff., 254 (Props and note); unity = his existing necessarily 66; will is asylum of ignorance 143; Kingdom 7; Love

of himself = our Love of each other 152

God or Nature 47, 230 note, 254–56 (Props. 36, 37)

Goethe, W., and rediscovery of BdS ix

"good" and "ill," relative terms 41, 54, 128, 177, 226–27 (Defs. 1 and 2)

good, the highest, knowledge of union 55

good and ill, drama of 8–9, knowledge of inadequate 128–9, unless an Affection 232–3 (Prop. 14); relative 156–7; see also sundry propositions in P. IV, motion

government 3–5, 45–6, 47, 133–4, 142–3

grammar, and notion of substance 73–4, Sp's effect on 105–6, 151–2, 204 note, 225 note, 250 note; affected by idea of unity 67–71, 74–6, 172; to be thrown by, in the case of attributes 197 note; when important and when not 204 note, 250 note

growing up, and identity 96; and dependency 127; and free will 142–4, and consciousness 153

Hakuin, on enlightenment 92

"has," goes with properties 84; as "is" 212 note, 256 note

Hate, Def. 124; overcome by Love 135, 139; an impediment to true knowledge 135; and be-ing 146; when not capitalized 221 note; sundry propositions in Parts III, IV, V in Appendix

Hayes, F. A., tr. 39, 167

Hebraic influence on BdS 37–8, 42, 48, 56–7; see *Hebrew Grammar,* language, and Spinoza, B.

Hebrew Grammar, of whole language not just Scriptural 38, and that language 48–9

Hebrew language, philosophical import of 38, 48–9, 75, 106

Hebrews, development of 5–6

ETHIC the work of 161; is indirect awareness 113, 155–6; a source of the mind-body distinction 114; is primarily physical 119, 146–7; is passive 133; and passions 125; and order 177; and Body 146, 201 note; and immortality 145, 150; Sp's def. of 212 note, Sp on 201 note, 214 note, 234 note; and knowing intuitively 114; like dreaming 116; of little moment 153; *beings* of 177; when confused with understanding 177; see also Elwes, memory, moral responsibility, names, substantive, understanding

imaginor 214, 234, 246, 252; tr. as "conceive" by Elwes 109

immortality, common view of 9; almost ridiculed 13; Desc. on 32; Sp on 38–9, 43; Plato on 19, 72; a confused idea 123, 150; and imagination 145; seemingly implied by BdS 145; impossible given unity 145; experience of 150; and notion of duration 152; part of the notion that thinking is incorporeal 32, 159, see unity

imperfection, problem of 25–7; see perfection

impossibility Def. by Sp 41; more than two attributes, an 84

impotence, human, causes of, Sp on 121, 230–3 (Props. 1–18); 127–9

inanimate, made animate 78ff., 156, 163, 218 note; see also rock, things

independent existence 31, and interaction 33, 62, 68, 72; being 127; see also *causa sui*, moral responsibility, substance, will, free

Individual Def. 198–9 (after Prop. 13), 52, 224–5 notes; word used 55, 78, 132, 156, 192–5 (Def. 8 and Ax. 3); see *ratio*

individuality, emphasis on, a consequence of Sp's insight 66; related to another way of knowing 66, 67; a false awareness of 90 (def. of

"ego"); see also determinism; knowing, always of individual things, though much of it mediated by images; knowing intuitively, not by means of universals

inhuman, being 134

insight, Sp's great and Prop. 5 64; and grammar 68; and philosophy and religion unified 85; and both attributes active 86ff.; and no faculty of understanding 104; and distinction of imagination and understanding 109; and all things have Affections 123; and the nature of the spiritual 131, and the modes of knowing not really distinct 139–40; various expressions of 107; in area of human conduct 126; and the Affections 127; two basic to ETHIC (unity and understanding) 121, 171, 254 note; see also unity, understanding

intellectus, tr. viii, 104–5, 234 note, 250 note; see also understanding

ipsa and *ipso* confused 242 note; see also Acquiescence

"is," as an active verb 67–9; and adverbs 172, 180–3 (all the Defs.); passim, e.g. 182–3 (Ax. 1), 204–5 (Prop. 34); is ambiguous between "to be" and "to exist" 64–5, 186–7 (Prop. 20), 234 note; see also "be, to," existing, *existendi, Jehovah*

-isms, freedom from all 160, 162

"it" to refer to a human being 122

jadah, to know and to love 38, 46, 107–9, 118

James, W., "thinking" equivocal 159

Jealousy, a Sadness 127; not a Love of be-ing 140

Jehova, as Being 6; or to be 38; or to be existing 65; as Sp's def. of "God" 57

Jelles, J., Sp's friend and publisher 36, 40; discussed 42; and TTP 45, 48; Preface to OP 48

mythopoesis, def. 1; Greek development from 2; Hebrew 5; both slow 7; in Middle Ages 9; and unity 78

Nagelata Schriften, De, NS, 42–3, contents 48; compared to OP 49–50; no capitalization in 53; and "imagination" 110; and preposing *Dei* 151; referred to in notes 177, 183, 186, 187, 188, 195, 197, 203, 206, 212, 230, 249, 251, 253, 255
name, God's proper 6, 49, 51, 57–8, 71
names, God's 6; in BdS and their gender 51; and imagination 173
naturalism, Sp's passim, but especially 101–2, 141–4
Natura naturans discussed 146; two ways of seeing things 149, 188 note, 194–5 (Ax. 5)
"nature," as used by BdS 47, 230 note; see *rerum natura*
nature, as corporeal world 26, 47; attitude toward: before philosophy 1, Greek 2, Hellenic 4, Medieval 8, Renaissance 12–14, Cartesian 28, Sp's 47, 78–9, 86–8, 144–54; 157–8
Nature, or God, 47; and unity 55; see also animate
Nature's laws, 55, see order
"necessary," Def. 182–3 (Def. 7, 188–9 (Prop. 32)
necessity, knowledge of and remedy and example 139; and unity 139–40; Sp on 41, 186–9 (Props. 32–36); see also determinism
neighbor, notion of changes 5–6, Sp's 132, notion now possible 155–6; see love thy neighbor
Newton, I., physics, 12, and the spiritual 12
Nietzsche, F. quoted 157, ix
nominalism, Desc.'s 24, def.; and Sp's 105; and the Affections 124; and universal notions 110, 206 note
no-mind 90, and understanding 92, 119
non-dualism, Def. 63; and attributes

72, 77–8, 81; and distinctions 82; and the whole of the ETHIC 79, 117, 172; and capitalization 122–3; and reference to Body 132; and moral problems 144; and knowing 148; as knowledge that there are attributes 149; and language's changes 151–2; and attitude toward nature 158; and physics, art and psychology, and wisdom 159; and no system of philosophy in BdS 161–2, and 196 (Prop. 7 and note); throughout Parts III, IV, and V 132; Sp and 194–9 (Props. 1–13), 246–7 (Prop. 1, cf. Prop. 7, P. II); see also dualism, Postscript, unity
nothingness, and no-mind and egolessness 90–2; see also Bayle on Buddhism
notion, a common defining substance, "no property is of nothing" 20; as Desc.'s 2nd def. of substance 58; and language 67–8; and science 69; and grammar 73–4; Sp abandoned it 58–9 (but see 69); see also identity, substance
notions, common, also called "axioms" 56; in Def. of reason and example 110, 206 note and Props. 37–39; universal, and nominalism and source for in BdS 105; in Def. of reason 110, 206 note; as parts of universal knowledge 152; source in imagination 177
nouns, as adjectives 151; see adjectives, Body, Mind, names, substantives

objective being or reality, of ideas 22, 196 (Corol. and note)
Occam, William of, 11
Oldenburg, H., BdS meets 39–40; Letter 1 43; BdS to about EU 104; BdS to about oriental languages 38, 106; asks about Bacon and Desc. 106
Old Testament, OT, see Testament

thority 11; on thinking 19, 73, 107; and "idea" 79

plurality, and Prop. 5, P. I 59ff.; not multiplicity 63, 140, 250 note; and the attributes 83; *Being* not a plurality 145; see also unity

plus, tr. as "plural" passim but espec. 59ff. (and corresponding propositions in the Appendix), 75, 250 note

polis, "city" 3; city-state, political unit 10

Political Treatise, TP, discussed 47; no capitalization in 53; in OP 48, 166; civic body in 238 note

Pollock, Sir F., for Sp's community 35

Pompanatius, and immortality 13

positivism, logical and philosophy ix, 159–60

possible, 226–7 (Def. 4)

possum, root of and cognates 174

Postulates from ETHIC used in text: from P II, Post. 4 132

postulates, nature of 55, see also axioms

potency, for acting, contemplating brings Joy 149; meaning of 174; see also knowing intuitively; Mind's a

pragmatism, and effect of Darwin ix-x, and quest for certainty 160; Sp's x-xi, 159–60, 177, and *beings* of reason 111, and *beings* of imagination 177, passim; see also notions, universal

praise and blame, BdS on in children 95; and moral responsibility 142ff

preconceptions and prejudices (including delusion), Desc.'s turning from 15; in the schools 16; BdS and Desc. on 50–1; ours in reading BdS 50–1, 100–2; of dualism 77; and the notion of attribute 81, 82–5; of the ego 90, 93; about identity 96–8; and sense of the self 103; and the article "the" 104–5, that the EU is about science 106; and being clear on "idea" 123 (see

also Freud); about religion 120; as image of God 140–1; and notion of self-caused 141; of dualism and reading BdS 144–5, 147, 151; and the attributes 196 note; ours and God 252 note; and killing animals 156 (see animals)

Preface to OP, relates ETHIC to TTP 42–3; 48

preposing of genitive case, passim but especially 175, 196 note, 197 note

prepositions, use of 172–3, 218 note, 254 note

prescriptions of reason 130; summarized 131–2

Pride, Self-love and understanding 127; an impediment to true knowledge 135; and Ambition 138; and Fortitude 151; improper 156; Def. of 240 note (and Props. 55–57)

Principles of Philosophy, Desc.'s, and *Meditations* 15, and *cogito* 21; and immortality 32; where written 35; quoted on universals 24; on substance 31, 58; and the soul 16 (quote), 32; BdS on 40, 56; and attributes 72–3; and distinctions 81–2; and extension 85ff.; compared to ETHIC 117

Properly speaking, of God 63; of existence 64; of God's unity 66; of substance 66; of "to be" 68; things properly said of God 98ff.; and more properly speaking 161; see degrees

properties, are of substances 20, 58, 64, 69–70, 84; and objective reality 22; a thing is its 59–60; God has no 63, 76; necessary vs. accidental 66, 139 (see determinism); and identity 59–61, attributes are not 76, 84–5; notion of changed 69; notion of attribute stems from notion of 84; see "has"

Prophets and prophecy 5–6, 94, 134; for BdS on in TTP 45

Prop. 5, P. I, originally first proposition of ETHIC, stated 59 (see also 184–5); analyzed 61–3, equivalent to Prop. 11 63–4; and God's unity 66; and identity 59–61, 96–8; called illogical by Bayle 96, 150; and free will 137; = all things constantly changing 61; and future life 145

proportional, example of, misleads about knowing intuitively 111; why BdS was pleased with 117

propositions, nature of 55–6

Propositions used from ETHIC in text: *from P. I: 1*/64, 75; *5*/59, 60, 61, 62, 96, 97, 98, 137, 145, 150; *6*/63; *4*/70, 78; *7*/63, 116; *8*/64, 71, 75, 168; *9*/64, 75, 83, 84; *10*/64, 75, 83, 84; *11*/64; *12*/98; *13*/59, 98; *14*/67, 68, 87, 97, 98; *15*/100; *16*/80, 87, 100; *17*/94, 100; *18*100; *19*/100; *20*/100; *21–24*/100; *25*/100; *26–27*/101; *28–36*/101; *30*/146

from P. II: 1–13/114; *3*/80; *7*/80, 116; *8*/80, 145; *11*/38, 80; *13*/77, 100, 132; *36*/115; *40*/105, 108, 109, 110, 112, 115, 152; *41*/140; *41–47*/112; *42*/140; *48*/105; *49*/95, 117, 147

from P. III: 2/116, 141; *11*/124; *29*/142; *57*/123; *58*/125; *59*/124, 125

from P. IV: 14/129; *17*/128, 129, 130; *18*/131, 133; *20*/133; *37*/133, 139; *37–46*/135 (on true life & religion); *39*/134; *43*/134; *44*/134; *45*/134; *50*/134; *54*/134; *67–73*/134 (on Freedom); *73*/135, 136; *37*/142; *68*/141, 154

from P. V: 2/138; *3*/138; *4*/138; *6*/139; *10*/139; *15–20*/140, 146; *17*/152; *19*/152; *20*/145; *18*/146 *21–42*/107, 118, 141, 146; *21*/146; *22*/147, 148; *23*/147, 148; *24*/148; *25*/148; *26–46*/107; *26*/126, 136, 148; *27*/148, 149; *29*/149; *30–32*/149; *32*/150, 152; *33*/151; *34*/123, 150, 152; *31*/146, 150; *35*/144, 152; *36*/152; *37*/152; *38*/153; *38*/95, 153; *40*/154; *41*/154; *42*/154

psychology, contemporary advances in 158

ratio, vs. *modus* 183 note; see Def. of Individual 198

reality, vs. appearance, distinction dissolves in the new outlook ix–x; and in BdS 70; Def. as perfection 123, 192–3 (Def. 6); relation to *Being* and "thing" 258; seen as *Being* 25; objective, see objective

reason, vs. theology 45; or understanding in Desc. 27, their alternation in BdS 139–40, 141; confused with understanding 106 (see mental, the); and identity 96–7; function of imagination 108; Def. by BdS 206 note; as second genus of knowledge 110; in EU and ETHIC compared 112, 126, 136; as between imagination and understanding 112, 136; BdS on 208–9 (Prop. 44); in Affections Chs. 8 and 9 (see p. 137); also plays a role in understanding 141; see also prescriptions of reason

reason's dictate, phrase examined 112; in a Def. of understanding 112, 126; in Def. of Generosity 125; summarized 131–6; as moral commandments 135–6, 154

reductio ad absurdum, Sp's favorite proof 62

religion, Hebrew 5–6; Christian 7–8; its original message 131; Def. by BdS 133, 258 (and see Prop. 41 on 256–7); as lived in imagination 46; not a branch of knowledge 31; and superstition 120; and nonvirtues 134; a first thing 154, 256–7 (Prop. 41); things that look to 135; Sp's 250–7 (Props. 21–42); see spiritual, the; humanities

"remains" = "left over" in Prop. 23 and note 252

remedies for Affections 137–41, 246–251 (Props. 1–20); discussion

[275]

of illuminates understanding 139–40, 252 note

Renaissance, humanistic 10; religious 10; scientific 10–12; philosophic 12–14; Ch. 2

rerum natura, in, discussed 188 note, 255 note

res, thing and reality 258

responsibility, see children, moral responsibility; will, free

Reverence, no virtue but useful 134

revolution, philosophical ix, 161; see philosophy

reward, and punishment, educative and civilizing 142–43; virtue's 154, 256–7 (Prop. 42); see also praise

riches, as a goal 54

Rieuwerts, Jan, Sp's friend and publisher 39, 40, 45, 53; his son and refusal to reprint 49

right 4–5; of government 45; sources of 133–4; of living 142–3, as might or authority 141–4; see also children

rock (stone), and feeling 79; its "mind" 79; its mode of being mentally 156; a pet and feeling 123

Russell, B. ix

Sadness, Def. 124, overcoming 139; mistranslated 224 note; sundry propositions from 21–257

sapience, actions of 134, 244–5 (Prop. 67)

satori, steps in awakening 92; see degrees

scepticism, in Greece 3–4, 7; in Renaissance 13, 14; as outcome of Desc. 33; see dualism

Schriften, De Nagelata, see *Nagelata*

Schuller, C. H., Sp's doctor and friend 48

science, Greek view of ix–x; born 2–3; empirical in Renaissance 10–12, 13; in Desc. 30–31, 117; and identity 69, 96–7; a function of imagination 108; its propositions

are media not knowledge 116; not precisely what BdS calls "reason" 126; and Desc.'s def. of "substance" from a common notion 69; and religion brought together xi; and dualism 157

self, know thy, see know; understood by idea of God (as an image) 95; and Love of God and Affections 140; consciousness of and living 153; understanding and experiential ground of Sp's thinking 94; and Acquiescence in oneself 127; and loving God 140; and *Being* 149–50, 151–2; understanding and the language of BdS xi; selfishness and altruism not a real distinction 133; see also identity

Self-love, as Pride or as Acquiescence 127, 240 note

sense, common, the 108; and G. E. Moore ix

sentio, translated as "feel" or "think" 123, 151; used as "think" in the title of Ch. XX, TTP 45–6

Servitude, Def. 127; wages of according to the vulgar 132; is living according to imagination 133; in the OT 136; causes of 128–9

Shakespeare, W., quoted 163; on word and thing 107

Short Treatise, tr. by Wolf 35, 168; probably spurious, 37; possible source of 40; when appeared 49, 168

signs, knowledge by 109–10; example 111; knowing intuitively not from 149 (see demonstrations, more than needed); 206 note

singular things, knowing always of 113, 116–7 (see knowing, though much of it mediated); to know, is to understand God 148; knowing, is better than universal knowledge 152; Def. 192–3 (Def. 7); see nominalism, thing

Smith, D. D., tr. and *mens* 144, 165, 224 note

(religious life), 129, 136, 143–4, 228 note; Sp quoted on 16; Sp on 188–9 (Props. 30, 31), 234–7 (Props. 26, 27), 250–7 (Props. 21–42) see also EU, imagination knowing intuitively, Love, moral responsibility, reason. [Since BdS on understanding expresses one of his two basic insights (which see), understanding should be kept in mind throughout the book.]

understanding Love, God's 38, 151–4, 254 (Props. and note)

union, of Mind and Nature 55, 58, 78, 150; of religion and philosophy 120; of religion and science xi; experience of 150–1; of Mind and Body, and the attributes 75–6; with God 151; and a true idea of 153–4; a clear statement of 254 note; see unity

unique, properly uniquely, see God, identity, plurality, Prop. 5, substance

unity, first statement of 55; second 57; and Prop. 5 59ff.; of Mind and Body 66–7; and a new way of knowing 66, 67; insight into = insight into *Being* 70; and grammar, see grammar; as acceptance of being 87–8; and the need for experience 93–4; penetrating notion of to true idea 113; and impotence 128; and talk of Affections for conveying insight into 127; penetration into, downwards not upwards 131; as identification with others 135; concrete expression of in Parts III, IV and V 122; of God 58, 63, 140–1 (see also God is uniquely); and the attributes 84–5; various expressions of 107; and necessity 139; and thinking 141–2; grammatically considered 172; and the illusion of immortality 150; and the illusion of morality 228 note

unity, idea of, implies no immortality 38–9, 43, 145; vs. notion of 67, 68–9; becomes unity 112–3, 150; effect on Sp's view of the Affections 121–4; and whole person and Affections 238 note; concretely expressed Part III (e.g., 125), Part IV (e.g., 134–6), Part V (e.g., 153–4) and Prop. 42 pp. 256–7; see union. [Since BdS on unity expresses one of his two basic insights (which see), unity should be kept in mind throughout the book.]

universals, see nominalism; notion, universal; *beings* of reason, *beings* of imagination; Affections def. by no number 124; Desc. on 24; mistaken as objects of knowledge 107–8, 113, 114–7, 132, 155–56

variety, see motion

verities, eternal, Sp on 55; and understanding 129, def. 144; see also Annot. 34, commandments

virtue, its foundation 132–4; meaning of the word 131–2; Def. 228–9 (Def. 8); Sp on 234–5 (Props. 22, 23), 244–5 (Prop. 69), 250–7 (Props. 21–42); non-virtues, some useful 134, 204 (Props. 50, 53, 54 and note); see also Annot. 34, commandments

Visalius, and experience 51

Wang Yang-ming, on knowledge and action 130; and *zazen* 169

Wedeck, H. E., tr. 41, 167

well-being, or being well, Ch. 9 passim

what is, 2; is *Being* 64, 84; as reality 86; new view of 155; but see 161–3 after "more properly speaking"

White, W. H., tr. 165, 224 note

will, and intellect in Desc. 25; and understanding same for BdS 115, Sp on 108–9 (Props. 48, 49 and Corol.); terms not the same for God and humans 256 note

will, free, sources of notion of 93–4,